PROBLEM FATHERS
AND RENAISSA

Fathers are central to the drama of Shakespeare's time: they are revered, even sacred, yet they are also flawed human beings who feature as obstacles in plays of all genres. In *Problem Fathers in Shakespeare and Renaissance Drama*, Tom MacFaul examines how fathers are paradoxical and almost anomalous characters on the English Renaissance stage. Starting as figures of confident authority in early Elizabethan drama, their scope for action becomes gradually more restricted, until by late Jacobean drama they have accepted the limitations of their power. MacFaul argues that this process points towards a crisis of patriarchal authority in wider contemporary culture. While Shakespeare's plays provide a key insight into these shifts, this book explores the dramatic culture of the period more widely to present the ways in which Shakespeare's work differed from that of his contemporaries, while both sharing and informing their artistic and ideological preoccupations.

TOM MACFAUL is Fellow and Departmental Lecturer in English at Merton College, University of Oxford. He is the author of *Male Friendship in Shakespeare and his Contemporaries* (2007), *Poetry and Paternity in Renaissance England* (2010), and many articles on Renaissance poetry and drama. He is also the co-editor of *Tottel's Miscellany* (2011) with Amanda Holton.

PROBLEM FATHERS IN SHAKESPEARE AND RENAISSANCE DRAMA

TOM MACFAUL

CAMBRIDGE
UNIVERSITY PRESS

CAMBRIDGE
UNIVERSITY PRESS

University Printing House, Cambridge CB2 8BS, United Kingdom

Cambridge University Press is part of the University of Cambridge.

It furthers the University's mission by disseminating knowledge in the pursuit of education, learning and research at the highest international levels of excellence.

www.cambridge.org
Information on this title: www.cambridge.org/9781316505274

First published 2012
Reprinted 2013
First paperback edition 2015

A catalogue record for this publication is available from the British Library

Library of Congress Cataloguing in Publication data
MacFaul, Tom.
Problem fathers in Shakespeare and Renaissance drama / Tom MacFaul.
pages cm
ISBN 978-1-107-02894-4
1. Shakespeare, William, 1564–1616–Characters–Fathers. 2. Shakespeare, William, 1564–1616–Criticism and interpretation. 3. Fathers in literature. 4. English literature–Early modern, 1500–1700–History and criticism. I. Title.
PR2992.F3M33 2012
822.3′3–dc23
2012015668

ISBN 978-1-107-02894-4 Hardback
ISBN 978-1-316-50527-4 Paperback

For Sally

Contents

Acknowledgements

This book began with a lengthy reading project – a chronological survey of all surviving Elizabethan and Jacobean drama. I am particularly grateful to the staff of the English Faculty Library in Oxford for granting me special loans which enabled the relatively swift completion of that reading. I have also had very useful conversations with many colleagues at Oxford about the progress of the project, including Richard McCabe, Emma Smith, Laurie Maguire, David Norbrook, Jonathan Thacker, Steven Gunn, Helen Moore, John Pitcher, and Glenn Black. Thanks are due to John Lee and attendees at the University of Bristol Renaissance Graduate seminar, where I presented some of my ideas as the first draft of the book was completed. Sarah Stanton at Cambridge University Press has been a model of patience as this book went through its various revisions; the anonymous readers for the Press were insightful and very helpful, giving me valuable advice on pruning what had threatened to become rather an unwieldy book; thanks also to Fleur Jones and Christina Sarigiannidou for seeing the book through the press, and to Chris Jackson for his careful copy-editing. I am grateful to Merton College for a research grant covering the cost of the index. Amy Waite gave invaluable assistance in checking quotations. Most of all, I would like to offer heartfelt thanks to my undergraduate students over the years, particularly at Corpus Christi and Merton Colleges: their fresh and imaginatively engaged perspectives on the great literature of the past is a constant reminder of the real audience for our scholarly endeavours.

CHAPTER I

Introduction

In his *Brief Lives*, John Aubrey retails an amusing anecdote whose truth is less important than what it reveals about the tensions between fathers and sons in Shakespeare's times:

Sir Walter Ralegh being invited to dinner with some great person, where his son was to goe with him; He sayd to his son, 'Thou art expected to stay at dinner, to goe along with me; but thou art [so] engaging in quarrels that I am ashamed to have such a Beare in my Company'. Mr Walter humbeld himself to his Father and promised he would behave himselfe mighty mannerly: so away they went . . . he sate next to his Father, and was very demure at least halfe Dinner time: Then, sayd he, 'I this morning, not having the feare of God before my eies, but by the instigation of the devill, went to a Whore; I was very eager of her, kissed and embraced her, and went to enjoy her, but she *thrust* me from her, and vowed I should not, "for your father lay with me but an hower ago"'. Sir Walter being strangely supprized, and putt out of countenance at so great Table, gives his son a damned blow over the face; his son, as rude as he was would not strike his father, but strikes over the face of the Gentleman that sate next to him, and sayd, '*Box about, 'twill come to my father anon*'. 'Tis now a common used proverb.[1]

Although there is something of the jest-book here, the tale is significant: the son feels that there is a definite barrier to any actions against his father, whose person is really thought of as sacred, but still needs to assert himself; there is no question of who the joke is on – the son will ultimately displace his father, and the taboo of filial aggression is got round with relative ease. Ralegh's sense of his own dignity as being dependent on his son's actions makes him vulnerable to insult and loss of status, whereas his son is relatively protected. The father–son rivalry over a whore is a distillation of larger tensions based on the son and the father being strangely invested in one another. This investment or identification is more a matter of Oedipal tensions: it seems to be driven by larger forces such as the devil which Walter Junior (a.k.a. Wat) mentions, which are beyond the ken of the individuals involved. There is something deeply problematic in the paternal relation, something rich and strange which is a bizarre mixture of the demonic and the sacred. The relationship, which ought to be a proper performance of dignity at the great man's table, becomes a farcical knockabout into which the son's bearish nature surprisingly intrudes; yet the father is no more dignified – he too is lustful, and driven by the demonic (his blow is a damned one, after all). It is a moment of revelation and recognition, as the private relationship becomes public.

There was a more clearly tragic sequel to this comic moment, in that young Wat was killed on the Orinoco river, having disobeyed his king and his father in attacking a Spanish station, an action that ultimately led to Ralegh senior's own execution. The story distils both the comic elements of paternity and the tragic possibilities that are implicit in them. The graceful loops – boxing about the table, as it were – of comedy and the stifling hyperidentifications of tragedy both rely on the sacredness of fathers, a factor that this book contends is central to the power of Elizabethan and Jacobean drama. In comedy, a whole community can be brought in to diffuse the tensions between the generations (in romance, supernatural forces may also intervene); yet diffusing the tension does not defuse it: it is spread into the atmosphere of such plays, leaving a sense of uneasy compromise. In tragedy, the need for sons and fathers to invest their sense of identity in one another leads to competitions that cannot be resolved. Only in history plays can there be a sense of secure continuity, but there it comes at a considerable cost to individuals.

Fathers are paradoxical figures on the English Renaissance stage. Being a father was in some sense a precondition for full masculine selfhood; yet once a man has reproduced, his subjectivity and scope for action usually seem to be attenuated in literary representations, which have a tendency to estrange the father, both from his offspring and from himself, for he possesses a dignity that he cannot quite own. The attenuation of selfhood is managed in different ways in different periods and genres of the drama; it not only makes for great dramatic movements, but demonstrates that there is no monolithic notion of patriarchy in the period. The father is divided between his private, emotional self, and his public, sacred role, and different kinds of dramatic plot attempt to unify that self, with varying degrees of success and failure.

Four major phases of the dramatic representation of fathers can be identified. In early Elizabethan drama, fathers are presented, with considerable nostalgia, as figures of restraint, or 'stays' – a key word in *Gorboduc* – but this also leads to them being tragically impotent figures; when they act they usually precipitate disaster or humiliation; this phase culminates in *The Spanish Tragedy*, where a father finally finds a mode of legitimate (though anguished) action. In the drama of the 1590s, the representation becomes more complex: excessive reverence and father–son identification starts to seem grotesque, leading to absurd tensions in comedy and ultimately to stifling impasses in tragedy; such plays are full of moments and scenes of excruciating paralysis, culminating in *Hamlet*. After *Hamlet*, drama starts to press at the limits of the father–child bond, in plays like *King Lear*, but plays of this period, including prodigal-son comedies and emergent tragicomedy, start to find ways of limiting, effacing, or even purging the power of the father; this is based, I think, on a half-stated sense of uncertain paternity, an issue that is generally ignored (or repressed) in Elizabethan drama; this phase reaches its greatest heights in *King Lear* and *The Winter's Tale*, and culminates in the hard-won but gracious acceptance of uncertainty and limitation in *The Tempest*. That uncertainty becomes more explicit in later Jacobean plays, particularly in the tragicomedies that follow *The Tempest*: the new dominance of the tragicomic mode involves a gradual and often grudging acceptance of the limitations of paternal authority, and a concomitant need to find new sources of authority and identity, crucially founding selfhood in ideas of honour and virtue that are detached from mere *nature*. This acceptance is one of the keynotes of the last phase I deal with, later Jacobean drama, where fathers gradually withdraw from importance, setting the stage (as it were) for Caroline and Restoration drama's increasing indifference to fathers. The drama of this period tries to disentangle the private/emotional and the public/sacred roles of fathers, but in doing so it ultimately emphasizes the destructive tendencies of patriarchal ideas. Social and political change often underlies the changes in the drama, but the development of dramatic genres also has its own logic, frequently anticipating rather than reacting to political events.

Judith Haber has demonstrated that the idea of patrilineality is frequently invoked in drama as a way to introduce the causal and teleological elements of dramatic narrative and history, pushing aside tendencies to 'pointless play' that frequently emerge in drama's more lyric moments.[2] However, strange loops of dramatic structure and human emotion emerge even when causality and teleology seem most urgently in place. Even as ends are invoked by the prioritizing of paternal roles, so are limits and impasses which require drastic inventiveness on the part of dramatists and their characters. This inventiveness gives rise to the most striking instances of 'the vertiginous dramatic moment' (to adopt Simon Palfrey and Tiffany Stern's phrase),[3] such as Edgar in *King Lear* leading his blind father to an imaginary cliff. Here we find something different from Haber's pointless play, but something which is equally subversive of normative structures. Hence one has to quarrel with Stephen Greenblatt's view that identity in the Renaissance is less 'a final goal than . . . a way station on the road to a firm and decisive identification with normative structures';[4] such a decisive identification is never quite managed, and always needs the mediation of another individual, who may well seem more important than the normative structures he represents. Fred Tromly's recent work on fathers in Shakespeare shows how a son's potential aggression against his father may be resolved through the idea of rescuing him;[5] the individual is always more important than the structural.

It is certainly true, as Lisa Jardine has demonstrated, that the representation of gender relations on the stage reflects 'the patriarchy's unexpressed worry about the great social changes which characterize the period', particularly worries about women subverting lines of male inheritance.[6] Yet that worry is projected at least as much onto the representation of fathers as onto unruly women, and fathers take on an emotional ambiguity whose richness derives from more than merely materialistic concerns. The present study should serve to complicate Linda Bamber's view (in what is otherwise perhaps the subtlest account of Shakespeare's gender politics) that 'For Shakespeare the issue of the feminine is much more problematic than the issue of the father.'[7] Masculinity, for Shakespeare and other dramatists, is an ideal whose power derives at least in part from its unattainability;[8] the ideal of the father is perhaps the most acute instance of this. Peter Erickson shows that, while men tend to prop up one another's identity in drama, there is a developing need, which seems to increase over the course of Shakespeare's career, 'towards a possible accommodation with women', particularly in their roles as mothers.[9] That accommodation goes hand in hand with an increasing sense of fathers as a problem. Catherine Belsey has described 'the incursion of anarchy, cruelty and death into what is legal, affectionate and life-giving' in Shakespearean family life.[10] Yet we shall see that cruelty and affection tend to be deeply linked in the drama's developing sense of human possibilities. The precariousness of manly honour in the period means that it can hardly be otherwise,[11] and fathers most acutely embody this problem.

Fathers are crucial figures in the process of dramatic recognition, a process which is not as teleological as it might initially seem. The father being, in a very vivid sense, a sacred figure at this time, this means that any action on his part may imperil the whole system of sacred order. However, being sacred also makes a figure taboo – and taboos are wonderful resources for drama. They put limits on action, and thereby give structure. Fathers therefore enable a large variety of tense dramatic set-pieces, most of which involve kinds of recognition – Aristotle's pivotal moment of dramatic intensity and release (*anagnorisis*).[12] Recognizing the father is particularly powerful, as it is an affirmation of the deepest ideas of identity available at the time. Yet recognitions are also a very eerie and controversial feature of drama.

As Northrop Frye puts it, in both tragedy and comedy 'what is recognized is seldom anything new; it is something which has been there all along, and which, by its reappearance or manifestation, brings the end into line with the beginning'.[13] It is clear that a father is a perfect instance of this in Renaissance drama (for the Greeks, the appearance of a god might be better). What happens in moments of recognition is a crystallization of identity that is deeply paradoxical: on the one hand, that crystallization is momentary and contingent, destined to be swept away by the larger progress and process of drama; on the other, it constitutes an epiphanic glance into eternity, the realm of sacred continuity. There is a tension between the illusion of completeness that *anagnorisis* brings, and our knowledge of limitation.[14] To put it another way, recognition is an impermanent recognition of permanence.

It is clear that *anagnorisis*/recognition is a crucial aspect of aesthetic experience as well as being an essential cognitive pleasure, but its role in tragedy in particular is harder to explain.[15] We enjoy seeing someone move from ignorance to knowledge partly because we have generally anticipated that movement, and can feel superior;[16] in the best detective fiction, we often guess the solution *just* before its revelation, so that our pleasure is one of confirmation rather than real discovery;[17] this effect may help to confirm for us the coherence of the fictional world and therefore even the existence of the external world. The representation of recognition also affirms for us the continuity of the fictional character who does the recognizing;[18] though the previous ignorance of that character indicates the limitation of human knowledge, the recognition prioritizes knowledge and continuity, and suggests that the connection of two points in an individual's life is enough for our faith in continuous selfhood to be justified. The fact that we ground our belief in the existence of other minds on such moments is hugely significant: the movement from ignorance to knowledge (what developmental psychologists call 'theory of mind') is in some sense proof of our own humanity as much as proof of fictional characters' reality, because we may have faint recollections of our own development from infantile solipsism to acceptance of other people's different understanding of the world.[19] Perhaps this is why recognition of other people is always more striking than recognition of things and facts; but perhaps this is also why it is coloured with something tragic: even as we recognize someone else, in doing so we recognize that they are fundamentally inaccessible.[20] Even when we encounter recognition in comedy, it is more likely to be coloured with sadness than with real joy: people bring together the burdens of their sufferings, yet at the same time realize the incommensurability of those burdens.[21] Recognition of a father is, furthermore, apt to be a primal instance of this: if there is something symbiotic about the mother–child bond,[22] the father is apt to be the first true 'third person' in human experience. He is therefore the symbol of all that is unknowable even as he is also the symbol of knowledge; he can only be an object of sympathy, never of empathy, and yet the ideology of a patrilineal society asks boys at least to identify with their fathers, while demanding respect for them which might preclude sympathy. This may be the essence of the tragic double bind.

There may be several ways of cutting this knot in Renaissance England, all of them rather magical: the first is a simple faith in names, the superstitious belief that similarity of name ultimately allows real identification, and so naming becomes a key aspect of recognition; the second is the act of revenge, which constitutes proof of one's relation to the patrilineal family; the third is the idea of the paternal blessing, which is the one remaining licensed ceremonial magic in the family;[23] indeed, the ideal father is perhaps most powerfully felt in moments of paternal blessing. By this means, acknowledgement (one of the other meanings of *anagnorisis*) gets the performance it requires – it cannot be merely internal.[24]

Of course, this is a major feature of Biblical portrayals of patrilineal identity (most notably in the story of Isaac, Jacob, and Esau), but it seems to have acquired new meaning and force in Renaissance England. Indeed, the idea of the blessing seems to have gained in importance, being mentioned more frequently in drama, and often treated as the paradigm of earthly bliss – e.g. in Fletcher's *The Pilgrim* (c. 1620), where a state of contentment is compared to 'the blessing of a father' (II. ii. 325).[25] The emphasis on paternal blessings may have to do with protestantism's abandonment of intercessory saints, making fathers into the only source of connection to the divine.[26]

Freud's myth (one might call it a just-so story) of a band of brothers ganging up to kill their father is highly suggestive, if deeply speculative. For Freud, this moment is the origin of totemism and taboos, and ultimately of all religion.[27] The inability of any one son to embody the murdered father necessitates the creation of an ideal father who will be a patriarchal god.[28] The whole myth relies on an idea of collective repression, though, and is therefore completely unverifiable; nor does it really help explain particular social constructions of the idea of the father and the idea of patricide. It is also highly speculative, of course, for me to suggest that the Reformation brought about a comparable sense of guilt at killing a primal father, at rejecting the authority of the Pope, or even of God Himself. If nothing else, the Reformation certainly increased the value of individual fathers, perhaps making them *too* important, making them bearers of a range of value and meaning that they could not in everyday life sustain.[29] This must have contributed to a greater level of ambivalence about fathers (Freud's key point), and a sense of fragmentation between ideal and reality that drama could work through.

The taboo status of fathers can be most clearly seen when the taboos involved come close to being broken. In Jonson's *Every Man out of His Humour*, Sogliardo says that he will not trust his heirs to build his grand tomb; Carlo Buffone pretends to assent to his position, saying 'heires and executors, are growne damnably carelesse, specially, since the ghosts of testators left walking' (II. i. 77–9).[30] The joke reflects an important reality: since the protestant abolition of Purgatory, the place from which ghosts could explicably return, there is no way for the dead to pressurize their sons and other heirs. The fear that one's children will not respect one's wishes after death, and that they will rejoice in one's death, becomes a dramatic commonplace. In a play celebrating charitable deeds, *2 If You Know Not Me*, this motivates charitable actions during life, Hobson saying 'Heauen grant that I may liue, that, when I die, / Although my children laugh, the poor may cry' (1: 278).[31] Increasingly in the early seventeenth century, characters in plays repeat the idea of sons rejoicing at their fathers' deaths as if this were becoming a paradoxical proverb: in Middleton's *The Puritan Widow* (1606), for example, a play which opens with some allusions to *Hamlet*, the bereaved son is very different from the Danish prince, saying 'I protest I am glad he's churched, for now he's gone I may spend in quiet', and 'a fair riddance. My father's laid in dust. His coffin and he is like a whole meat pie, and the worms will cut him up shortly' (I. i. 48–9, 136–8), and the idea of laughing at a father's death is repeated later in the play by other characters (III. v. 92–4, IV. i. 19–20).[32] Similarly, in *Your Five Gallants* (1607), Middleton has his hero Fitzgrave ask the titular rogues 'Are your fathers dead, gentlemen, you're so merry?' (IV. vii. 246–7). Taboo-breaking gives way to commonplace comedy with only the mildest shock value.

Yet the taboos associated with fathers never entirely lose their force. In the depths of misfortune, people may curse their nurses, their homelands, their mothers, and even their parents in the plural, but they seem never to curse their fathers specifically. And they very rarely kill their fathers, as we shall see. Nonetheless, fathers tend to be treated as objects or ideals rather than as subjects in themselves. Coppélia Kahn argues that Shakespeare's 'male characters are engaged in a continuous struggle, first to form a masculine identity, then to be secure and productive in it'.[33] Yet it is actually rare for any father to be productive: their selves seem *achieved*, and the priority of security – of preserving the peak of *being* that they have arrived at – seems much greater.[34] Rather like a woman preserving her chastity, a father seems only able to preserve his sense of honour,[35] and this can make his position as precarious as a virgin in the woods. In reality, it seems that many men searched for other forms of self-realization as an alternative to the family,[36] but in drama the familial seems primary. We must be wary of attributing too much anxiety to the condition of patriarchal masculinity in the period,[37] but the fact that the position of the patriarch was so important – even central – to the culture of the time means that a great deal of dramatic energy goes into protecting it. This makes the position of fathers crucial to our under-standing of dramatic form.

Something similar is at work in Greek drama, but the differences are as revealing as the similarities.[38] In Aeschylus' *Eumenides*, Orestes is pardoned for matricide on the basis that avenging his father takes absolute priority: Apollo, who had ordered the vengeance, takes his authority from 'the power of the Father', Zeus, and says:

> Here is the truth, I tell you – see how right I am.
> The woman you call the mother of the child
> is not the parent, just a nurse to the seed,
> the new-sown seed that grows and swells inside her.
> The *man* is the source of life – the one who mounts.
> She, like a stranger for a stranger, keeps the
> the shoot alive unless god hurts the roots.[39]

Yet despite the importance of fathers as motivating principles – Agamemnon must be avenged in *The Libation Bearers* and Sophocles' and Euripides' *Electra* plays – fathers are not treated with great respect in Greek tragedy, a contradiction that might subtly and indirectly inform Renaissance drama. Pentheus in Euripides' *Bacchae* can abuse his abdicated grandfather Cadmus for his ridiculous Bacchic attire (lines 250–2); whereas in *Orestes* Electra expresses doubt as to whether her father Agamemnon was really glorious (line 17).[40] This may have something to do with the fact that in Greek myth one can have two fathers: Heracles, Theseus, and Helen, for example, have both human and divine fathers (and Heracles' human father in Euripides' play admits his own feebleness). Perhaps there is bound to be less pressure on the idea of paternity in a polytheistic, kin-based culture where the range of obligations is spread more broadly than in a monotheistic culture beginning to adopt nuclear familial patterns; yet some of that Greek doubleness of paternity may find its way onto the Elizabethan and Jacobean stage. Of course, fathers for the Greeks are figures to whom one is obliged in various ways. In *Iphigenia in Aulis*, Menelaus appeals to Agamemnon to make the sacrifice of his (Agamemnon's) titular daughter on the basis of their common paternity, but when he (ineffectually) changes his mind and decides that the girl shall live, his pity for his brother is based on their common maternity (lines 404, 501). This idea of the father as conferring obligation, the mother as bringing pity is shared by Elizabethan and Jacobean drama; but it does not share very strongly the idea of the cursed family which is so important in Greek tragedy and which there dissipates individual obligation to a father.

The greatest scenes of direct paternal pressure in Greek tragedy come in Euripides' *Hippolytus* and Sophocles' *Women of Trachis*. In the former case, Theseus falsely believes that his titular son has raped his wife (the boy's stepmother) Phaedra, and therefore curses the son; despite his rage, he does not kill his son himself (killing a son seems as unthinkable to the Greeks as patricide does to the playwrights of Shakespeare's day).[41] In the latter, stranger, and more brilliant case, the dying Heracles makes huge, seemingly illegitimate demands on his son Hyllus, para-doxically insisting that their fulfilment will be proof of the son's legiti-macy: the poisoned Heracles has Hyllus take him to a mountain-top and burn him up, and adds the further command that the boy must marry Iole, a woman he admits that he has himself slept with; in thus demanding both patricide and a kind of incest, Heracles is obliging a dutiful son to commit precisely the sins that were signs of a cursed unfilial nature in Oedipus. Rather than acting as the embodiment of the Law, the father here comes to represent the caprice of an utterly lawless nature; but this is because he is becoming a god. The gods can transcend human laws, it is clear (the play ends with a choric insistence that all that has gone wrong should be attributed to Heracles' father Zeus); like

Oedipus at the end of *Oedipus at Colonus*, the figure of the sinful father
gains a kind of apotheosis that transcends and purges human sinfulness.
Rather than being models for emulation, these Greek hero-fathers are
warnings, figures that go beyond human limits, men at whom we can
merely wonder.[42]

Perhaps one might conclude that fathers in Greek tragedy are rather
taken as literary *exempla* than as people with deep human connections,
the familial drama usually taking place in their absence: the absorption
of this attitude, when put alongside Protestantism's ambivalent valori-
zation of paternity and an increasingly humane sense of the relations
between fathers and children, may account for the extraordinarily various pressures which emerge in the dramatic representation of fathers in
the Elizabethan and Jacobean period. Greek tragedy, however indirectly
and incompletely absorbed, created another model to which dramatic
fathers had to rise.

Tragic catharsis – purgation – can be more than the removal of pity
and fear: it can also involve the cleansing and recovery of women. In
Euripides' *Helen*, for instance, the sins of the titular character are taken
away as we learn that she was replaced by a phantom and that the
Trojan War has been all for nothing; the latter aspect of this may be
tragic, but Menelaus' recovery of a pure wife is a happier catharsis.
The discovery that Iphigenia is not really dead in *Iphigenia among the
Taurians* is a similar cancelling-out of tragic causation;[43] as is the
recovery of Alcestis in her eponymous play. These plays are the ultimate
root of tragicomedy – but it is worth noting that the tragicomic norm is
for women to be purified and recovered, not men. Hence Leontes in
The Winter's Tale can recover his daughter, and even his wife, but
cannot recover his son. The reason for this is, I think, based on an
inversion of the sexual double standard: a woman, in a patriarchal
society, can never recover her honour/virtue if she is unfaithful, whereas
a man can (his honour/virtue being based on something more than sex).
The unfairness of this double standard is obvious to us, but I think it
was also half-consciously recognized in earlier ages, and the tragicomic
purgation of women is a way around it; the strange corollary of this is
that men cannot recover their honour in tragedy as they can in other
genres. Our only response to them is pity and fear. The father is, as
Apollo says, the one who mounts (in many senses), and that means that
he is one who must always elude comprehension. In Renaissance
drama, particularly of the early Jacobean period, the purgation of the
father tends to lead to his erasure.

In one of the best accounts of gender relations in Shakespeare, Marianne L. Novy argues that:

In both comedy and tragedy, Shakespeare's women gain their dramatic power because they seem to live so close to the conflict between the desires to keep and to lose the self, between individuality and merging with others, between integrity and flexibility, which is part of the basis for the human interest in the theater.[44]

The human interest in fathers, by contrast, is more problematic: they are less able to perform their identities, and remain elusive, precisely because the distance between their private, individual selfhood (which may be flexible) and their sacred, public patrilineal identity (which must be fixed) is so great, creating greater tension and even mystery.

The most elusive father in Greek tragedy is the Oedipus of *Oedipus at Colonus*, the man whose grave must remain a secret. His defiant acceptance of his fate makes him the most *completed* figure in all tragedy – from the beginning of the play, he asks for little, but it is *enough* (lines 5–6). He is able to confer blessings on Athens because of this, but he remains a mystery, in the most radical sense. Due to an oracle promising safety to a city that possesses Oedipus, his sons want to treat him as an object, something to be kept as a talisman, but not welcomed as a person; Oedipus responds to this with the marvellously gnomic ' ὅτ' οὐκέτ' εἰμί, τηνικαῦτ' ἄρ' εἰμ' ἀνήρ' (line 393) – when I *am* no longer, then I am a man?[45] Yet he is prepared to accept this position in relation to Theseus, to whose city (Athens) he offers himself, if not to his sons. That offer allows him *enough* subjectivity, even as he becomes an object, a figure as impotent but pivotal as a king at chess. This strange doubleness of fathers is something that we will see throughout Renaissance drama. Sophocles' play is full of such paradoxical tensions: Oedipus is objectively guilty of patricide and incest, but subjectively free from guilt, as he was ignorant (and, for that matter, he *knows* that he was ignorant); he is cursed, but a blessing to others; yet despite his sense that his passion is spent, he persists in cursing his sons; he transgresses the sacred ground of the furies, but he also guards against them; the man who once solved the riddle of the Sphinx is now the most mysterious riddle of all; even as he most fully becomes himself, he must die; but the death is not wholly to be welcomed: Antigone, his daughter, can finally say that there is a love that persists even in the midst of suffering/evils (line 1697). Human emotions exist and persist despite the existential pressures brought to bear. Oedipus' wise acceptance of the limitations of his position anticipates the position of Shakespeare's Prospero. In both cases, there is a participation in nature which

cancels out the fearful presumption of the paternal subject, an acknowledgement of a 'thing of darkness' without an attempt to explain it away.

Of course, Renaissance attitudes to paternity and theories of its role
and importance were different from those of the ancient Greeks. Firstly,
protestantism placed new pressures on fathers, making them more
authoritative in spiritual and micro-political senses than they had been
before.[46] Secondly, newly competing theories of biology made people
genuinely uncertain as to the kind of investment a father had in his
children.[47] Thirdly, changes in the organization of society meant that
there were fewer intermediate loyalties between the state and the family,
enforcing a stronger analogy between them even as the disjunction
between them grew.[48]

My previous book, *Poetry and Paternity in Renaissance England*,
showed how writers in various genres used the idea of fatherhood to
focalize an embattled process of self-realization; the role of paternity in
drama is very different; the plots of drama focus on certain problems
that can be avoided in poetry: in particular, we may wonder whether
drama can manage what Charles Taylor calls the 'affirmation of ordinary life',[49] or must it rely on one of Taylor's other axes of moral worth,
such as the insistent respect for hierarchy or a sense of divinely sanc-
tioned universal order? My answer in this book is that the figure of the
father is a key object of contention between such different moral models,
a figure of strange doubleness: he is a representation of Taylor's 'attitu-
dinal respect',[50] and is also a symbol of the proper functioning of the
cosmos; yet he is also, inevitably, part of day-to-day being, and there is
no legal fiction, such as that of the King's Two Bodies,[51] which could
resolve the tensions between his modes of being. That strange doubleness is
also founded on a conflict between the private/emotional self and the
public/sacred self. The dialogic structures of Renaissance drama highlight
the contingency of hierarchy and cosmic order while not necessarily
privileging ordinary life in their stead. As Alastair Fowler compellingly
demonstrates, 'Shakespeare's natural world is not ours', and multiple
representational strategies were needed to integrate the representation of
an individual: 'character is partly distributed among personal mirrors or
surrogates'.[52] The father is the fullest surrogate for an individual because in
a sense the son is a surrogate for him: father and son paradoxically both
displace and guarantee one another. The ethical discontinuities involved in
this issue seem to force a kind of mannerist representational strategy onto
drama,[53] which tries to unify the discontinuous self of either the father or

the son. Renaissance dramatic forms may constitute a method of supplying unification that was missing from the ideology of the times.

This imaginatively fruitful problem is rooted in the politicizing of social and familial structures. Alexandra Shepard concludes that 'Discussions of generational difference served to define patriarchal manhood, and firmly claimed it for the middle-aged householder',[54] and D. M. Palliser observes that Elizabethan society 'was composed of households; and only the heads of those households constituted the "commonwealth" or political nation. The rest of the population was subsumed (to adopt an ugly but necessary term) under those heads.'[55] Such subsumption is an important element of dramatic economy, but there were bound to be tensions, partly based on the problems men had in defining women's roles. Antony Fletcher argues that:

> men's long-established and traditional conception of womankind as the weaker vessel, it seems, left them [women] in possession of sources of power which men found mysterious and threatening. Meanwhile men's overall conceptions of gender, in terms of hierarchy rather than incommensurable difference, gave them an insufficiently competent means of imposing a patriarchal order rooted in nature.[56]

It may be that the 'journey [of masculinity] ended, if the moralists had their way, with the sober manhood of the little patriarch ordering his household of wife, children and servants',[57] but the world of drama, much less of real life, did not necessarily conform to the moralists' narrative: the patriarch is always aware of his littleness, and his position of authority frequently only gives a greater chance of his being humiliated. The father's responsibility for his children's actions – and those of his wife and servants, for that matter – came close to being codified in law;[58] the effect of this was bound to be more burdensome than empowering. Crucially, in drama, the idea of life being defined by productivity (of whatever kind) is not as pressingly present as it is in poetry,[59] leaving the father at rather a loose end. Yet that loose end does have a role.

In Dekker's *Satiromastix* (1601), we get a classic statement of the analogy between kings and fathers, but the dramatic situation undermines it. The king (William Rufus) tells the newly married Sir Walter Terrill that his wife is:

> now thy fadom, thy new world,
> That brings thee people, and makes little subjects
> Kneele at thy feete, obay in euerie thing,
> So euerie Father is a priuate King.   (II. i. 161–4)[60]

Yet the king is using this rhetoric to flatter Terrill, as he has *droit de seigneur* designs on the bride; the analogy becomes a justification for rapacious desire: if the husband can play the role of the king, the king can play the husband's. Significantly, it is the bride's father who gets her out of having to sleep with the king: he gives her a sleeping draught, telling her that it is poison, thus enabling her to keep her chastity while her husband can keep his oath to the king. The actual father has a real authority here that transcends that of a tyrannous monarch: as he says, he bears 'the chiefest part' in the drama (V. ii. 98).[61] Yet, at the same time, he is only a 'private king': the idea of privacy in the Renaissance still suggests deprivation rather than privilege. He is always the lesser man, and this applies particularly acutely after the succession of James in 1603. If fathers had some sense of privilege, of being at the top of a hierarchy under Elizabeth, that fantasy was clearly exploded after the queen's death.

Even in Elizabethan drama, though, the key role that a father can play is a restraining one. The concept of a 'stay' is crucial to many earlier Elizabethan dramatic presentations of fathers and their relation to their children: the word has a fruitful ambiguity, in that it can mean both support and restraint; yet there is also an imbalance in the proper uses of this ambiguity, for while fathers can both support and restrain their children, children can only support but not restrain their fathers. The asymmetry of the relationship is nicely conveyed in this, and it can be the source of some important tensions. By the time of the late Elizabethan drama, however, it is the son who becomes a 'stay' on his father: as in *Wily Beguiled* (Anon., c. 1602, pub. 1606, line 338).[62] The obligation for a father to be a 'stay' to his children means that he must also be 'staid' – that is, sober and restrained. Yet a further implication of this seems to be that fathers cannot act very much at all: and in drama almost all direct paternal action is presented as disastrous. One crucial effect of this is that paternal and filial feelings frequently lead to scenes of vacillation and even impasse – developed perhaps most fully in the whole structure of *Hamlet*.

The presence or absence of fathers plays a key role in our sense of a young man's position in the world of a play. In allegorical interludes such as *The Marriage of Wit and Science* (c. 1569), as in Spenser's *The Faerie Queene*,[63] the hero who must realize his virtue tends to have a mother but no father, as a father would represent the virtue as already achieved. An exception is Francis Merbury's *The Marriage between Wit and Wisdom* (1579), in which Wit's father Severity is introduced from the first; this is an interesting variation, as the figure of Severity is often the judge in such interludes, punishing the sinners and the Vice towards the end of the play. Such a position also pushes the mother aside: whereas *Wit and Science* has Nature as the mother, here the mother is Indulgence – a figure who constitutes a critique of maternal coddling. Despite his importance, however, Severity only appears at the interlude's beginning and end: Wit must be on his own in the central plot struggles, even if he is consistently helped by his tutor Good Nurture. As the drama matures in the later Elizabethan period, it is striking how absent mothers are. Indeed, as mothers are most commonly introduced along with very young children, the presence of a mother is generally a sign that the son is not fully mature, a fact that may have some importance for *Hamlet*.[64] The father is a validating and judging presence, whatever his personal motivations, and this contributes to our sense of his doubleness.

Doubleness, however, may entail the threat of nothingness. In *The Three Lords and Three Ladies of London*, the titular ladies Lucre, Love, and Conscience have an adopted father who is a central figure of authority to all in the play's world; yet he is called Nemo ('No One'), suggesting that such a father figure is a mere notion – wholly disinterested, and even less a person than the other allegorical characters.[65] In some ways, he takes on the queen's role (this is a play which celebrates the defeat of the Spanish Armada); rather than present her directly, it seems preferable to displace her authority onto a cipher of a father. It is unusual for a tragic figure to have a living father: the appearance of a protagonist's father might therefore seem to be a guarantee of a happy ending, acting as a blessing, even. But when the father plays such a role, his own personality may be effaced.

Although this book will give a good deal of attention to fathers and daughters, it is clear that the pressures of that relationship are somewhat less than those that obtain between fathers and sons: the daughter must to some extent renounce and be renounced by her father when she marries, as her husband must become her be-all and end-all; but there is no such attenuation of the father–son bond in marriage. In a sense, a father will always be more important than a wife, and can only be displaced by a son. Yet daughters often represent familial emotions that sons struggle to express; due to the sheer ideological pressure on sons, there is seldom room for much emotion to be expressed between fathers and sons.[66] A father of a daughter may represent the father in his private aspect, a father of a son in turn embodying the public aspect. Accordingly, drama rarely presents a father of both a son and a daughter: Titus Andronicus is one obvious instance, as is Polonius. We shall see that Titus is presented as acutely torn between his public and private roles – killing his daughter may constitute a choice of the public role. Polonius, meanwhile, is a curiously limited figure: his original name (in the First Quarto) seems to have been Corambis, which implies that he has a double heart. Being a father of both a son and a daughter almost doubles the self, because the self is partly invested in others.

What we must constantly bear in mind about Renaissance drama (as Stanley Cavell, Charles Taylor, Harry Berger, and Alastair Fowler all emphasize in different ways) is that moral representation takes precedence over the psychological: this does not mean that people of the Renaissance were fundamentally different from modern people, but that their priorities and interests came from different angles, focussing on the tensions between what one ought to do and what one does rather than on what kind of person one is; nor does it mean that this drama is less human, or that its interests are less in individuals – it is simply that the individuals' moral position was often taken as more generalizable (even if often alarmingly discontinuous), and therefore more likely to implicate the audience.

Some degree of confusion is therefore inevitable in Renaissance drama's representation of a valorized self: as Harry Berger argues, the subject is 'a project of (self) representation that shuttles between the deictic poles of self and other driven by a never fulfilled and perpetually renewed desire for identification – for "the armor of an alienating identity"';[67] in other words, the more important someone is in the drama of the period, and the stronger his (usually his) sense of self, the more he needs to find someone else to be his guaranteeing other; sometimes this is a friend, sometimes a lover or hero, but most often a son or a father.[68] Strangely, though, the armour of this other person can also be an Achilles' heel. By allowing someone else to be the validator of one's identity, one becomes vulnerable to the vagaries of that person's subjectivity. Sons are vulnerable through their fathers, fathers through their sons *and* their daughters. Paternal and filial bonds may allow for the practice of virtue, but they also limit it, and often lead a man into courses that are anything but virtuous.

The range of texts covered in this book is designed to give a cumulative sense of a general dramatic pattern, one which illuminates the practices of the playwrights who are most studied by considering their relationship to more minor or unfairly neglected drama. There are few literary forms in which it is feasible to read the entire surviving corpus, and doing so gives fascinating perspectives on what is really important and unusual in the period. Setting the major plays of the Renaissance in this larger context is perhaps the only way of getting at what is typical and what atypical in those great works. It also throws attention and, I hope, light on a large number of plays that often are, if not *King Lear*, at least quite startling and interesting – some of them are even very good. There are good reasons for calling a halt at 1625: that year sees the death of James I, and also that of the most important dramatist of the second half of his reign, John Fletcher; several hugely significant plays also appear in that year or the next: Jonson's *The Staple of News* (discussed in *Poetry and Paternity*), Heywood's *The English Traveller*, Webster and Rowley's *A Cure for a Cuckold*, Webster's *Appius and Virginia*, and Massinger's *The Unnatural Combat*. Middleton also died two years later, and it is reasonable to think that a distinct phase in the theatre ends in the mid 1620s.

Though genre is central to this book, I have chosen to take a more broadly chronological rather than a wholly generic approach in the organization of chapters; despite the immense uncertainties of chronology, this illuminates key trends and the way these interact with changing social and political circumstances; perhaps more importantly, though, I don't want to separate tragedy and comedy too radically – there is an intensely rewarding oscillation between the comic and the tragic in Elizabethan and Jacobean drama's presentation of the condition of paternity, and this dynamism is perhaps unique to the period. There seems to have been a genuine sense of a theatrical repertoire at the time. In such plays as *Mucedorus* (a comedy, pub. 1598; probably perf. 1590 or earlier) and *A Warning for Fair Women* (a tragedy), the genre's presiding deities appear as chorus, and in their epilogues they promise the appearance of other genres the next day.[69] This metatheatrical awareness of an alternating generic repertoire (with the appearance of history as a third genre, at least in the prologue to *A Warning*) enables a sense of give and take between the different kinds of drama. I would further suggest that this enables each genre to act as a kind of catharsis to the emotions stirred in the other, thus licensing certain dissatisfactions and irresolutions *within* each play. The idea of a repertoire (even a canon) forces originality of plot onto later playwrights – something particularly evident in the moot-court plot contrivances of Fletcher's later work (many derived from Senecan legal thought-experiments). It also helps to explain the movement towards tragicomedy as the dominant mode: it is easier to be at least superficially original with a mixture (as one can vary the way in which one mixes things up); it is also possible in the mixed genre to incorporate a sense of the wider repertoire itself, allowing the part to reflect the pattern of the whole. Fathers are crucial figures in the early stages of tragicomedy around 1610, but the genre's development increasingly marginalizes them.

The interaction between the genres gradually increases the range of possible action in both: if a son can desire or welcome the death of his father in a comedy because that genre guarantees a happy outcome, this has the effect that such desires become more commonplace and can ultimately be realized in tragedy as the grandest intergenerational conflicts (e.g. those of *Hamlet* and *King Lear*); in turn, tragedy's pressing of the pathos of paternity may ultimately give more serious weight to a father's feelings in comedy (e.g. *The Tempest*). Even as the drama relies on father figures as a steady centre, it starts to imagine more flexible roles for them.

If a son's identity in some sense resides in his father, and a father's in his son, the very idea of patrilineal identity may be a self-sustaining fiction, or even a phantom. Drama continually pushes characters towards the awful recognition of this – in tragedy – or towards the acceptance of this – in comedy. The promised end is never quite the self-realization that is expected. The role of fathers in drama is rather like the role of kings in chess: they are crucial to the structure of the game, yet their scope of action is limited; much of their value comes from their vulnerability, and the necessity of either defending them (in comedy), or attacking them (in tragedy). Yet the rules about fathers do vary in the different theatrical genres. It is a key contention of this book that the rules of these genres are not only affected by historical events, hopes, and fears, but by the playing of the games – the playing out of tragedy affects comedy, and *vice versa*. One need hardly add that Shakespeare is the most skilful and influential player of these games, and that a significant part of his influence is in his ability to imbue the games with emotional meaning and political force. Only when we understand the rules and limits of the dramatic games he and others were playing can we understand more fully the force and meaning of his greatest plays.

Like Sophocles' aged Oedipus, and like Nemo in *Three Lords and Three Ladies*, the father is 'a kind of nothing' (to use the phrase from *Coriolanus* – V. i. 13). Yet everything comes from that nothing. The ghost in Hamlet is 'nothing at all', according to Gertrude (III. iv. 132). Nothing, also, is the insistent keyword of Leontes' jealousy in *The Winter's Tale* (I. ii. 292–5), as well as the only response that Cordelia can give her father. The word is often associated with femininity, specifically with the female genitals, yet this book will contend that the drama of Shakespeare's time more insistently suggests that fathers are the real and original nothing. There are many different kinds of nothing: the father evolves over the course of the Elizabethan and Jacobean periods, and as a result the form of drama changes too.

CHAPTER 2

Staying fathers in early Elizabethan drama: Gorboduc to The Spanish Tragedy

The roles of fathers in earlier Elizabethan drama are circumscribed: the limitations of their roles are partly affected by generic expectations, but, in turn, social rules about fathers help to mark out the developing rules of dramatic genres. Paternal action frequently results in disaster in tragedy and humiliation in comedy, but fathers are initially protected from these outcomes by being marginalized in various ways. Much early comedy, however, derives from romance norms, which push closer to tragic outcomes than comedy proper (or at least in its more obviously classical modes) would, and romance plays give more of a role to fathers (if not much more agency), enabling us to see how they might react to potential disaster and humiliation. The genres affect each other's sense of what is possible/representable, and given that fathers are taboo figures they often act as determinative limits on the generic game. This chapter will start with a discussion of early tragedy's pushing at and setting up of limits, then consider the apparently safer ground of romantic comedy, with a brief excursion into more straightforward/classical comic modes, before returning to the tragedies that become increasingly dominant in the late 1580s/early 1590s: such plays are, I shall argue, inflected by the romance mode of the plays that had dominated the previous decade. The result of this is that fathers are or ought to be comforting figures in these tragedies, but begin to have an almost meta-tragic awareness of their own status as non-agents, a process that culminates in *Titus Andronicus* and *The Spanish Tragedy*.

The crucial development here is that fathers start off as merely notional exemplary figures in early tragedy, but gradually, through their roles in romantic plays, acquire emotional significance, enabling them to become more complex objects (and subjects) of recognition in later Elizabethan drama, even if their practical roles are increasingly circumscribed. In other words, what we see is the slow gestation of the father's selfhood, where earlier he was a mere notion or idea; yet the almost sacred idea of the father continues to operate even as he becomes more individual. This process culminates with the carefully licensed but strangely alienated revenge action of Hieronimo in Kyd's masterpiece, *The Spanish Tragedy*, and would ultimately have an enormous effect on Shakespeare's generation, for Shakespeare himself never forgot the fashions of his youth, to which he contributed, forcefully and ironically, in *Titus Andronicus*.

EARLY TRAGEDY

Sackville and Norton's *Gorboduc*, praised by Sidney in *The Defense of Poesy*, is the starting-point for the major tradition of Renaissance English drama, and it is no accident that it is centred on the relation between a father and his sons. The conflict between the generations, indeed, is nicely expressed in the fact that the second edition of the play is named *Ferrex and Porrex*: whether the old generation or the new is the true focus of dramatic interest is a key question throughout the dramatic tradition considered in this study. Drama, as the word's etymology implies, involves movement and action, but the father is insistently presented as a 'stay': the word, whose meanings include anchoring restraint, peacemaker, protector, and preventer of action, is used hundreds of times in the play.[1] If a true father is really bound to be a successful stay on action, dramatic form almost *requires* that such a figure be displaced, for he is alien to drama. On the other hand, the root meaning of the word, a rope supporting a mast, may suggest that a 'stay' allows some sort of movement, while preventing that movement from getting out of hand: the father, like God, is the guarantor of all action; indeed, the word has strong Biblical resonances – e.g. 'The Lord was my stay' (2 Samuel 22.19 – Geneva Bible). *Gorboduc* is concerned with how easy it is to lose such a stay, which results in chaos for the realm, and for the form of drama.

The authors' chief ideological concern was evidently to urge Queen Elizabeth to name a successor, demonstrating what might happen to the kingdom if there was no certainty about the matter.[2] Yet most elements of the play are not strictly necessary or even appropriate to the promulgation of that message. The debate in Act I is over two questions – whether the king should abdicate, and whether he should divide his realm between his sons – neither of which had any relevance to Elizabeth's position in the 1560s. Only the chaos of Act V, in which Fergus of Albany (Scotland) tries to take the throne, relates to contemporary fears – that rule by the heir presumptive, Queen Mary of Scotland, would entail the ruin of England. The core of the play is more abstractly concerned with how a father may influence his sons, even once he has lost his nominal authority; if the king is reduced to the mere *idea* of a father, without direct power, can he still provide a moral centre? This question is pertinent to Elizabeth's own time, of course, in that the notion of centralized masculine authority had to be attached to a woman who was not even a mother, much less a father. Gorboduc's actions, then, may relate more to the problems created by Henry VIII than to Elizabeth's own situation, though even that is not a matter of straightforward allegory. Henry had hardly abdicated prematurely, though he had perhaps compromised the basis of his authority with his religious vacillations and associated marital caprices; he had also obviously not divided the kingdom spatially, but perhaps had done so in more temporal terms, by having three children who ruled successively without producing successors themselves. In some sense, Henry had fragmented the centralized notion of patriarchal power, and paradoxically had done so by being so central a patriarchal figure himself. As we shall often see, the more powerful the father figure (Henry V, for instance), the more problematic a legacy does he leave to his successors, whose failures to live up to their progenitor are made particularly acute by the comparison. Whether this involves a cyclical attitude to history, or a slightly different sense that Providence compensates for any excessive successes, it is clear that most drama of the time presents a powerful predecessor as more ominous than reassuring to the present.

It is not clear whether Sackville and Norton consider Gorboduc's abdication and division of the kingdom as acts of hubris. Unlike Shakespeare's Lear, to whom he is obviously a forerunner, he is supported by at least one of his council: his 'purpose' (I. i. 132) is not dark like Lear's,[3] but rationally argued out. Arostus supports both aspects of the plan, and Philander supports the division of the kingdom; only Eubulus argues against both the division and the abdication – and though his name suggests that his advice is right, and this is supported by events, the arguments in favour are strong. Arostus argues that the abdication will be good because 'Your lasting age shall be their longer stay' (line 169) – following from Gorboduc's own point that they will best learn to rule while their father is still around to supervise; both he and Gorboduc give less in the way of clear reasons for the division of the kingdom, which seems to be based on the not fully articulated position that the two sons will be mutually supporting – an idea conveyed in the image of tied faggots being unbreakable in the initial dumb-show – and the rather ingenuous idea that fathers should share things fairly. There are in fact hints that the abdication is only necessary because of the division rather than *vice versa*: there will be greater need, says Arostus, for:

> Your eye, your counsel, and the grave regard
> Of father, yea, of such a father's name,
> Now at beginning of their sundered reign,
> When is the hazarde of their whole success. (lines 179–82)

In fact, it is the division rather than the abdication that causes the problem, as the first scene presenting the elder son Ferrex's jealousy suggests. Unlike in *King Lear*, there is no hint that Gorboduc has a real favourite child, but it is clear that the mother Videna does favour Ferrex, and she accuses her husband of being 'In kind a father, not in kindliness' (I. i. 18) because he is giving equal shares to sons who are apparently equally virtuous. Maternal jealousy rather than paternal division of the kingdom might in fact be seen as the root problem: in a play where the princes are driven to civil war by bad counsellors, and which clearly suggests that warning against bad counsel is a major didactic theme, perhaps Videna is simply the first to give bad, jealous, emotive advice that steers a young man away from the staid position of his father. Even in arguing against the abdication, Philander recognizes that both sons are 'Undoubted children of so good a king' (line 286); how, then, if they are such perfect representations of their father, do they descend to vice? It can only be because of their mother. In the end, it is her killing of Porrex that prompts the people to rebel, killing her and Gorboduc, and turning the nation to anarchy. Even Videna, however, is not blamed too much for killing Porrex: she is described as driven by the furies, and thus not in control of herself (IV. Chorus); but that is the supposed problem with women, who do not base their actions on reason. The ills of emotive femininity may be the play's central target, then, getting close to an indictment of female rule such as Elizabeth's. However, if women here are treated as putting the spanner in the works, later drama, particularly in the Jacobean period, will start to present them as the solvers of problems.

As we tend to read the play through the lens of *King Lear*,[4] we may tend to blame Gorboduc more than the authors intended. His action is not selfishly based, but founded on the desire to do good to 'our country, mother of us all' (I. ii. 140); this maternal interest is holistic and unifying, in contrast to the selectively loving Videna. It is Gorboduc's desire to unify which, paradoxically, drives his desire to divide the kingdom: his initial case for abdication suggests that the relationship between father and sons is a kind of zero-sum game, but not a direct competition. Yet we

might detect an underlying sense that two sons add up to one of himself –
it is in this, perhaps, that his motives are egotistical. He tells the court that
the gods

> Gave me two sons in my more lusty age,
> Who now in my decaying years, are grown
> Well towards riper state of mind and strength,
> To take in hand some greater princely charge.
> As yet they live and spend their hopeful days
> With me, and with their mother, here in court.
> Their age now asketh other place and trade,
> And mine also doth ask another change,
> Theirs to more travail, mine to greater ease.   (lines 118–26)

If these sons, conceived as outgrowths of the self, growing ripe as he
decays, are not to 'spend' themselves unnecessarily, they need a task;
Gorboduc believes that he is engaged in rational husbandry of resources.
Their later conflict with one another is not fundamentally founded on
anything their father does, but on their failure to take advice from him;
unlike Lear, he remains a figure to be reckoned with, one who could still
punish them, as even the parasite Hermon recognizes (II. i). He could still
'stay this hatefull strife' (III. i. 86), and would have 'stayed this mischief'
had either son sent to him for help or advice (line 92); Gorboduc is still, in
Philander's terms, 'the only hope of stay' (line 130). In contrast to emotive
motherhood, paternal rule is shown to be calm and rational: Gorboduc,
though very angry at Porrex for killing his brother, is prepared to 'stay our
will' (IV. ii. 112) and listen to a defence. This ultimate stay contrasts
strongly with Videna's vengeful passion.

Written under a female ruler, *Gorboduc* evinces a nostalgia for male
paternal rule (even if the last example, Henry VIII, had not exactly been
clement), but cannot dramatize its re-emergence with any emotive force.
Eubulus, after the death of the royal family, wishes that the people would
pay attention to their *fathers'* warnings against rebellion (V. ii), as that
would be the only way to 'stay their lewd rebellious hands' (line 173). As
the royal stay has been lost, however, nothing can bring about resolution,
no true successor can be named, and the play cannot have anything like a
satisfactory ending. This problem is not Gorboduc's fault, or at least not
directly: if he has a tragic flaw (and one should be suspicious of such a
notion), it is his indispensability. This is a different kind of tragedy, in
which terrible things happen because one man was too good. It will often,
at least in the early Elizabethan period, be the keynote of tragic (and
sometimes comic) dramatic fatherhood.

The presumption of paternal goodness drives much early Elizabethan tragedy, and perhaps accounts for some of its dramatic limitations (limitations here being more a weakness than an aesthetic necessity). In *Apius and Virginia*, by 'R. B.' (probably Richard Bower), the father Virginius kills his daughter to prevent her being ravished by the tyrannous Apius. Though the play is a strong candidate to be regarded as the worst written in the period, it highlights some important issues:[5] the paternal killing is regarded as entirely legitimate, even heroic, and the father's action is wholly independent of the family structure with which the play begins – his loyal wife disappears in the later acts. The righteous authority of a father is asserted against the power of a tyrant, and it is important that the rights of an individual are encoded in this way, for only as a father is one an individual with sufficient credit to defy the state.

The play begins with a family happy to the point of idealized perfection (they even sing songs about how happy they all are, which gives a pretty good hint that they won't be for long). That perfection is emphasized by the deployment of what would become a standard comedic trope: the father eavesdropping on his family. Contrary to the proverb, Virginius hears only good of himself – there is no subversion to be found among his womenfolk, and perfection is only to be unsettled by external desires of Apius, assisted by the Vice Haphazard. The lack of any tension within the family deprives us of real drama here, emphasizing the public but not the private role of the father. Virginia is not only willing to be sacrificed, but actively so, saying, 'Oh father mine, refraine no whit, your sharped knife to take, / From giltles sheath, my shame to end, and body dead to make' (lines 952–3).[6] Apius may call Virginius 'carll vnnaturall' (line 1048), but the allegorical figures of Justice and Reward enter to condemn the tyrant instead, and Fame celebrates the father's deed. The play leaves no room for doubt as to the justice of Virginius' actions – there is no dissentingly 'natural' voice from the mother, for example. The right to preserve family honour is in no way challenged. It is for this reason, as much as for the inclusion of comic scenes of familial quarrelling among the servant class, that the play is called a 'Tragicall Comedie': Virginius' preservation of his honour constitutes a happy ending, its mood being more characteristic of comedy than tragedy. He can be regarded as almost proverbially the ideal father, a point that has important implications for *Titus Andronicus*, as we shall see.

At this stage, dramatists were still casting around for classical precedents to enable fully tragic selfhood in a father, yet the versions of the Oedipus myth chosen at this time focus on the hero's role as a son more than that as a father. Alexander Neville's version of Seneca's *Oedipus* (1563) is the major English exemplar of the classic myth in the sixteenth century. Already much more laborious than Sophocles' great play, its anguished moralizations are further complicated by the translator's attempts to accommodate the original's stoic ethic with a protestant world-view. Oedipus' fated crimes are considered as illustrative of a state of predestined original sinfulness; indeed, the crimes are almost considered as being punishments for the state of sin from which Oedipus cannot escape, rather than as causes in themselves ('*Vnto Apollo knowen he was, / or euer he was borne*' – Biv[r]).[7] As such, they do not impinge much on the personality of the protagonist, who is simply a prototype of man in a state of sin. His self-punishment and exile, however, do operate cathartically, clearing the air for his people. The predestined sinner is therefore made into a scapegoat figure – a fact which may offer implicit justification for God choosing to damn some people before their birth.

The people are 'in a fearfull staye' as the play begins, for 'the plage cannot be stayed' (Avii[r]); paradoxically, the cause of all these problems will become their stay and stay their troubles, by destroying himself. The Chorus conclude that 'As fates, decrees, so things do run. / no man can make them stay' (Ev[r]), but the attempt to learn lessons here seems rather futile, amounting to 'Aduyse the well and staye' (Ev[v]). The play's moral seems to be that all action is suspect. Even when blinded at the end, Oedipus adds to his crimes when Jocasta throws himself onto his knife. Seneca's addition to Sophocles is also an addition to the prophecy against Oedipus; as such, it seems so excessive that it pushes beyond the tragic into the comic: in the end he even has to tell himself 'Stay. / Lest on thy Mother thou do fall' (Fi[v]).[8] No action is possible for man in such a condition.

Yet Oedipus' deed in mutilating himself is ultimately treated as admirable. What Seneca added to the Greek original was a strong sense of paternal anger, which becomes a motive for action: as Creon reports, having descended to the underworld, Laius is furious with Oedipus for killing him; in Sophocles, the sense of Nemesis is more abstract – the order of nature being wronged and the gods offended rather than the father being vengeful. Hence, perhaps, the need for excessive violence in Oedipus' self-mutilation: he is acting as a personal avenger for his father rather than just trying to set right a world that is out of joint. He wants, so the Nuntius tells us, to 'recompense [his] fa- / thers death sufficiently' (Eii[v]); the unusual stretch of the word 'father' over the line-break suggests an unusual strain in being both avenger and criminal. The need for sufficient recompense causes excess; he not only blinds himself, but chews and stamps on his eyes, mutilating his face, raging 'more than nedes' (Eiiii^r). He calls this act 'My Fathers rites' (Evi^r), and once it is done he is in some sense vindicated.

One of the play's most extraordinary moments comes when the Senex reports the death of Oedipus' adopted father; the son responds 'And is he deade in dede? Not slayn? / What joye may I conceyve?' (Div^r). Such an unfilial moment would be shocking to an Elizabethan audience, but the real irony comes in the word 'conceive', which hints at the hero's desire to conceive a proper family. That, precisely, is what Oedipus cannot do: in killing his father he has denied himself the opportunity to be a true father himself. It is significant that his children do not appear on stage in this version: perhaps, being incestuously begotten, they are too horrific a sight, but their absence indicates Oedipus' lack of the self-realization that paternity supposedly brings. Having taken his father's place, he can only realize his father, not himself.

Oedipus is genuinely puzzled that Polybus and Merope should have adopted him, asking:

> What vauntage shuld it be to her
>   adopted Sonnes to haue?
> SENEX. A kyngdom she shall gayne therby.
>   Her Husbande layde in graue.
> The chiefest prop to stay her Realms
>   from present Confusion,
> Is Children for to haue: and hope
>   of lawfull succession.   (Dv^r)

The standard terms regarding children are used here (Tiresias had earlier called his daughter 'myne onely prop and staye', meaning this quite literally, due to his blindness – Bvii^r), but they have some contemporary force for Neville, given the parliamentary efforts of the time to get Queen Elizabeth to marry. It is significant in this light that Creon is Oedipus' successor, rather than his children. Oedipus, who ought to be a patriarch, is reduced to being a 'Paracide' (Evi^r). The parricide is a parasite, the pun implies, but he has enough of his father's spirit in him to remove the interloper. Being a son, he cannot be a father.

The story of Oedipus comes again to the Elizabethan stage in a version of Euripides' *Phoenissae* translated by George Gascoigne and Francis Kinwelmersh called *Jocasta* and derived from an Italian version of that name by Lodovico Dolce. As in Euripides' original and Dolce's intermediate version, Oedipus, that most dubious of paternal figures, is marginalized.

Owing to his (accidental) crimes, he lacks the regal authority that should be his, but he also seems to lack paternal authority over his sons and daughter (the other daughter Ismene does not appear); this may be due to the fact that he is as much a sibling to his children as a father, though the play does not state this directly. In fact, the one thing he is explicitly described as being guilty of is the murder of his father – this act may have destroyed all notions of paternal authority in the play-world. As the title given to the play by Dolce and Gascoigne implies, it is Jocasta who is the more important figure here. Oedipus has been imprisoned by his sons, for the odd reason that he 'Should reape no joy of his unnatural fruite' (I. i. 145),[9] and he has cursed them for this unfilial act. Late in the play Creon describes him as 'here on earth the onely soursse of evill' (V. ii. 36). In contrast to the 'giltlesse' Jocasta, Oedipus is called 'giltie' even by the loyal Antigone (V. iii. 43), principally, we infer, owing to his killing of his own father: the unwitting incest is morally if not divinely forgivable, but the patricide, though also unwitting (and having taken place in war and not as a result of anger as in the now more familiar Sophoclean version), cannot be mitigated.

The play's preoccupation with and marginalization of fathers is further accentuated by the scenes in which Creon is told that his son Meneceus must be sacrificed to save the city. Here Dolce alters the original in having the son insist on dying and the father resist this, so that we have a scene of ultimate filial piety in which Meneceus expresses his desire to sacrifice himself for both his father and his city. Unlike Creon he is prepared to put city before self, as Creon's refusal to kill his son is conceived as selfish. This is a crucial starting-point for the common idea in Renaissance drama that a son may be more virtuous than his father, while still having to revere that father. The play's argument calls Creon 'the type of Tyranny' (line 21), and though this seems a little unfair, it is clear that fatherhood has become infected with the vice of tyranny. On the other hand, the play's other father Oedipus is too lofty to descend to quarrels with Creon (as he says, 'Do what thou canst I will be *Oedipus*' (V. v. 53)), yet this may also reflect his loss of a real paternal position, at least in the private, emotive sense. Antigone's strength looks forward to Cordelia, and Oedipus' weakness to that of Lear. Like Lear he remains every inch a king, but has been ruled out of any effective sphere of action.

The focus on sons of powerful fathers continues in John Pikeryng's *Horestes* (1567), the earliest English revenge tragedy, which probably allegorizes contemporary Scottish politics, particularly the murder of James VI's father,[10] and seems to suggest the need to punish Mary Queen of Scots for her involvement. Yet the play seems rather limited by its agenda.

Horestes is driven to kill his mother not out of a passionate need to vindicate his identity as his father's son, but as an agent of justice: so keen is the playwright to insist on the lawfulness of punishing Mary that no passion can be introduced. Indeed, the passion of revenge is dismissed along with its avatar, the Vice who pretends to be Patience and Courage, but turns out to be Revenge. Horestes has been inspired by the gods, not by a paternal ghost; rejecting the counsel of Nature (presumably female), he is validated by all the men around him, particularly the kings Idumeneus and Nestor. Clearly proposing a similar outcome for Scotland, the play concludes with the restoration of masculine amity; even Menelaus (who for some reason has been irked by his brother being avenged) is appeased, marrying his daughter to Horestes. Agamemnon, whose memory haunts the Greek plays on this subject, is thought of very little here; perhaps because the allegory makes him equivalent to Darnley, from whom James did not derive his regal status, he is not really presented as a model for his son; indeed, Idumeneus' council say of Horestes that he does not follow 'his fathers steppes, in feates of cheuallrey', but rather imitates Achilles (line 346).[11] Masculine emulation is everything in this world, and Horestes has many alternative models/fathers supporting him. He may rue killing his mother, but this is soon forgotten as he goes on to be a model ruler. The play concludes with Revenge insisting that endless vengeance is only really a feminine trait: masculinity, if one imitates the proper models, can do without such passion. Only by removing the father from revenge drama can the situation of the son become unproblematic.

As in classically inspired plays, the restraint of passion is pivotal to plays which use Biblical models of fatherhood for tragic purposes in the early Elizabethan period. Theodore Beza's *Abraham's Sacrifice*, translated by Arthur Golding in 1575, offers an essentially Calvinist line on the classic story of a father subordinating paternal feeling to godly duty. Beza adds little to the Biblical account other than having Satan on stage (dressed as a catholic monk) to offer some rather half-hearted temptations, but the play's language shows how much of a preoccupation the possession of a male heir could be. Satan hopes to make Abraham 'a sonne of mine', and questions that 'If stedfastnes him faile / To hold out still: what shall his hope auaile?' (p. 10)[12] – the word 'hope' being used so frequently for sons becomes a kind of metonymy: the father must be steadfast in being prepared to lose his hope. Abraham is indeed phlegmatic in his woe, as his response to the angel's demand indicates: though he thinks his task 'straunge and irksom', he says 'What! burne him! burne him! wel I wil do so' (p. 11). The most significant consolation Abraham can give himself is that God's demand for the sacrifice is incompatible with the Promise he has also had of endless descendants, a thought that almost tempts him into disobedience. His 'hope' (p. 33) is for a whole nation, embodied in Isaac, but he is still prepared to kill him, unnatural as that is. Sons are presented as the greatest of all consolations, bringing one the hope to live 'in ioy and pleasure' (p. 34) – but of course the truest pleasure is to be found in his son's obedience and his own, which secures '*much more happy yssue*' (p. 46), without, of course, finally having to make this bargain. Abraham gets to have his son and his obedience too, and so remains a paradigmatic instance of the good father, one whose public and private roles are in full accord.

Wicked or at least excessive fathers do gradually emerge. In moral interludes, the Vices are often presented as sons to Satan: Ill Report in Thomas Garter's *The Virtuous and Godly Susanna* (1569) is amusingly presented as an inversion of the loyal son, abusing his 'Dad' as a 'shitten slaue' (lines 54, 61) and being praised for it, receiving in return a fond blessing made up of traditional curses (lines 118–30).[13] Sometimes, as in *Like Will to Like*, the Vice is Satan's godson, a term that can only be used ironically in such a context. In Nathaniell Woodes's *The Conflict of Conscience* (1581), Satan asserts that:

> The mortall men by natures rule is bound
> That child to fauour, more then all the rest,
> Which to himselfe in face, is lykest found:
> So that he shall with all his goodes be blest.   (lines 31–4)[14]

He uses this 'natural' argument to justify his own love for his favourite son, the Pope (who does not actually appear in the play). This ironizes the issue of paternal love, particularly when claims are later made for the Pope's paternal authority (lines 1164–8). A truer sense of what paternal example might mean is given at the end of the play, when Philologus' devilishly inspired earthly prosperity is marked by his sons' gratitude, and they then witness his debate with Theologus (whom they have called to his aid) about his salvation. In one version of the play he cannot repent, though he does so in a revised text: in both cases the presence of his sons serves to point up his case as an example (either to be shunned or followed). Paternal salvation should mean more than prosperity; as Philologus says, even if he is not to be saved, 'My sonnes, my sonnes, I speake to you, my counsell ponder well, / And practise that in deedes, which I in wordes shall to you tell' (lines 2228–9). Although this is a play about *individual* salvation, it is given wider resonance by the fact of its protagonist being a father. Yet what is missing here, still, is a sense of emotional connection with the father. That connection will emerge in comedy.

COMEDY AND ROMANCE

Like tragedy, English comedy starts with the assumption of paternal dignity and restraint, but it is able to go further in eroding its own premises. If *Gorboduc* is the wellspring of the major tradition of English tragedy, George Gascoigne's *Supposes* – a freely expanded but basically faithful version of Ariosto's *I Suppositi* – starts the hare of comedy in England. As in *Gorboduc* the father is a central figure who becomes marginalized from the plot; in fact, the play ultimately presents three fathers, all of whom are defeated by the younger generation, but without being humiliated in the process. The first father, Damon, is betrayed by his servant and daughter, who have engaged in 'petty treason' against his authority.[15] However, we do not encounter Damon until he has seen through this subterfuge, so that there is no scene in which he appears as an ignorant fool. In a passage added by Gascoigne, Damon also shows the self-awareness to realize that the betrayal is partly his own fault: he recognizes that his daughter would have been better brought up if his wife had lived, and goes on to condemn 'my wretched selfe the caytife and causer of all my cares'. The basis of this is the fact that children only owe obedience, whereas:

the parents are bound, first to beget them, then to bring them foorth, after to nourish them, to preserve them from bodily perils in the cradle, from daunger of soule by godly education, to matche them in consort enclined to vertue, to banish them all ydle and wanton companie, to allow them sufficiente for their sustentation, to cut of excesse the open gate of sinne, seldome or never to smile on them unlesse it be to their encouragement in vertue, and finally, to provide them mariages in time convenient, lest neglected of us, they learne to sette either too much or to litle by themselves. (III. iii. 46–61)[16]

The overbearing weight of parental duties, rather than being cause to condemn the child, is used here to suggest that parents are more responsible for their children's actions than the children themselves are, as they have many more fields in which they could fail; Damon goes on (as in Ariosto) to observe that all this has come about because he did not marry his daughter off when he could first have done it. In shouldering the blame thus, Damon garners audience admiration as most later comedic fathers would not. Although he imprisons his servant for seducing

Polynesta, Damon does not fly into a grand rage with his daughter; rather, he has to become complicit with her to some degree, concealing her sexual laxity in order to secure her a marriage (V. vi). The lack of rage means that he does not bring the play anywhere near to tragedy, and that he cannot become ridiculous in the comic ending.

Cleander, Damon's chosen suitor for Polynesta, is the play's other father. An ageing doctor of laws, he only wants to marry the young girl in order to produce offspring, as he lost his only son many years before. When his lost son turns up, Cleander withdraws his claim – acquiring a son puts him back into his proper generation, and rules him out of the play's erotic economy: now that he has a son to leave his estate to, he does not need to remarry; property issues are central to paternalistic desires. Early in the play Cleander doubts the supposed Erostrato's ability to marry Polynesta, saying 'how can he make any dower, and his father yet alive?' (I. ii. 88–9). A father is here presented as an obstacle to marriage, and the essential plot of the play is to remove this problem. Erostrato's father Philogano finally gives his whole property as dowry in order to pay off his son's sin against Damon (V. x. 14–16); all the play's rebellions, by sons and servants, have to be adjusted by paternal negotiation. In this light, it is significant that Erostrato, though the play's romantic hero, does not appear in the final scene, and Cleander's son has a very basic recognition scene, saying only 'O father' (line 34). The fathers, though their wishes have been subverted, retain their authority, without an emphatic triumph for the younger generation such as we will see in later drama.

The generic conventions of romance mean that fathers need to have a more central position before they move aside for the younger generation.[17] The chivalric romance *Clyomon and Clamydes* (Anon., c. 1570, pub. 1599) involves a conflict between knightly duties undertaken on behalf of a lady and those imposed by a father; the latter take precedence throughout for both heroes.[18] Clamydes has to kill a flying serpent in order to win his beloved Juliana, but his father insists that he first hunt down and discover the identity of the disguised Clyomon, who has nipped in and 'stolen' Clamydes' knightly dubbing – until and unless he does so, he is not to look upon his father again. Clyomon's slightly absurd crime is significant in that it constitutes a kind of theft of paternally derived identity (like Jacob taking Esau's birthright). He himself has promised his father that he will not reveal his name unless he is defeated in combat, a vow that causes him considerable problems in his amours with Neronis, the princess of the Strange Marshes. The irony is that his lack of secure identity is driven by the need to retain his 'fathers grace' (line 193);[19] he must gain renown of his own before he is able to claim the paternal blessing that will make him a worthy suitor of a princess. Only an agreement to delay their combat (and some further entanglements) enables the knights to pursue their love-plots; whenever they have the choice, they put their paternal duties first. The play seems to imply that identity is a purely masculine business: though the knights are able to recognize each other, even in disguise, and though there is no confusion in Clyomon's re-encounter with his father, the ladies are unable to see through the simplest disguises. Underpinned by paternal duties, and secured by knightly endeavour, masculine identity is a matter into which women have no insight. Women may be the rewards for chivalric endeavour, but must not be prioritized over the masculine sphere that is the real arena of men's lives.

Paternal absence is therefore a key problem in romance. Possibly the silliest play of the sixteenth century (and that's saying something), the anonymous romance *Common Conditions* is inhabited by singing tinkers, pirates in desperate need of a captain, and a female 'natural' fool in search of nappies for her beloved doll. The play is built around the crazily capricious machination of the Vice Conditions, whose changes of agenda drive the romantic characters to continual escapes and disguises which result in an averted brother–sister incest plot and an inconclusive scene in which a father (probably) tries to kill his daughter. All of these absurdities, however, are only possible because the father figure has been unjustly exiled from his homeland, and has failed to return and take responsibility when he might have done. The exile of a father is a signal of weakness, often associated (as in Plautus' *The Rope*) with loss of one's children.[20] This, of course, would become the central subject of Shakespeare's late plays, which are more informed by early Elizabethan romantic drama than by the theatrical trends of the early Jacobean period. The figure of the exiled father is presented as a teasing dramatic paradox: he is to be reverenced from below, but has no status in the upper political world; a key link in the patriarchal chain has been broken.

Galiarbus begins the play making his blessing conditional on his son Sedmond's abiding loyalty to his sister Clarisia (lines 31–2), and charging him to be a 'stay' for her (line 35).[21] Sedmond fails in this paternal role, running away (admittedly at Clarisia's urging) when they are attacked by the tinkers, thus precipitating all the later plot developments. The brother–sister relationship seems only mediated by their common parenthood: they bicker as to how much grief they should feel for their father's exile; and

Sedmond laments the loss of his sister mostly because he feels guilt at the loss of a jewel truly belonging to his father (line 456). Yet the father is as inadequate as the son: Galiarbus becomes wealthy in his exile, but decides he must 'refraine' and 'forgoe' his children, for the rather flimsy reason that the king who exiled him will imprison them if he sends for them (lines 507–9). Later, in disguise as Leostines,[22] Galiarbus adopts Metrea (really Clarisia) as his heir, but has made no efforts to find his real children. The irony of adopting one's real daughter is pointed – she is to accept him as her 'only sier' (line 1598) – but she in turn betrays him for her lover Lamphedon. Meanwhile, Sedmond, disguised as Nomides, has fallen for Metrea, who fortunately resists his unwittingly incestuous advances.

The play's plot may enact in some rather oblique way the kind of chaos presented more directly in *Gorboduc*, a chaos apparently caused by the absence of paternal authority and sure successors, and whose presentation in other plays constitutes a critique of Queen Elizabeth's refusal to marry – and even perhaps an implicit critique of female rule. The ending of the play does seem to have been censored, and its epilogue pointedly wishes the queen well; but we cannot know what aspect of that conclusion could have caused offence. The closest we get to Elizabeth is in the scene where Metrea–Clarisia persuades her adopted father to let her stay a virgin – a vow she immediately reneges on when her lost lover reappears. This might imply that Elizabeth's vows to Parliament were empty, predicated only on a desire to marry the earl of Leicester once opportunity served.[23] Perhaps the name of the titular Vice, who represents opportunism and equivocation, also hints at this possibility. Yet none of the parallels are particularly pointed in the play as we have it; it may well be that the play, having reached a point where we can guess its ending, tails off in the *pretence* of censorship, in order to give an air of intrigue that the resolution of romance strands would not have in themselves.

As Conditions says several times, his plots and the plot of the play have come to a 'stay' (lines 1746, 1805), the word here meaning a pretty pickle rather than a comfort or support. He also uses the word ironically when Clarisia is tied to a tree by the tinkers (line 436). Absence of paternal support has led to captivity and tangled-up plots. At the very end of the play, Nomides–Sedmond, still in love with his sister, tells Leostines–Galiarbus to 'stay' his hand, as he is about to kill Metrea–Clarisia (line 1888);[24] the son takes on the paternal role (for the wrong reasons) and prevents his father's infanticidal desires, thus allowing the play to be 'A pleasant comedy'. What seems like an impasse fairly obviously contains the route to a resolution. All that remains is for disguises to be doffed, the poison given to Lamphedon to turn out harmless, and Sedmond to accept the love of Sabia (whom he earlier rejected). Absurd as he is, Sabia's father, the Spanish doctor Mountagos, would surely play a part in this conclusion: his complete support for his daughter's love, including the ability to prepare love potions for her, contrasts with the derelictions of Galiarbus. Paternal care is needed to resolve comedies, which otherwise threaten to run out of control. The paternal 'stay' is needed to prevent things being at a 'stay'. The play's inconclusion may therefore be an oblique comment on the absence of such a healingly paternal figure in English politics.

Fathers play a more positively emotional role in *The Rare Triumphs of Love and Fortune* (Anon., pub. 1589; probably perf. 1582). The duke/king Phyzantius opposes his daughter Fidelia's love for his poor ward Hermione, but not as vigorously as his son does: whereas the prince Armenio fights with Hermione and later seeks his utter ruin, acting on behalf of his own sense of his father's honour, Phyzantius himself is only prepared to exile the young lover, even after he has hurt Armenio in a fight. Hermione's own father turns out to be the hermit Bomelio, who was unfairly exiled from court many years before, and this revelation of gentle identity, along with the intervention of Venus and Fortune, is enough for all to be forgiven and the lovers to be happy. Fidelia, who had earlier refused to save her brother's life at her father's insistence, is easily persuaded to do so by her new father-in-law. The superiority of romantic love to birth family enables the restoration of happiness for the lovers, but distinctly undermines paternal authority, suggesting the primacy of private emotion over public position.

If Phyzantius seems ineffective as a ruler and father, Bomelio is much more active, though in decidedly contradictory ways. When he first meets his son, their meeting offers some 'recompence' for the son's apparent loss of Fidelia (Diii[v]),[25] and Bomelio's patience in his long misfortunes seems to provide a model of stoicism for his son. However, Bomelio is not just a foreshadowing of *Cymbeline*'s Belarius, but also of Prospero in *The Tempest*:[26] he has engaged in magical studies in his cave, and uses these to curse Armenio, making the prince dumb. This serious act of vengeance is then turned to comic purposes when Bomelio disguises himself as an Italian physician, in order to gain access to Fidelia and restore her to his son, a process that also enables the aforementioned refusal of the princess to help her brother (her blood is, we are told, necessary for this). In fact, Bomelio is at the centre of the play's very peculiar generic mixing: his magic may help resolve the problems, but it is also very clearly recognized as illegitimate and dangerous to his soul. When Hermione discovers his

father's magical texts, he calls them 'vile blasphemous Bookes', wondering
'What gaine can countervaile the danger that they bring, / For man to sell
his soule to sinne, ist not a greeuous thing?' (Fi ᵛ), and so destroys them to
save his father. The effect, however, is to drive Bomelio mad, as the books
have prevented devils from tormenting him; this is a weirdly serio-comic
madness that undermines his dignity as well as underlining the illegitimacy of his intervention on behalf of his son. Yet in the same speech that
contains Hermione's filial disapproval of magic, he praises his father as a
model of how to bear misfortune:

> The better borne the more his magnanimitie:
> The scarcer sight, the deeper wound, the more vndaunted he.
> So I perceiue it now, I well perceiue it heere:
> What I my selfe could not, I learne by thee my father deere.

Clearly, a father can be a fine model for a son, but it is a father's *past* that
is the object of imitation; present actions are less legitimate as a means of
resolving dramatic problems.

Ultimately, both fathers in *The Rare Triumphs* are shown to be impotent,
even as their position is treated as worthy of respect. The duke, pondering
his need to persuade Fidelia to save her brother, reflects in very standard
terms on the anxieties of paternity: 'He that hath felt the zeale, the tender loue
and care, / The feare the greef that parents deer vnto their children bare / He
may, and only he conceiue mine inward woe' (Eiiiᵛ). Punning on sexual and
intellectual conception, he asserts the privileged emotional understanding
of a father. Yet it is hard to take these sentiments (or *sententiae*) terribly seriously:
Armenio is merely dumb, and surely therefore a rather comic presence on the
stage. Lip-service is given to the importance of fathers, but all action seems to
make them become ridiculous or at least to lose authority. It is significant that
female goddesses provide the solutions at the play's end: though they are
instructed to do so by the ultimate male authority of Jupiter, their intervention
solves problems which might be implicitly caused by the absence of mothers
from the play. As such, the play provides some fascinating precedents for
Shakespeare's late romances, in structure if not style. If things are to turn out
well, fathers must simply be patient, and must abandon their magical powers.

What a father must not abandon, though, is his position as father,
something attempted by the hero of *Guy of Warwick* (?1590s, pub. 1661).
Recently married, Guy makes a vow not to see his wife, who is pregnant, for
twenty-seven years, and dies before he can manage a proper recognition
scene with her and his son. Romance structures prevent the affirmation of
ordinary family life. Meanwhile, Guy's servant, the clown Philip Sparrow,

goes adventuring with him because he has got a neighbour's daughter in the family way. Sparrow's position undermines that of his master, highlighting the absurdity of chivalric vows. Sparrow says that:

my Mistriss *Parnell* is as precious to me, as your Lady *Phillis* is to you, we have gotten them both with child; and all the difference is, that *Phillis* is your wedded Wife, and *Parnell* is my unmarried Mistris, and we must needs run up and down killing of Dun Cowes, Dragons, Wild-boars and Mastiff Dogs, when we have more work at home then we can well turn our hands to. (lines 340–6)[27]

Although Guy's pilgrimage achieves more than these absurdities – he liberates Jerusalem and England from invaders – his failure to obey the laws of marriage is more dubious than Sparrow's abandonment of a mere mistress. It smacks of catholic devotion and an associated devaluation of marriage. Allowing one's public/sacral role to take priority over one's private life no longer seems as valid as in earlier ages.

Guy does meet his son, but without there being a recognition: with a common irony, they address each other conventionally as 'father' and 'son' (merely reflecting their relative ages – lines 1485–98). The son Rainborne has a more extensive colloquy with Sparrow, who reveals that he is Guy's servant, and argues that he might well be Rainborne's father:

> indeed, when I came out of *England* I left a Wench pretty and
> plump, thou may'st be my Son, if thou beest, kneel down
> and ask me blessing, and i'le give thee two pence.
> RAINBORNE. Away you base slave.
> SPARROW. Why dost thou think scorn to ask me blessing?
> RAINBORNE. I Sir that I do.
> SPARROW. Then I think scorn to give thee my two
> pence.   (lines 1266–74)

This may be comic, but the loss of the continuity provided by paternal blessings is a serious matter in this play. Rainborne ultimately only gets a squeeze of the hand from his dying (even dead?) father (lines 1549–53), and this seems very close to tragedy. Early in the play, by contrast, Sparrow's father gives him a malapropistic blessing, offering 'Gods malediction' (line 238). The play suggests, finally, that such adventuring as it seems to celebrate may be a cursed activity that seriously compromises the solid basis of patriarchal society. As a result, the play does not give us the paternal recognitions and blessings that would later become central to romantic comedy and tragedy.

The romantic comedies of John Lyly fuse some of the tendencies of early tragedy, romance, and comedy, adding some emotional weight by introducing a sharper focus on daughters. *Gallathea* (?late 1580s) centres around paternal irresponsibility. The plot is driven by two fathers' attempts to prevent their daughters being sacrificed to a sea-monster, who must be fed the region's most beautiful virgin every five years in order to satisfy Neptune. Both Tyterus and Melebeus begin the play by disguising their daughters (Gallathea and Phillida) as boys so as to avoid this fate, after which action both fathers disappear from the scene until the fourth act. The absence of fathers from the central action of the play is under-lined by the fact that in the decidedly disconnected subplot Rafe, Robin, and Dick, shipwrecked sons of a miller, wander around looking for work without their father ever appearing. These lads do not encounter Gallathea and Phillida, who inevitably fall in love with one another in their masculine disguises, a problem that is solved by Venus promising to transform one of them permanently into a boy.

The absence of responsible male figures in the play, whether as fathers or as lovers, is the central point at issue, perhaps reflecting the feminized court of Elizabeth (at which the play was performed) as well as the fact that the theatrical company concerned was the Blackfriars Children; no psychosexually mature male can be constructed from such materials. The classical gods take on authority roles instead of men, but they are not on the whole figures of real, consistent authority: Venus and Diana are women, one concerned for her maiden entourage, the other for her son; Cupid is a boy; even Neptune is a figure of 'subtle' caprice (II. ii. 26) and even bestiality.[28] Although between them the gods resolve all the prob-lems, they only do so as a result of compromise between their various perverse (or at least non-patriarchal) priorities.

The human fathers' irresponsibility is highlighted in the fact that their daughters take on their fathers' names when they dress as boys: in some senses, the girls – who only reluctantly obey in donning the disguises, and thus seem more dutiful than the men who should instruct them in duty – displace their fathers in doing so. The excessive fondness of the fathers is also construed as potentially incestuous, if not actually so: Melebeus begins with the decidedly ambiguous formulation 'I know that which I most desire and would least have, that thou art fairest' (I. iii. 4–6); more explicitly, Tyterus accuses him of giving her 'infinite kisses, with affection (I fear me) more than fatherly' (IV. i. 40–1); Melebeus' response is intended as part of a pretence that he has no daughter, but its effect is to give some credence to the allegation: 'Did you ever see me kiss my daughter? You are deceived; it was my wife' (line 52). Though no such charge is explicitly made against Tyterus, Melebeus' generalizations about the attractiveness of youth implicate him too. Excessive fondness for a daughter, in turning them against the interests of their 'country' (here a regional reference, but with nationalistic overtones for an Elizabethan audience), necessarily becomes a kind of incest. Gallathea soliloquizes thus: 'Thy father doteth, Gallathea, whose blind love corrupteth his fond judgement, and, jealous of thy death, seemeth to dote on thy beauty, whose fond care carrieth his partial eye as far from truth as his heart is from falsehood' (II. i. 4–10); a dutiful daughter, she cannot wholly condemn Tyterus, but she sees that he has lost his 'truth' to his country, a sin he himself recognizes in hypocritically accusing Melebeus of being 'careless of your country' (IV. i. 29). Neptune hammers home the charge with the judgement that 'so overcareful are fathers to their children that they forget the safety of their country, and, fearing to become unnatural, become unreasonable' (IV. iii. 3–5). It is hard to accommodate both one's public duties and one's private emotions. At the end of the play it is made clear that the daughters have been saved not by their fathers' care, but by the intervention of the quarrelling Diana and Venus: as Neptune says, 'your deserts have not gotten pardon, but these goddesses' jars' (V. iii. 116–17). The pardon, however, seems in some ways a punishment to the fathers: when Venus decides to transsexualize one of the girls, Tyterus insists 'Gallathea, I will keep you as I begat you, a daughter', and Melebeus replies 'Tyterus, let yours be a boy, and if you will; mine shall not' (lines 161–4), both hinting at a persistently dubious desire for their daughters, though Tyterus does say he wants her to stay female so that his (unpresented) son will not be disinherited. The question of which will be changed is left beyond the play's end; satisfying as this will be for the girls, both fathers are left with the potential of loss. Of course, the acquisition of a son would normatively be regarded as a definite gain, but the play's dizzying sexual dynamics have thrown the valuation of masculinity, particularly of the patriarchal variety, into serious question. As in Lyly's other romance-oriented comedies, *Love's Metamorphosis* and *Midas*, daughters are seen as more able to offer resolution than sons, who are presented in more conflictual terms.

The more realist mode of Lyly's *Mother Bombie* allows some of the fullest expressions of paternal anxieties we can find in Elizabethan drama, while still injecting a degree of flexibility into the idea of paternity, suggesting that fatherhood is not as fixed a relationship as the ideology of the time would insist. It begins with the marital schemes of four fathers: Memphio wants to marry his foolish son to Stellio's daughter; Stellio likewise wants to trick Memphio's son into marrying his foolish daughter; Prisius and Sperantius have a daughter and son, respectively, who have no prospects, but who are in love – their fathers therefore want to marry them off to the richer offspring of Memphio and Stellio. All employ their trickster servants as agents in these plans, which of course results in the partial subversion of the schemes. Foolish offspring are a real concern, introducing doubt into the idea of paternity:

> MEMPH. I maruell he is such an asse, hee takes it not of his father.
> DRO. He may for anie thing you know.
> MEMPH. Why villain dost thou think me a foole?
> DRO. O no sir, neither are you sure that you are his father.
> MEMPH. Rascall, doest thou imagine thy mistres naught of her
>   bodie?
> DRO. No, but fantasticall of her mind, and it may be, when this boy
>   was begotten shee thought of a foole, & so conceiued a foole, your
>   selfe beeing verie wise, and she surpassing honest.   (lines 29–40)

Dromio's irony here is clear enough, given that he is going to trick his 'wise' master, but the key idea that a woman's imagination can alter a man's offspring is striking, even if it is not taken entirely seriously. Lyly is fond of the rhetorical deployment of biological ideas, and it is hard to be sure whether they are considered to have any purchase on reality; they are 'conceits' of a sort, notions that may or may not help to explain the individual's relation to the world. Dromio goes on to say that 'your sonne may be a bastard and yet legitimate, your selfe a cuckold, & yet my mistres vertuous, all this in conceit' (lines 44–6); this gnomically phrased idea resembles the prophecies of Mother Bombie herself, which will help resolve the play's problems. Paternity is not as simple a matter as the fathers think, being coloured by an element of feminine mystification. The fool Accius will turn out *not* to be Memphio's son – and not due to infidelity or 'conceit' but due to an exchange made by his wetnurse. This may be the best form of misconception about paternity, but we might wonder how well it dispels other anxieties based on wifely infidelity: the idea of swapped children in some way displaces and defuses the concern that men cannot be sure about their paternity. Conceit, in the sense of understanding, or of how one looks at the world, is everything. It is a crucial kind of recognition associated with paternity – one which gives the illusion of certainty and truth.

   Candius, plotting to marry against his father's wishes, insists that his wit is better than his father's, saying ironically 'when my face is bedaubed with haire as his, then perchance my conceit may stumble on his staiedness' (lines 275–7), a position that runs against the traditional association of beards and wisdom: staidness is a stumbling-block. Paternal restraint is treated as a trivial obstacle when confronted with the greater conceitful understanding claimed by the younger generation, yet as the plot develops it will not be Candius himself, or his beloved Livia, that will subvert paternal intentions – instead, the servants will be the ones who make things turn out for the best. Though the play seems to be set in Kent, the servants' actions are driven by the desire, as in Roman comedy, to earn their freedom: they are fatherless boys whose ingenuity will earn independence. As such, their rebellions are not exactly unfilial, and the advantages they bring to the younger generation of the core families are to some degree incidental, though symbolic of their own emancipation. The play nicely articulates the conflicts between fathers and children, Livia saying:

In deed our parents take great care to make vs aske blessing and say grace when as we are lyttle ones, and growing to yeeres of iudgement they depriue vs of the greatest blessing, and the most gracious things to our mindes, the libertie of our minds: they give vs pap with a spoon before we can speak, and when we speake for that wee loue, pap with a hatchet: because their fansies beeing growen musty with hoarie age, therefore nothing can relish in their thoughtes that savours of sweet youth: they studie twentie yeeres together to make vs grow as straight as a wande, and in the end by bowing vs make vs as crooked as a cammocke. (lines 307–19)

The 'euphuistic' balance of Lyly's sentences here conveys the paradoxical and double-edged qualities of paternal care with particular precision. This passage is itself balanced by Sperantius' protest shortly afterwards: 'the sonnes must be masters, the fathers gaffers, what wee get together with a rake, they cast abroade with a forke, and wee must wearie our legges to purchase our children armes' (lines 414–17). Of particular interest is the idea that to be a 'gaffer' (grandfather) is undesirable – such a position rules a man out of his proper sphere of action. The young ultimately triumph, and the older generation are little compensated: Memphio and Stellio acquire non-idiot offspring (who are already in love with each other); Prisius and Sperantius simply have to accept their children's marriage, as they have unwittingly witnessed their betrothal. The servant Risius sums up: 'this all stoode vppon vs poore children and your yong children, to shewe that olde folkes may be ouertaken by children' (lines 1965–7). Though the fathers may not have fools as children any more, they have been shown to be less wise than they thought.[29] The impetus for action must come from the young, who are more flexible than the staid old men. The main generic lines of Shakespearean comedy are being drawn up here.

The limits of paternal action are set up powerfully in *A Knack to Know a Knave* (c. 1592), a comedy strongly influenced by Lyly. The play contains a very peculiar scene of exemplary justice, in which a father demands the king punish his disobedient son Philarchus, a royal favourite; despite this son's repentance, and the king's pleading in his favour, the father will not forgive him, and the king asks that he take on the role of judge; he then banishes his son, despite his own pity. Disobedience to the father here is taken as a primary sin, from which all other sins arise: 'wilfull children, spotted with one ill / Are apt to fall to twentie thousand more' (lines 487–8).[30] Indeed, he has not only denied his poor father, but struck him back when beaten in punishment for his pride. The father, though the one offended against, cannot forgive, because the sin is against an idea of paternal authority that transcends him as an individual. Both king and father are divided between their personal affection for Philarchus and their public duties as judge, but give precedence to the latter. Banishment, however, is presented as a mild punishment in this play (whose modes of justice are generally harsher). The vacillation of this long scene is typical of its time – paternal feeling and paternal duty are set in conflict and cannot be happily resolved, even by an appeal to the king. Here comedy starts to set up conflicts that will be realized in later tragedy.

All this is set up in contrast to the bad father the Bailiff of Hexham, whose four sons are the play's principal knaves; a conycatcher, a farmer, a courtier, and a priest, all are given deathbed paternal advice to act with utter selfishness and ignore any consequences in the afterlife, and prefer this counsel to the obvious warning given when they watch their father being taken off to hell by a devil. The tensions between the idea of the judging father and the judged father are sharply worked out here, in a way that anticipates later dramatic developments;[31] balancing tragic and comic outcomes enables the emergence of fuller tragic possibilities for the father.

A similarly judicious but even more peculiar role is created in Greene's *James IV* (1590–2), which puts its key father Bohan in a curious (in all senses) metatheatrical supervisory position: he and Oberon, king of the Faeries, watch and comment on the (fictional) events of seventy years earlier, into which Bohan's sons Slipper and Nano have somehow been inserted.[32] The father here escapes from his timebound condition, indicating that the public/sacral role of the father is somehow connected to the eternal. The paternal surveillance, through Oberon's agency, ensures that all turns out well for the sons and, through them, for the kingdom. The play is thus a perfect instance of the father's *indirect* action guaranteeing familial and national success. His position may constitute a benign rewriting of the role of Andrea in *The Spanish Tragedy*, for a father's presiding spirit enables national cleansing without the vengeful impulses unleashed by the friend in the earlier play; there, as the father Hieronimo has to act directly, he can only do so vindictively; here, he can be impersonal and magnanimous, while still retaining his fatherly feeling. Yet all this is founded on Bohan's misanthropic withdrawal from the public world, symbolized by him living in a tomb. Unlike Philarchus' father in *A Knack to Know a Knave*, he has both his honest and his more knavish son saved: he is the indulgent judging father, but is only able to be so because his sons' actions do no real harm to the nation.

The play's other father figure is the unnamed English king: although the play is decidedly unhistorical, its precise setting in 1520 indicates that Henry VIII is indirectly intended, especially given that king's wars with Scotland. He intervenes when James IV plots to kill his queen (the English princess Dorothea). His presence is a nostalgic reminder of paternalistic kingship which was typical in writing of the 1590s: Nashe's *Unfortunate Traveller* and Deloney's *Jack of Newbury* similarly present such a rose-tinted vision of Henry VIII as a guarantor of a happy nation. Of course, Henry VIII did not have a daughter called Dorothea, and it was his sister who was married to James IV (a marriage which gave James VI his claim to the English succession). Cutting through the mixture of history and fiction, an allegorical intention emerges: Dorothea indirectly represents Elizabeth, and James IV represents his whole dynasty, including James VI, his sexual sins being his son's, his murderousness that of his granddaughter Mary Queen of Scots, and his favouritism (possibly) that of his great-grandson. James VI himself was anxious that the sins of his grandfather in particular might have cursed his family, urging his own son towards purity in order to expiate them (in *Basilikon Doron*).[33] The play enacts such an expiation: the marriage of James IV and Dorothea represents the anticipated union of the nations; her forgiveness represents Elizabeth's acceptance of James as successor, while asserting a certain superiority in the marriage that the English would need; the presence of Henry VIII as guarantor of the union, after his successful invasion of Scotland, allows the English to feel that they have absorbed Scotland rather than *vice versa*, while also appealing to a desire for a masculine, martial king. James IV can be forgiven because of his youth, as Dorothea repeatedly says (V. vi. 140, 160), and because he has been misled by favourites; if he listens to counsel from older statesmen, who will act as 'stays' (line 197), he can be a good king, and the union between the kingdoms can 'command the world' (line 103).[34] These words come from the elderly Sir Cuthbert, who is respected by the English king, thus allowing him to stay paternal rage (line 104). The benign and restraining presence of fathers and old men, like the metatheatrical presence of Bohan, has guaranteed national success.

What emerges from these mixed-genre romance-based plays, with their essentially comic optimism, is a new range of possibilities for representing the figure of the father: he can be redemptive, but only in limited ways, exercising quasi-magical influence rather than having direct powers to intervene; he can be a powerful judging figure, but he can also be judged; above all, he is now allowed to have feelings – even feelings that relate to the limitation of his power and to his potential culpability. His import-ance for dramatic recognition, both as subject and object, has therefore been thoroughly enriched, giving him a worthy role in tragedy.

THE DEEPENING OF TRAGEDY

Despite the power of fathers in romance, the romantic idea of magic inhering in fathers may have ironic qualities:[35] it is an attempt to recover the kind of spiritual authority that more avowedly realistic tragedy insists we must do without. As tragedy comes into its own in the period 1587–92, it does so with remorseless savagery, throwing out the false comforts of an older romantic tradition. This tragedy turns to the distant British past, to the Islamic world, to ancient Rome, and to the present enemy Spain as alien places where anything goes – including, for a brief while, the possibility of patricide that is ruled out during most of our period.

Thomas Hughes's *The Misfortunes of Arthur* (1587) was presented before Queen Elizabeth – rather daringly, since it seems, as Richard McCabe argues, to welcome the imminent end of the Tudor dynasty, and to criticize the queen for too much indulgence of her kinswoman Mary Queen of Scots;[36] of course, it makes its implications deniable by insisting at its beginning and end that the civil wars of Arthur's times have been replaced by Elizabethan peace, but its sense of ending is clear enough. Beyond its current political implications, however, it presents a fascinating example of the paternal dilemma, and the problem of over-identification between father and son. The latter problem is signalled by the fact that Mordred is Arthur's incestuously begotten son (this follows Malory, whereas most other aspects of the play derive from Geoffrey of Monmouth).[37] The overdetermination of their relationship has made Arthur too indulgent, just as its sinful basis (Arthur having 'delighted in his [twin] sister Anna' – Argument), not fully acknowledged until the play's end, has made Mordred bad, inclining him to rebellion and an incestuous affair with Guinevere.[38] The upshot of all this is that in a final battle Mordred kills himself by throwing himself on Arthur's sword, in the process giving his father's death-blow; the combined suicide and patricide not only neatly cuts the knot caused by incest, but simultaneously expresses the overidentification between father and son that has made Mordred take his father's possessions.

The play's great horror is of civil war – which of course was the greatest fear as to what would ensue on the death of Elizabeth. It suggests that civil war is not so much prevented by a secure dynastic line as prompted by it. Fathers and sons killing one another is not just the horrific consequence of civil war here (as it is, say, in *Henry VI Part 3*); the patrilineal tension is presented as the problem. It is significant that Arthur and Mordred are described in the epilogue as 'vanquisht by themselues' (p. 46), perhaps configuring Arthur's death as an aspect of Mordred's suicide rather than a true patricide. Excessive valuation of a shared patrilineal sense of self is the essential issue. The overdetermination of the relationship caused by incest is therefore not so much a root cause as a logical expression of the problem. The only end to this can be complete destruction of the family, though the epilogue admits that life must go on, blandly saying 'men must needes be borne, and some must rule' (p. 47). This suggests that the fetishization of individuals and their dynastic families should end – that such overburdened patrilineal emphasis can only lead to tragedy.

Before the battle (and even after it), the play is framed as a series of debates, the most important of which are arguments as to whether Mordred should defy his father and whether Arthur should surrender to his son. The peculiar thing about these is that the obviously 'right' course (which would involve the father being vindicated and the son submitting) is not presented as the most practical or even admirable. Mordred's defiance is treated with some sympathy, and Arthur's anger comes to seem like a fault. Mordred's sense of the need to compete with his father as to 'whether is the fitter of vs two' (p. 14) gives a certain honour to his rebellion. Meanwhile, the depth of Arthur's paternal love is emphasized, making him refuse to spill his 'proper blood', and causing him to reject Howell's consolation that 'time may send you kine and sonnes inough' (p. 23), because he believes that 'To spoile my sonne were to dispoile my selfe' (p. 24); so he decides to abdicate in Mordred's favour. The fact that he suddenly turns from this lengthily articulated reasoning to intense anger seems rash; he himself later regards it as his tragic mistake. He believes that he should forgive Mordred, because he has given his son precedent for sin, and has provided a cause for envious emulation by being such a successful conqueror. This moral complexity contributes to the play's being the best of its kind – synthesizing the tradition of classical imitations and of political-familial tragedy following *Gorboduc*, the play nonetheless avoids the nostalgia for secure paternal leadership that haunts its predecessors.

Rather, it is haunted by the ghost of the wronged Gorlois, who wants revenge for Uther cuckolding him to beget Arthur (and perhaps also for Uther killing him) – if he is to have no descendants, nor must Uther. The ultimate tragedy may be having no offspring, but there is a sense of purgation in that condition, as the first Chorus suggests: 'In *Brvtain* warres and discord will not stent: / Till *Vther's* line and offspring quite be spent' (p. 11). This idea of childlessness as in some sense fortunate is similarly articulated by Francis Bacon, whose *In Felicem Memoriam Elizabethae* tries to present the queen as having reached a condition of perfection which may resemble Arthur's: childlessness being arguably 'the crown and consummation of felicity, because that happiness can only be accounted perfect over which fortune has no further power; which cannot be where there is posterity'.[39] Arthur's final childlessness also allows his memory to be unimpeachable; as he says in his lengthy dying scene, 'goe we not inglorious to the ground: / Set wish a part: we haue performed inough' (p. 44). Few speeches of tragic catharsis are so sufficient; perhaps they are only possible for the childless.

Perhaps, also, the sense of potential (if only memorial) return is only possible for them. Arthur plays nicely with the tradition of himself as once and future king, spinning this into a threat:

> Yea: though I Conqueror die, and full of *Fame*:
> Yet let my death and parture rest obscure.
> No graue I neede (O *Fates*) nor buriall rights,
> Nor stately hearce, nor tombe with haughty toppe:
> But let my Carkasse lurke: yea, let my death
> Be ay vnknowen, so that in euery Coast
> I still be feard, and lookt for euery houre.

This is remarkably eerie – the ideal king is an object of sinister terror. Yet Arthur's firm sense of a fully realized and eternal self depends on leaving not a rack of offspring behind. Mordred shares this sense that there can be 'No better end', for 'His last mishaps doe make a man secure' (p. 16); the play several times makes the distinction between safety – that is, real freedom from danger – and security – freedom from cares and concerns; the latter is to be preferred, and can only be attained in childlessness. This is an issue that would return in a very different form in *Macbeth*. Calm of self, all offspring spent – one might say; ultimately, then, the play may be more admiring than critical of Elizabeth's virginal position.

The paternal transmission of power and its associated potential for tragedy is central to *Edmund Ironside* (Anon., c. 1588–92), like *The Misfortunes of Arthur* a play set in the distant British past. Edmund's efforts to get back the throne that his father lost clearly mark him out as admirable both in filial and English-nationalist terms; however, the political rights and wrongs of this – the debates between possession and inheritance, conquest and natural right – are only touched on briefly. More important is the sense of each character needing to vindicate himself as part of his patrilineal line. Early in the play Canutus insists he will see his people right as 'yet the spirit of my father Sveyn / runs in these veins, which I will shed/even drop by drop ere I will see you harmed';[40] this idea of blood as a familial resource stored up to be deployed in certain causes gives quite a powerful sense of identity to characters who might otherwise be mere cut-outs. It is as if the yearning to become oneself is dependent on realizing one's father. Oddly, though, this goes alongside a lack of concern for sons: when Leofric and Turkillus decide to return to Edmund's side, the latter wonders:

> what shall then become of our two boys
> who are our pledges? They shall surely die.
> LEOFRIC. Tut, 'tis no matter, if they die, they die.
> They cannot suffer in a better time
> nor for a better cause, their country's good.
> We gave them life, for us they shed their blood.
> TURKILLUS. He that sent them can send us more again.
> Then let us hence, delay of time is vain.   (lines 269–76)

It is significant that *two* men are making this judgement: it makes it seem a norm, rather than an exceptional act of devotion; but it also makes it seem like a norm that has been created by homosocial peer pressure. There's something perfunctory about this – Turkillus' final sentiment resembles the king's in Peele's *Edward I* (see Chapter 3, below). Not caring about one's sons has become a macho norm that paradoxically makes for tougher (therefore better) sons. At the end of the play, these men's attitude is shown to be less disinterested than it would initially seem: peace having been reached between Edmund and Canutus, these two still hold a grudge, saying they 'wait upon occasion for revenge. / A day of mirth begins a woeful year / as sudden storms do follow sunshine clear' (lines 2036–8). Mind you, their sons were treated horribly – hands and noses cut off, and then laughed at, all in vengeance for their fathers' tergiversation; the loss of the noses in particular seems like a symbolic castration, thus threatening the manliness of the whole family. Such injuries to the patrilineal notion of manliness mean that there can be no peace.

Given this moral emphasis, it is ironic that the play's central focus is on a man of no significant family. Edricus is a both-sides rogue, an '*Ambo-dexter*' (line 330), a man of humble birth who has become duke of Mercia; he will try to stay with the winning side, but

> indeed to say the very troth
> rather of both I love Canutus best;
> for Edmund's father first did raise me up
> and from a ploughman's son promoted me
> to be a duke for all my villainy,
> and so as often as I look on him
> I must remember what he did for me,
> and whence I did descend and what I am –
> which thoughts abase my state most abjectly.   (lines 316–24)

This is a succinct expression of a systematic ingratitude, in which a lack of integrity is associated with a lack of patrilineal honour – what he *is* is still low: 'for all my villainy' is nicely ambiguous, meaning both 'for the sake of all my wickedness' and 'despite my low status'. This is realized again when he denies his parents a few scenes later; such scenes are common ways of presenting the viciousness of the courtly mushroom (Joan in *Henry VI Part 1*, Radogan in *A Looking Glass for London and England*, Philarchus in *A Knack to Know a Knave*), but this is perhaps the liveliest example. Edricus starts with abuse of his father: 'My father, grouthead? Sir knave, I say you lie, you whoreson cuckold, you base vagabond, you slave, you mongrel peasant, dolt and fool; canst thou not know a duke from common men?' (lines 491–5). His mother then proudly admits: 'By my troth I learned him all these names to call his father when he was a child, and see if he can forget them yet. Oh, he is a wise man, for in faith my husband is none of his father, for indeed a soldier begot him of me, as I went once to a fair' (lines 496–500); this is intended to vindicate Edricus' view of himself as superior to his father, but in fact it means that he cannot even be regarded as an honest ploughman's son – the comic moment undermines the larger tragic picture. The father he denies is therefore not so derogated by having such a son, and therefore, of course, the offence against him is the greater. In any case, Edricus also denies his mother; if she has made him a kind of nothing by her boast, she can gain nothing by it. His lack of identity, the play's whole structure implies, makes for all the trouble between the truly noble princes (about whose paternity there is no doubt). Not only does Edricus stir the pot throughout the play, but he ends it promising further revenges. True men like Canutus and Edmund can become friends by proving themselves in combat, but an Edricus has no self to prove. In this, he obviously anticipates Shakespeare's Edmund in *King Lear*, but he also resembles Edgar in the same play: once one has lost one's position as a son, one becomes 'nothing' (*King Lear*, II. iii. 21). As in the case of Mordred's suicide–patricide, conflict with one's father undermines the basis of one's identity. Push too hard at the idea of proving oneself, and one may destroy the basis of all identity.

This problem becomes particularly acute when the father is too striking a model for a son. This is the case in Peele's *David and Bethsabe* (c. 1588–94), which focusses on Absalon's decidedly undermotivated rebellion against his father. In concentrating on the problems created by polygamy, the play probably reflects obliquely on Henry VIII, but lacks the wit to make anything stick.[41] David's desire for Bethsabe is 'unstaid' (line 31), but despite it being unbecoming of a king and father, it can hardly be said to cause his son's rebellion, which emerges, as per the Biblical account, from fraternal tensions.[42] Crucially, though, Bethsabe's husband Urias does – drunkenly, and without much motive – tell Absalon 'Your father is a better man than you' (line 522), indicating perhaps that this is the real problem: a great and famous father, who cannot be imitated, can only be rebelled against. David's essential tragedy is that 'to thee is left no seed / That may revive thy name in Israel' (lines 854–5) – yet he says this prematurely, reflecting mainly on the death of Bethsabe's child and of Amnon; Absalon is still alive (if fratricidally 'unkind and graceless' – line 1077), and Solomon will succeed, despite David's preference for the former, more lovable son. David's mourning for Absalon (lines 1839–42) reflects a *private* sense of paternity: as king, he may be happy in his sucession, but not as a private father; the play seems to acknowledge the validity of the latter emotion, but suggests that it must not be tangled up with politics. The strange doubleness of fathers here prevents plot resolution, as the public and the private roles of the father are incommensurable.

The two parts of Marlowe's *Tamburlaine* articulate both this doubleness (the individual and the father) and the pressures of paternal glory. The focus is on one meteoric individual in the first part, but the second becomes particularly concerned with succession. Tamburlaine's initial concern is with 'That perfect bliss and sole felicity, / The sweet fruition of an earthly crown' (*Part 1*, II. vii. 28–9), and has no interest in further fruition at this stage.[43] By the end of the second part, as the dying Tamburlaine laments that he has not conquered the whole world, it is clear that such perfect power will ever lie tantalizingly out of reach. He hopes that his sons will 'finish all my wants' (*Part 2*, V. iii. 126), but it is obvious that they will not do so. His successor Amyras ends the play with a sense of fruition as finality rather than endlessness, praying 'Meet earth and heaven, and here let all things end! / For earth hath spent the pride of all her fruit' (lines 250–1). Tamburlaine fears that his son will be a doomed Phaethon or Hippolytus: both myths imply the son improperly leaping into his father's seat, the first as inept manager of the Sun's chariot, the second suspected of adultery with his step-mother. However well the father wishes his offspring, the suggestion is that no one can rightly adopt this father's role. Like the audience, the sons can do no better than to 'View but his picture in this tragic glass / And then applaud his fortunes as you please' (*Part 1*, Prologue, 7–8). He is a mirror for admiration, not for imitation.

Throughout the second play, Tamburlaine has put immense pressure on his sons: this is an almost satirically extreme version of a model education for masculine, martial youth. Tamburlaine begins the play contemplating them at their mother's side, admiring 'these my sons, more precious in mine eyes / Than all the wealthy kingdoms I subdued' (I. iii. 17–18). But their lack of martial qualities 'Would make me think them bastards, not my sons, / But that I know they issued from the womb / That never looked on man but Tamburlaine' (lines 32–4). His attitude to these sons proves that he does not really value them more than conquests, as will become starkly evident later. He despises them for amorousness, but this conveniently forgets his own grand passion for Zenocrate; that passion in turn is put into confusion here: he blames his wife one way or another, in that she has either through nature or nurture introduced something effeminate to them, as infidelity on her part seems unthinkable. Although Celebinus and Amyras are willing enough to prove their martial prowess, Calyphas has no interest, and would rather stay with his mother; this prompts the re-emergence of the thought that Tamburlaine dismissed above, calling Calyphas 'Bastardly boy, sprung from some coward's loins / And not the issue of great Tamburlaine' (lines 69–70). The fact that he can insist on this without any genuine suspicion of Zenocrate seems a little problematic, but it shows how a son can be disowned verbally while biological issues are finessed away.

The implicit or repressed tension between husband and wife may be ironically displaced into the incongruous scene in which Tamburlaine gives his sons, who are mourning their just-deceased mother, a long and detailed set of instructions about the management of sieges (III. iii); such hyper-masculinity must seem rather absurd, but it points forward to the play's most truly tragic moment. Whilst Amyras and Celebinus are happy to 'follow ... our father's sword' (IV. i. 4), Calyphas is, quite subtly, aware of Tamburlaine's self-sufficiency, reflecting that 'My father needs not me' (line 15).

This may in part be an excuse for idleness, but he is surely right to see his father's pleasure in his brothers' martial prowess as merely a commonplace pleasure in childish *imitation*: in the play's scheme of things, no one but Tamburlaine can really be a man, and we might see something more truly manly in Calyphas' independence.

Renaissance parents enjoyed watching their children playing at being adults, but that does not mean they took them as seriously as they would real adults.[44] Even when Amyras and Celebinus are successful, it is clear that they are still being 'trained in arms and chivalry' (line 81), still merely mimics of their father's majesty. Calyphas, by contrast, is an 'Image of sloth and picture of a slave' (line 91): he is an inadequate representation of his father (the charge of bastardy is still in the back of his mind here), and therefore must be destroyed like a bad portrait. He is 'A form not meet to give that subject essence / Whose matter is the flesh of Tamburlaine' (lines 111–12). This indicates that the idea of Tamburlaine (what other literary character speaks his own name so often?) can never be wholly contained in the world: 'earth and all this airy region / Cannot contain the state of Tamburlaine [*stabs Calyphas*]' (lines 119–20). Killing his son is a way of killing the inadequacy of matter and the material world; how much aggression there is in this towards the dead *mater* (mother) is another matter. Yet excessive filial piety (such as that displayed by the son of Balsera's Captain – III. iv. 26–7), which runs against the natural order of things, is a keynote of the play: when Tamburlaine is dying his son Amyras wishes he were dying in his stead (V. iii. 209–10). A father who can provoke such feelings is admirable in a way, but he surely prevents any further fruition in his sons. Such a model of masculinity, the play implies, is counterproductive.

The role of fathers as a problematic precedent is extended further in a vogue for plays set in the Islamic world which follow on from *Tamburlaine*. Robert Greene's *Alphonsus King of Aragon* seems like a bland attempt to cash in on Marlowe's success with *Tamburlaine*, but it does at least supply an initial motive that is missing in the greater play. Alphonsus is inspired to his military exploits by his father's tales of being usurped in his kingdom. However, when he recovers the throne, he does not give it to his father (who has promised to 'spend his daies with praiers and horizons' 'in this sillie groue' (lines 177–8), perhaps indicating some sort of abdication);[45] indeed, he doesn't even keep it for himself, giving it to his supporter Albinius – because he wants to obtain other kingdoms, and perhaps because, like Tamburlaine and like the princes in Sidney's *Arcadia*, he feels it 'a greater greatness to give a kingdom than get a kingdom'.[46] He ends up winning the throne of Turkey and riding around with several kings' heads in his canopy; all this happens because he needed to compensate for his father's humiliation.

As something of an afterthought, Alphonsus' father Carinus does get to act, taking revenge on the very minor figure of the duke of Milan, who – we are told only at this late stage (IV. ii) – connived in Carinus' exile and deposition. The appearance of this scene may be an attempt to compensate for Carinus' rather embarrassing passivity before the play's opening, which might be thought to reflect badly on his son. When Carinus comes, dressed as a pilgrim, to greet his son, he does worry that his presence is a 'disgrace' (line 1945); though this fear is dispelled (Alphonsus insists that his father's arrival is a greater 'pleasure' than all his conquests – lines 1934–7), the underlying anxieties take more effort to extirpate. Even though he has been defeated, Amurack of Turkey has refused to marry his daughter to the 'beggers brat' he believes Alphonsus to be (line 1811). Alphonsus is piqued by this and imprisons the whole Turkish royal family, ignoring their change of mind; notably, it takes a request from his father to make him relent. Once Carinus has intervened, Amurack is prepared to acknowledge that '*Alphonsus* is the sonne vnto a King' (line 2069). The reappearance of the father is necessary to resolve this 'Comicall Historie'. Though Alphonsus has political authority, his father is still worthy of his respect, and is 'the Loadstone of his life' (line 1951).

In *Selimus* (pub. 1594, possibly by Greene), the Islamic context licenses an absolute amorality, associated with popular conceptions of Machiavellianism, taken if anything rather further than in Marlowe.[47] At its centre is the rebellion of the titular anti-hero against his father Bajazeth, which inspires a similar rebellion by Selimus' brother Acomet. Though such rebellions are insistently presented as 'unnatural', their prevalence gives the lie to that pious sentiment; familial ties come to seem the cause of conflict rather than as bulwarks against it. Turkey seems like a through-the-looking-glass world in which 'Christian' norms of good and evil are inverted, but this may constitute a genuine challenge to those norms. As in *King Lear*, the level of casual cruelty (including an on-stage blinding) seems to be reflecting on the true horror of human nature, making appeals to natural standards of goodness seem hollow.

All of this subversion of norms centres around the problematic relation between fathers and sons, with the complications of sibling rivalry merely accentuating the issue. It is normal enough in the drama of the time for brothers to be presented as necessarily in conflict,[48] but here the father is just as much a necessary target for envy. Selimus justifies his rebellion by saying that he is rebelling against his father's decline, claiming, extraordinarily, 'I tooke armes vnkind to honour thee, / And winne againe the fame that thou hast lost' (lines 621–2); this comes closer than any other position in the drama of the time to suggesting that a father and son cannot exist side by side and are in a fundamental zero-sum competition. Where one rises the other must fall. An attempt is made to present father and son as equals: on his behalf Hali contends that:

> Tis lawful for the father to take Armes,
> I and by death chastize his rebell sonne.
> Why should it be vnlawfull for the sonne,
> To leauie Armes gainst his iniurious sire?   (lines 885–8)

This is dismissed as sophistry, but it reflects the problematic asymmetry of the relationship. Selimus may also be justified in resisting Bajazeth's favouritism: his deceased eldest son Alemshae was once 'the comfort of my dayes' (line 62),[49] and now the amorous Acomat is favoured over his older brother the philosopher Corcut and the youngest, martial Selimus, who accordingly rebels. On this subject, his father tells him:

> Well hoped I (but hope I see is vaine)
> Thou wouldst haue bene a comfort to mine age,
> A scourge and terrour to mine enemies
> . . .
> But thou like to a craftie *Polipus*,
> Doest turn thy hungry iawes vpon thy selfe,
> For what am I *Selimus* but thy selfe?   (lines 582–4, 592–4)

This notion of the father as another self actually feeds into Selimus' egotism, suggesting that they are struggling over not only sovereignty but the possession of the very self.

The rebuke also constitutes a summary of the standard tropes of paternity – comfort, hope, and vindication – but these essentialist longings have been subverted by the nominalist scepticism of Selimus, who thinks such concepts are designed to cow the individual, and condemns 'the foolish names, / Of father, mother, brother, and such like', which he thinks 'are but a policie, / To keepe the quiet of societie' (lines 340–6). This radically sceptical line of thought impels Selimus throughout. He never expresses doubts about what he is doing, and goes from murder to murder with brisk efficiency. He does, however, at least try to cover up his patricide. Whereas he kills his brothers, nephew, sister-in-law, brother-in-law, and sister openly, he hires a Jewish poisoner to do in his father, and then pretends grief and denies accusations; clearly, some shame attaches to the murder of a father even in this world, though there is some precedent for patricide offered in Selimus comparing himself to Jove (line 1671). The other rebellious son Acomat never actually encounters his father, but he displaces his rage against him by removing the eyes and hands of his messenger; this is followed by the most extreme expression of filial hostility in the dramatic canon:

> would I had my doating father here,
> I would rip vp his breast, and rend his heart,
> Into his bowels thrust my angry hands,
> As willingly, and with as good a mind,
> As I could be the Turkish Emperour.   (lines 1456–60)

Such feeling is clearly intended to put these characters way beyond the pale of civilization, but the only corrective offered comes from the unambitious third son Corcut. He has been converted to Christianity by a shepherd, and emphasizes the paternal nature of his new God:

> if we do like head-strong sonnes neglect
> To hearken to our louing fathers voyce,
> Then in his anger will he vs reiect,
> And giue vs ouer to our wicked choyce.   (lines 2148–51)

Neither this nor Mustaffa's warning that he is destroying his father's entire line (lines 2190–4) affects Selimus in the slightest. He accomplishes his aim – 'Now am I King alone and none but I' (line 2511) – and this is sufficient. Though there is the promise of a sequel, telling of 'greater murthers' (line 2563), there is no evidence of one having been written; after all, it seems unlikely that one can trump patricide. The effect is to leave the play without any sort of moralization. It has a sense of finality, in that Selimus has no offspring in the play, but the title page reminds us that Selimus was 'grandfather to him that now raigneth'; there is to be no end to this violence, we may infer. The bad, patricidally violent son is a model of absolute evil, resulting in endless savagery. Yet a savagely violent father can be a model of virtue.

Titus Andronicus is a revenge tragedy which emphasizes the paternal rather than the filial perspective on identity; its savagery is in keeping with the dramatic trends of 1587–92. It is also unusual in the Shakespeare canon in that it presents a man being cuckolded and an illegitimate heir born; Tamora's affair with Aaron threatens to undermine the imperial lineage, though the fact that the child is black and cannot therefore be imposed on the emperor actually mitigates this even as it brings out miscegenation as the ultimate objective realization of wifely infidelity.[50] On the other hand, Aaron mentions another mixed-race couple who have produced a white-skinned son – a child he plans to impose on Saturninus (IV. ii. 154); this raises the possibility of the royal family being tainted with bastardy and racial otherness. Aaron later tells his son 'Had nature lent thee but thy mother's look, / Villain, thou mightest have been an emperor' (V. i. 29–30). The Moor may mostly lack motive, but this would be a form of self-realization for him. Aaron may be an utterly villainous character, but he has considerable affection for his son; this affection is due to his certainty that the child is his. The skin-colour which mortifies Tamora's other sons delights him – 'Look how the black slave smiles upon the father, / As who should say, "Old lad, I am thine own"' (IV. ii. 120–1); he even calls his son 'this myself' (line 107), as if he were a perfect copy of him. He protects this son, planning to foster him out, but even he notes that the mother is 'the surer side' (line 126). In the end, he betrays all his and Tamora's sins to Lucius precisely in order to save his son's life. Aaron's *natural* feeling is in complete contrast to the hero's unnatural sense of public duty.

Titus himself paradoxically asserts his paternity by sacrificing many of his sons to the Roman cause, and even killing one with his own hand (as well as his daughter), thus following the supposedly virtuous model of Virginius. Yet there is some hope here: the fact that one son of his survives the play's carnage indicates that such sacrifices may ultimately lead to familial success. The first thing to say about Titus is that he is a *good* man, at least according to the standards of the play-world. Much plot contrivance is needed to assert his goodness, firmly linked to the Roman idea of *pietas*, the key Virgilian virtue, which links public service and filial piety: he has even been given the cognomen Pius to emphasize this (I. i. 23), and he is described as 'Patron of virtue' (line 65). However savage the play gets, at no stage does anyone question Titus' goodness, and the play's plot is carefully designed to augment it at every turn.

Through all the play's dizzying shifts of allegiance Titus is always on the *right* side, even though he is frequently judged by others to be in the wrong. I think this is why the play's effect is so emotionally baffling: if Titus must always be in the right, emotional considerations and alliances based on former connections must be brushed aside. This is the fundamental problem of insisting that the father always be good, even when he kills his own son. Though Lucius may call it a 'wrongful quarrel' (line 293), Titus' killing of Mutius seems to need no real justification: he is a 'villain boy' who bars his father's way, and must therefore be killed (lines 290–1). The absolute quality of this paternal standard brooks no questioning. Titus has been 'dishonoured by his sons in Rome' (line 385), and in a sense he never really recovers from this. He may accept his brother's and his sons' arguments that Mutius should be buried in the family tomb, but he is not actually convinced by them. So absolute are his standards, in fact, that they come to seem like passive instincts rather than active values: no process of self-questioning is required. The complete opposite of Hamlet in this respect, he is alienated from himself just as thoroughly as the Danish prince, but in his case it is because he does not have to think precisely on the event.

All the problems of this father in fact seem to come because he does not vacillate. He chooses Saturninus rather than Bassianus as emperor (and as husband for Lavinia) simply because Saturninus is the elder. Bassianus makes his claim on the basis of his 'desert' (line 16), but Titus does not even have to weigh the arguments, for his standards are simple. When Quintus and Martius are accused of killing Bassianus, Titus does not worry too much about whether they did it; he simply says that they are 'accursed' if they did (II. iii. 290–1). His subsequent appeal for clemency is based simply on his own merit and 'pity of mine age'. Yet he ultimately makes his arguments to an empty stage (III. i); this is not someone who really thinks he needs to argue a case. The only instance when he actually does so is when he asks Saturninus if 'rash Virginius'' murder of his daughter was 'well done' (V. iii. 36); having got the emperor's assent he can kill Lavinia with no pang. Following simple (though rash) standards of rightness in a strange way enables this father, like Virginius, to have his version of a happy ending. Though Titus refuses rule at the play's beginning, Lucius becomes emperor at the end; the father's virtuous denial reaps rewards for his son. As in the case of Aaron's thwarted hopes for his bastard lad, getting one's son to be emperor is the ultimate self-realization in this play; we can therefore say that Titus has a happy ending. Perhaps, like *Apius and Virginia*, *Titus Andronicus* is ultimately a 'comical history' rather than a tragedy.

The tensions between Titus and his sons do, however, seem more like the stuff of tragedy. What makes these particularly challenging is the way the play gives us sudden shifts of alliance without the characters talking through what has happened. For instance, Saturninus at one moment calls Titus 'father of my life' (I. i. 253), as he is to be his father-in-law and has just made him emperor; a moment later he is saying he doesn't need 'thee, nor any of thy stock' (line 300), despite the fact that Titus has just killed his own son for the emperor's sake. The emotional and moral discontinuity here extends into the relationship between Titus and his sons, particularly Lucius. Lucius calls Titus 'Dear father, soul and substance of us all' (line 374) when appealing for Mutius' burial in the tomb, but had shortly before been fighting his father, and no apology has intervened. When Lucius is banished, Titus does not commiserate, but calls him 'O happy man' (III. i. 52), because he is escaping the 'wilderness of tigers' that Rome has become (line 54). Lucius pitifully looks away from the ravished and handless Lavinia, only to be told by his father that he is a 'Faint-hearted boy' (line 65). The father–son relation is a series of moments rather than a continuous bond, and this series culminates in Lucius' instant vengeance on Saturninus for killing Titus, taking on some of Titus' simplicity when he says 'Can the son's eye behold his father bleed? / There's meed for meed, death for a deadly deed' (V. iii. 65–6). In the perfect version of the father–son relation, all is embodied in deeds.

Nonetheless, the play, perhaps surprisingly, has some of the most fully domesticated scenes in the Shakespeare canon. Peculiar though they are, they give us a real sense of continuous family life, approaching a grotesque sense of ordinariness. The scenes in question are at the centre of the play: the first is a banquet, but it is an exclusively familial affair. Eating is a bit tricky here, because Titus has only one hand and Lavinia none; the conversation, to which the tongueless girl cannot contribute, deals with her woes. Young Lucius wants Titus to 'Make my aunt merry with some pleasing tale' (III. ii. 47), and when Marcus kills a fly Titus speculates that it perhaps 'Came here to make us merry' (line 65); underneath the misery, then, is the possibility of familial merriment. In the next scene we see Lavinia chasing her nephew around, and though she frightens him Titus assures the boy that 'She loves thee . . . too well to do thee harm' (IV. i. 6); the ordinary tenor of familial affection is affirmed even as the plot is advanced in Lavinia's revelation of her rapists' names. Urgent as the play's plot mostly is, these scenes constitute a brief stalling of action that gives us a sense of the family norms which have been violated. Titus, having come near to his crisis, could only culminate a series of futile questions by asking 'What shall we do?' (III. i. 133), but rather than humiliating him, the slight stalling at the play's middle more firmly instals him as a familial patriarch.

Lavinia herself, though silent, is crucial to all of this. Not only is her feminine presence the marker of domesticity, she also embodies all the rewards and home comforts Titus has earned by his military exploits. If sons are sacrifices to the family honour, a daughter is the pay-off, the imbalance of virtue and reward perhaps being expressed in the fact that twenty-one sons have died in the wars (and three more die during the play), whereas there is only one daughter. Lavinia, however, is special to her father: she is 'The cordial of mine age to glad my heart', and her father wants her to 'outlive him' (I. i. 166–7). Her name, which is also that of Aeneas' Latin bride and of the land she brings Virgil's hero, identifies her with Rome, which has been 'Kind' to preserve her for her father (line 165). She is 'dearer than my soul' (III. i. 102) to Titus, who does not agree when Marcus argues that she's no longer herself after her rape (line 62). She represents all the personal emotion of the family, which may explain why such emotion is irrelevant in Titus' dealings with his sons. In this play's world, love only exists in relation to women and children (we are told that Titus loved his grandson well, and danced him on his knees – V. iii. 161–2). But still Lavinia must die. The expected pattern of sacrifice, then, is reversed in the end: Titus kills his daughter, and the pay-off is that his son will reign.

In *Titus Andronicus*, disclaiming one's paternal feelings is a way of asserting one's disinterested commitment to public service. The tension between public service and private feeling is still more complex in Kyd's *Spanish Tragedy*, which centralizes paternal feeling and puts it in opposition to both public duties and feelings of friendship. As such, the play develops the most rounded and complex tragic father figure in the drama before Shakespeare's Lear, yet all of the restraints we have seen earlier in this chapter are still in place; emotional power emerges from moral restraint. When told of his son Horatio's martial deeds, Hieronimo tells the king:

> That was my son, my gracious sovereign,
> Of whom though from his tender infancy
> My loving thoughts did never hope but well,
> He never pleas'd his father's eyes till now,
> Nor fill'd my heart with overcloying joys.   (I. ii. 116–20)[51]

Paternal pride can only come from public virtue. When the king gives Hieronimo a 'share' (line 125) in his son's victory there is a virtuous circle between father and son, a pleasing give-and-take; but this father has reached a peak of happiness and hope that cannot last. Fathers, it seems, can only suffer, can only react.

When the Viceroy of Portugal believes (incorrectly) that his son is dead, he blames himself:

> My late ambition hath distain'd my faith,
> My breach of faith occasion'd bloody wars,
> Those bloody wars have spent my treasure,
> And with my treasure my people's blood,
> And with their blood, my joy and best belov'd,
> My best belov'd, my sweet and only son.
> O wherefore went I not to war myself?
> The cause was mine, I might have died for both:
> My years were mellow, his but young and green,
> My death were natural, but his was forc'd.   (I. iii. 33–42)

The use of anadiplosis here, very characteristic of the play's rhetoric and its sense of tragic consequentiality, connects the people of the nation, its blood, and its treasure with one individual, the heir to the throne, who is a synecdoche for the whole. Personal and political feeling are deeply linked: the tragedy of the whole play relies on the fact that it is not 'natural' for a son to predecease his father, but also on the fact that the loss of an heir can throw a nation into hopeless chaos. Projecting this tragedy onto Spain, England's threatening enemy in the 1580s and 1590s, seems a way of compensating for the fact that it was really England that had no obvious heir to the throne.[52] The planned marriage between Balthazar, heir of Portugal, and Bel-Imperia, the king of Spain's niece, is set up as a way of securing peace between the two countries, but actually becomes the driving-force of the tragic events, as Bel-Imperia loves Horatio (having previously loved his friend Andrea). The friendly transfer of women from one man to another exemplifies the conflict of private feeling against familial and public duty; Lorenzo's murder of his sister's lover is a reassertion of his familial (and national) ownership of his sister. Hieronimo's laments for his dead son do not initially recognize this context:

> O poor Horatio, what hadst thou misdone,
> To leese thy life ere life was new begun?
> O wicked butcher, whatsoe'er thou wert,
> How could thou strangle virtue and desert?
> Ay me most wretched, that have lost my joy,
> In leesing my Horatio, my sweet boy!   (II. v. 28–33)

The great pity here, it seems, is that Horatio has not had the rewards – either financial or sexual – for his martial merit; things have not come to their due fruition. In fact, as this play is under the aegis of Revenge, true fruition will be in suffering. Revenge himself stresses this at the end of the act, responding to Andrea's complaint that the death of his friend can only 'increase my pain' (II. vi. 1): 'Thou talk'st of harvest when the corn is green: / The end is crown of every work well done' (lines 7–8).

The action of the rest of the play, particularly in the stalled movement of the long third act,[53] suggests the difficulty of coming to this harvest. Hieronimo complains of 'no life, but lively form of death' (III. ii. 2) and bewails the murder 'Of mine, but now no more my son' (line 8); as his son's achievements had given him joy, his death brings him only to negation. His repetition 'my son, my son' (III. vii. 43) indicates the sheer horror and disbelief that makes him unable to act; he sees his words as 'unfruitful' (line 67), an idea that ironically reflects on his childlessness. Fatherhood leads only to paralysis.

The anonymous *First Part of Jeronimo*, almost certainly a later-written prequel to Kyd's play, emphasizes some of these aspects of paternity. We begin with Jeronimo's installation as Marshal, the king even saying 'our kingdome calls thee father' (i. 40).[54] He brings Horatio in on this honour, telling him to 'Kneele by thy fathers loins' (line 7), and throughout the play he is keen to see his son's success as crowning his own. As 'wars tuter' (x. 150) he watches the battles with Portugal, declaring that 'Never had father a more happier boy' (xi. 5) when Horatio proves valiant and taking 'treble comfort' (line 184) in his deeds. For some reason, perhaps to do with the play being performed by a boys' company, or simply the use of a diminutive actor, Jeronimo is repeatedly presented as small, a fact which is taken as a paradox given his reverend status here. However, this enables him to end the play with a special pride, saying to the audience 'For my sons sake, grant me a man at least' (xiii. 14) – only in such proving can one's manhood be fully vindicated. However, the finest proof of Horatio's position comes when he and his father overhear plots against Andrea: the son's desire for revenge here (restrained due to respect for his father) is commended by Jeronimo, who says:

> I like thy true hart boy, thou lovest thy friend,
> It is the greatest argument and sign that I begot thee,
> For it shows thou art mine.   (iii. 86–8)

Here the two major masculine values of the time – friendship and filial piety – are bound up together, highlighting the consonance of those values in Kyd's play. Both values are in service of the public good, and their loss will lead to the most resounding tragedy of the age.

In Kyd's play, Hieronimo's role as Knight-Marshal of Spain puts him in a mediating position between the king and the people, between the public and the private – but while we might expect the public position, along with royal duty, to be disinterested, and the private grief to be partial, the play as a whole inverts this paradigm. In Hieronimo's sympathy with the 'Senex' Don Bazulto, who has also lost his son, we see his private feelings and his public duties coalesce in opposition to the royal family (III. xiii). Oddly, Hieronimo seems to need *reminders* of his son's death – his son's handkerchief, Don Bazulto, the tree on which Horatio was hanged. Perhaps this is because it is unnatural to have to remember a son; as Shakespeare's Lucretius says, 'If children predecease progenitors / We are their offspring, and they none of ours' (*Lucrece*, lines 1756–7) – premature death somehow cancels parenthood. This chimes with the play's general sense of alienation, a sense that one's actions are not quite one's own – a sense accentuated above all by the presence of Revenge on stage. The futility of human endeavour is central to the play's third act, but this is displaced in the final act, which drives forwards to the only harvest now possible – revenge.

Horatio's mother Isabella's tragic soliloquy is essentially personal, blaming the bower as Hieronimo does in the later fourth addition, but it also imaginatively has a cursing effect on the nation as a whole:

> Fruitless for ever may this garden be,
> Barren the earth, and blissless whosoever
> Imagines not to keep it unmanur'd!
> . . ..
> And as I curse this tree from further fruit,
> So shall my womb be cursed for his sake,
> And with this weapon will I wound the breast,
> *She stabs herself.*
> The hapless breast, that gave Horatio suck. (IV. ii. 14–16, 35–8)

Her curse and suicide impact on the climactic scenes that follow – her private woe surely affects not just the immediate garden, but the 'earth' of Spain as a whole.

Her *natural* passion is then acted out in the play Hieronimo presents, suggesting that passion comes to him in a second-order, alienated manner;[55] grief goes from private soliloquy into public performance, suggesting the difference between a mother's and a father's duty to the son. Hieronimo,

being a father, has to put on a probative public show, displaying Horatio's
body after the murderous play, with an accompanying speech:

> See here my show, look on this spectacle:
> Here lay my hope, and here my hope hath end:
> Here lay my heart, and here my heart was slain:
> Here lay my treasure, here my treasure lost:
> Here lay my bliss, and here my bliss bereft:
> But hope, heart, treasure, joy and bliss,
> All fled, fail'd, died, yea, all decay'd with this.
> From forth these wounds came breath that gave me life,
> They murder'd me that made these fatal marks.   (IV. iv. 89–97)

This highly wrought speech, with its anaphora being gathered into a
complex, overdetermined hypotactic hypozeuxis, its point rammed home
by deixis, holds a paradox – that the son gave the father life; this effect is
designed to justify killing his murderers. He has, as he says later, 'offer'd'
his life to his son (line 160). The ceremonial offering to a son's spirit is
against the proper, natural temporal order. But in fact it is not the son
who has specifically demanded vengeance: Horatio's ghost does not
appear – it is the ghost of Andrea who is the play's ultimate spectator;
friendship, not family, is taken as the play's main bond. Hence it is
that Hieronimo kills Castile, who has personally done him no harm: it
is Andrea who has been offended by Castile (who opposed his love
of Bel-Imperia), and it is for Andrea's sake that he must die, even if
Hieronimo doesn't know this. Andrea ends the play anticipating punishment for his enemies in the afterlife, and hoping to 'consort my friends in
pleasing sort' (IV. v. 16). These private desires, underpinned by the private
bonds of friendship, have overborne public priorities. The loss of heirs to
both thrones is a national tragedy; the king of Spain ends the play
lamenting 'My brother, and the whole succeeding hope / That Spain
expected after my decease!' (IV. iv. 203–4). It is also a personal tragedy for
the king, who (like Saturninus in *Titus Andronicus*) has done little active
wrong himself: 'I am the next, the nearest, last of all' (line 208). There is
something apocalyptic about this loss, compounded by the lament of the
viceroy of Portugal for 'our hapless son' (line 210); he asks to be tied on a
mast with his son and sent out to sea, ultimately to Hades. The only
future in this play is the afterlife – all earthly *hopes* have been destroyed.

Such hopes for the nation and its succession would need to be
entrenched in a new genre – the history plays that came to dominate in
the early 1590s. Yet they create their own problems, as we shall see in the
next chapter. *The Spanish Tragedy*, nonetheless, is a pivotal play, giving

fully meaningful subjectivity to a father, even while alienating his actions, dividing his public and private selves; we have come a long way from the dramatic token that was Gorboduc. Hieronimo, like Titus Andronicus, is a figure who fully embodies the strange doubleness of fathers, and the idea that a father is more deprived than privileged in his relation to political power. As tragedy matures, these problems become more acute, as we shall see.

CHAPTER 3

Identification and impasse in drama
of the 1590s: Henry VI to Hamlet

HISTORY PLAYS

History plays come into their own in the drama of the 1590s.[1] Here, continuity is everything, at least on the surface: Lawrence Danson, indeed, argues that the genre can be defined by the fact that characters have continuous existence from one play to another;[2] one might add that we are deeply aware of their relations to one another, particularly the question of their patrilineal identity, which is so foregrounded as to be the central thematic, political, and formal concern of such plays. Yet such insistent focus on the public importance of paternity tends to undermine it as an emotional principle. The totem of the society's ideology starts to seem grotesque as this drama goes on; ultimately the genre deforms into comedy and tragedy, but history's insistence on the primacy of paternity has its effect on those genres, filling them with anxieties about masculine identity that they could previously push to the margins. Comedies (more dominant at first in this period), romances, and then tragedies start to contain scenes of real impasse that history plays could manage more easily by appeals to larger providential patterns. Yet we also see scenes of strange recognition between fathers and sons in this period that enrich the emotional range of drama.

Henry VI Part 1 has the question of patrilineal identity very much at its centre. The play begins with the funeral of the heroic Henry V, and though this father figure does not cast as long a shadow as some dead hero-fathers (such as Gorboduc, Cyrus in *Cambyses*, Tamburlaine, or Old Hamlet), there are several references back to his age that suggest a definite decline in the present. His son, the king, does not appear until halfway through the play, and the central figure is really Talbot, who is presented as a better imitator of Henry V than his son will ever be. Meanwhile, Richard Plantagenet, later duke of York, is primarily concerned with vindicating the memory of his own father, who had been executed for treason – a motivation that will ultimately lead him to assert his right to the throne, thus starting the Wars of the Roses. If the concatenation of these issues does not finally amount to a very coherent play, this may be due to rather unusual circumstances of collaborative composition. On the other hand, the scenes most likely to be Shakespeare's do highlight the pressures of paternally derived identity as a central topic.

The most striking of such scenes are those between Talbot and his son; these add to the pathos of Talbot's death by having his son die with him, and emphasize the permanent loss of the values he embodies, while also presenting a dizzyingly intelligent reflection on the problems of identity. Talbot has sent for his son:

> To tutor thee in stratagems of war,
> That Talbot's name might be in thee reviv'd.
> When sapless age and weak unable limbs
> Should bring thy father to his drooping chair.   (IV. v. 2–5)

Wanting his son to be a future replacement for himself, he has ironically prevented this ever being the case; equally ironically, the revival of Talbot's name, as Nashe famously commented, came not from the son, but from the play itself.[3] For his son to survive and bear his name, Talbot argues, he must flee; but that, as the son replies, will call his identity into question – 'The world will say, he is not Talbot's blood, / That basely fled when noble Talbot stood' (lines 16–17). Therefore, despite his father's protests, it is impossible that 'Part of thy father may be sav'd in thee' (line 38). If the two are identified, part of one larger *idea* that is Talbot, they cannot be severed: the son concludes, 'No more can I be severed from your side / Than can yourself yourself in twain divide' (line 49).[4] Here is the tragic impasse of patrilineal hyperidentification in little; it will provoke deeper resonances and consequences in later plays, but this scene sums it up with extraodinary compression.[5] The next scene seems less loaded with typically Shakespearean problems of identity, but reinforces the issue: even now that the son has proved himself, he must carry on fighting alongside his father, for such proof needs to be ongoing. Significantly, young Talbot has been fighting the bastard Orleans, setting what his father calls his 'pure blood' against baseness (IV. vi. 23) – nonetheless, the father has had to rescue the son (this is very different from the refusal of Edward III to rescue his son – see below). Here, then, the son has no independent identity: indeed, in being rescued, he has been given life twice (line 6); the increase of obligation makes it impossible for him to flee.

The play's villains are less tied to patrilineal identity, and this gives them greater freedom. Joan of Arc's absolutely anomalous and puzzling nature is emphasized by the unusual strategy of having her repudiate her father.[6] This is more than a mark of her personal sinfulness, constituting a radical rebellion against patriarchy, and therefore against all of the values that underpin the men's actions in the play. Add to this her claims first to be a virgin, then to be pregnant (V. iv. 49–85) – both as futile efforts to avoid execution – and we can see that she embodies the idea of the mysterious woman who undermines all claims of paternalistic certainty. Of course, the play mostly seems to condemn her, but some confusion over this is probably caused by the collaborative composition of the text; the effect of this is quite powerful, however, in that she becomes very hard to pin down; uncertainty about her therefore reflects an uneasy uncertainty that all the patriarchally derived identities the men are fighting for may be mere illusions, reliant on the unknowable fidelity of women. Her claim to be nobly born (lines 8–9), or even 'issued from the progeny of kings' (line 38) may reflect on the apparently less arbitrary claims of royalty that will impel the Wars of the Roses. With the truly and securely patrilineal Talbots out of the way, dubious claims of paternity may become the order of the day.

Confusion about royal paternity sometimes rears its head in early history plays. Peele's *Edward I* presents the haughty, Spanish-born Queen Elinor as a source of corruption: in a climactic deathbed confession to her husband (who is disguised as a monk), she admits that her daughter Joan of Acon is really the result of her liaison with a friar. Once this information is passed on to Joan, she dies of shame at her base-born status. Among all these unhistorical histrionics, it is significant that the queen confirms that Prince Edward (who has been born, christened, and dubbed prince of Wales during the play) is definitely her husband's son; the foreign queen may be slurred, but the royal line must not be. Yet we may wonder whether the cat is not out of the bag here: despite attempts to repress the notion that patrilineal identity can never be entirely secure, the dropping of such hints betrays a larger anxiety that all the conflicts are over a fiction.

Greater security can be found, at least on the surface, in *Edward III* (1590–5, almost certainly by several authors, including Shakespeare), yet even here there are problems. The play is unusual in putting a father and son side by side as central heroes. King Edward and the prince are not only nostalgic models of military heroism, but, in their perfect agreement with one another, reflect a nostalgia for the perfect transmission of patrilineal virtue. Central to this is the scene in which the prince proves himself off stage, while his father ignores the nobles' emotional and urgent demands that he rescue his son, saying 'We have more sons / Than one to comfort our declining age' (III. v. 23–4). The son must prove himself here, without his father's aid: indeed, he is not to be knighted until after he has won the battle. Yet there is some irony in this scene of patrilineal proof: the prince may, as his father says, have 'prov'd thyself fit heir unto a king' (line 93), but of course we know that he never succeeded to the throne; we also know that the many other sons to whom the king refers would produce heirs who would fight each other in the Wars of the Roses. To have so many sons may not, in the long run, be a comfort, though to have one perfect son may be an intense present satisfaction (in this, the play reverses the dynamic of *Titus Andronicus*).

Despite all the play's military, masculine, paternal posturing (which is very good stuff of its kind), the most striking scenes – probably Shakespeare's – involve the amorous delinquency of the king-father with the countess of Salisbury. His crime is not only in the attempted seduction of a married woman, but in forcing her father to suborn her; that father, Warwick, does his duty as a liegeman in half-heartedly wooing for the king, but also his duty as a father in failing. The countess's rejection of his arguments therefore enables Warwick to give her his blessing (II. i. 454), and the scene thus becomes a paternal test of daughterly virtue, a process of proving that parallels the proving of the prince.

The prince is significantly tied in with the seduction episode in the next scene, where the sight of his face persuades his father to turn to virtue. The king begins this scene saying that the countess 'wins the sun of me' (II. ii. 68), punningly suggesting that his amorous defeat will taint his paternity. The prince's face, recalling that of his mother, 'corrects my stray'd desire' (line 77), an inversion of the normative father–son process which does not so much subvert the ideal relationship as emphasize its mutuality. However, once the countess enters, all this is proved to be insufficient; the king now comments, to his departed son, 'Thy mother is but black, and thou, like her, / Dost put it in my mind how foul she is' (lines 108–9). The proleptic irony here is telling, as we are reminded of the prince's future status as heroic icon – he will be the Black Prince who will bring his father fame. 'Black' here mainly means ugly, but it may have some minor racial connotations in order to suggest, if not illegitimacy (as in *Titus Andronicus*), then at least the idea that the son is not a perfect copy of the father. Yet Edward must, ironically, accept this fact if he is to have a perfect son and the good reputation this will bring. Just as it is the countess's virtue that prevents the king's lapse, and thereby enables him to go and defeat the French, so the good son is dependent on his mother (who, for good measure, arrives to witness his triumph in the play's final scene).

It may be that the original versions of the seduction scenes presented the king in an even worse light,[7] and it is important that this truancy from martial duty is redeemed more by the son than the father. After the Black Prince's first victory, the king can say 'Now, John of France, I hope / Thou knowest King Edward for no wantonness / No love-sick cockney, nor his soldiers jades' (III. v. 99–101); the class and gender references here affirm a masculine identity that can perhaps only be vindicated through one's son, black though he be. The failings of the father are made up for in the son, as will be the case in Marlowe's *Edward II* and Shakespeare's *Henry IV* plays. The son enables the father to be something of a prodigal, but without tainting the idea of fatherhood. The prince ends the play acknowledging that he has been 'the instrument to show thy power' (V. i. 219) in a prayer which seems to conflate his father and God – not claiming anything for himself, he affirms an abstract patrilineal virtue that is as much an object for emulation and imitation by future generations as a thing of value in itself. The perfect son must, in realizing himself, efface himself.

A curious and possibly misplaced speech rounds off the scene of the Black Prince's first victory (it may have been intended to go later, in the climactic scene of his capture of the French king). King Edward asks:

> What picture's this?
> PRINCE. [*Pointing to the colours.*] A pelican, my lord,
> Wounding her bosom with her crooked beak,
> That so her nest of young ones might be fed
> With drops of blood that issue from her heart;
> The motto, *Sic et vos*: 'And so should you'.   (III. v. 109–13)

The pelican, which supposedly fed its offspring with its own blood, was a traditional symbol of Christ, and it may be introduced here merely as a symbol of the analogous responsibilities of a king; however, to have this symbol presented by a son to a father – by a son, moreover, who has 'fed' his father's honour so – is surely significant. It suggests, along with the king's earlier willingness to sacrifice his son, that the prince is, perhaps improperly, perhaps necessarily, acting as a Christ-like figure, sacrificed to the honour of his father's larger family.[8] It may even suggest a mild rebuke to the father for acting so vicariously through his son. As in the case of Talbot and his son, the most honourable examples of father–son identification tend to be doomed: the Black Prince will die, leaving Richard II as his doomed heir. Yet, for a moment at least, there is this strange kind of recognition between father and son.

The issue of securing the succession in a son is obviously central to Shakespeare's grand cycle of English history plays, yet one key figure demonstrates scepticism as to the value of insisting on it. In *Henry VI Part 3*, the king, knowing that his 'title's weak' (I. i. 134), despite the precedent of his father and grandfather, adopts Richard duke of York as his heir; Clifford thinks this a 'wrong' (line 176) to his son, and Westmoreland that it makes him 'Base, fearful, and despairing' (line 178) – he is 'faint-hearted and degenerate', a man of 'cold blood' (lines 183–4), lacking the natural feeling that makes for honour; even the king himself knows that in disinheriting his son he is acting 'unnaturally' (line 193). He suffers contrastingly stinging rebukes (one vituperative, one ingenuously plain and direct) from his wife and the prince: the queen regrets ever marrying one who has 'proved so unnatural a father' (line 218), and insists:

> Hadst thou but lov'd him half so well as I,
> Or felt that pain which I did for him once,
> Or nourish'd him as I did with my blood,
> Thou wouldst have left thy dearest heart-blood there
> Rather than have made that savage duke thine heir,
> And disinherited thine only son.
> PRINCE. Father, you cannot disinherit me.
> If you be king, why should I not succeed?   (lines 220–7)

The mother's insistence that she has a greater natural affection for her son, and the attribution of this to her pains in childbirth and her nursing, are commonplaces that indicate the need to *prove* oneself a good father through action; this attitude of proof tends to be reciprocal: Henry's alleged degeneration and cooling of blood indicate a decline in his family, especially in comparison to his heroic father Henry V, signalized by the loss of France in his reign. The prince's question is more affecting, suggesting that a father *ought* to give straightforward precedent for a son: the emphasis is surely 'If *you* be king, why should *I* not succeed?' – suggesting an assumption of identity between father and son. The naivety of the attitude displayed here in the face of the bloody wars to come reminds us powerfully of how fraught an issue the transmission of paternal attributes can be. If patriarchy is the basis of this society, it is by no means as simple a basis as an innocent child might think. A few scenes later (I. iv), the queen demonstrates the power of maternal passion in her savage, taunting murder of York, a scene apparently played in the presence of her unspeaking son (though the Quarto texts significantly omit the prince from the list of entering characters in the stage direction at line 26). Seemingly unaffected by this, the prince later seems a throwback in some respects to Henry V (although in terms of Shakespeare's cycle he is more a throw-forward, the dead Henry V being the first on-stage image of *Henry VI Part 1*); he urges the feeble king:

> My royal father, cheer these noble lords,
> And hearten those that fight in your defence.
> Unsheathe your sword, good father; cry 'Saint George!'   (II. ii. 78–80)

Anticipating Henry V's invocations of St George, his is the one voice of goodness in an untrustworthy world, rebuking the master turncoat Warwick: 'If that be right which Warwick says is right, / There is no wrong, but every thing is right' (lines 131–2). Such a comment is founded on a firm sense of an inherent and essential *right*, but it is in fact Warwick (and later Richard of Gloucester) who is the presiding spirit of this play. The Prince's goodness is very marginal in a play which presents '*A son that hath kill'd his father*' and '*A father that hath kill'd his son*' (II. v. 54, 78 SD). Each of those symbolic figures of chaos has not *known* his father or son in killing him;[9] even the wise child cannot know his own father in these times (or *vice versa*); the son speaks of the wars as 'heavy times, begetting such events' (line 63) – the paternal metaphor ironically underpinning the idea that all this suffering comes when a king is an inadequate father, reflecting a belief that strong patriarchal lineages could protect the nation from catastrophe.

At the end of the play, the prince defiantly tells the newly crowned King Edward:

> Speak like a subject, proud ambitious York!
> Suppose that I am now my father's mouth:
> Resign thy chair, and where I stand kneel thou.   (V. v. 17–19)

This claim of identification with his father is futile: the Yorkists simply kill him. Catherine Belsey argues that Prince Edward's authority is 'unrealized' in the play, and that, despite our pity for his murder, his words to the Yorkist brothers are 'unappealing'.[10] But surely his words are his only authority; and his childishness is what gives them licence and force even as it deprives him of practical power. This is the inherent trouble of asserting that one is one's 'father's mouth' – for he is only a voice, without any practical power. Authority here is fundamentally divided, paternity merely theoretical supposition.[11]

In Marlowe's *Edward II*, however, the son of a murdered king is given real power, the youthful Edward III being able to push aside the rebel Mortimer and to punish his own mother who has connived with Mortimer. His authority comes from his 'loving father' (V. i. 40), whose voice he claims;[12] of course, his father's love was rather for Gaveston and other favourites than for his son, but once Edward II is dead that love can be translated into patrilineal terms, in a weirdly purgative kind of recognition. No supposition is needed here; as Judith Haber observes, the new king's 'painfully firm resolution is particularly striking in a play in which almost everyone else has been presented as "slack" or "drooping"'.[13] He affirms identity and unifies the doubleness of fathers. Yet Mortimer can call Edward III a 'paltry boy' (line 56), from whom he will ask no pity, and Edward weeps (though doesn't waver) at his mother being taken away; he ends the play saying 'let these tears, distilling from mine eyes, / Be witness of my grief and innocency' (lines 100–1) – the tears both prove that he is his father's son and repudiate the guilty example of his father. Haber sees this moment as 'a submission to history' on Marlowe's part, and certainly Mortimer reads his own story as the effect of 'Base Fortune' (line 58) rather than of Edward's power; but such submission in the end requires the purgation rather than the assertion of the father – this, we might suppose, is the reason Edward III can succeed where Prince Edward in *Henry VI* failed.

Prince Hal in the *Henry IV* plays is much less an essentialist of paternity than his earlier-written grandson. From the first, he punningly says that he will 'imitate the sun' (*Part 1*, I. ii. 197), considering the role of a son something that needs to be played, for he knows that paternity, like royal legitimacy, has to be negotiated. His father's attitude, from the first, suggests that he is right to play his long game: Henry IV envies Northumberland for being 'the father to so blest a son' as Hotspur (*Part 1*, I. i. 80), and laments his own son's riots, wishing:

> O that it could be prov'd
> That some night-tripping fairy had exchang'd
> In cradle-clothes our children where they lay,
> And call'd mine Percy, his Plantagenet! (lines 86–9)

Such a desire for *proof* of different paternity indicates the conditionality of paternal feeling in this context; the invocation of the changeling fiction points to imaginary possibilities of better fatherhood and a sense of radical paternal uncertainty.[14] Hal, of course, is going to be a changeling of a different sort in his planned reformation, but he plans this more for public consumption than to please his father – it is 'men's hopes' in general that he will falsify (I. ii. 211). Hope is the characteristic paternal emotion, but Hal does not focus on his father.[15] Hal's tendency to divert thoughts from his father is illustrated when a nobleman is announced coming from his father, and he responds 'Give him as much as will make him a royal man, and send him back again to my mother' (II. iv. 290–1); the joke is probably based on the fact that Hal's mother is dead,[16] but the more unsettling point is that anyone can be made into a royal man in this world, and it is unwise to think (like the prince in *Henry VI Part 3*) that simply being the son of a king will be enough to raise one up.

Hal is right to be wary of relying on paternal affection; this is a play in which even 'so blest a son' as Hotspur can be betrayed by his father; Northumberland's betrayal is about as far from giving a blessing as is possible. The negotiation of the king-father's blessing in this context is bound to be problematic. When Hal finally encounters his own father, he gives a rather cold 'submission' (III. ii. 28). Henry IV thinks him 'grafted' to ill company and pleasures which unnaturally remove him from 'the greatness of thy blood' (lines 15–16). He gives a lengthy and self-congratulatory speech contrasting their behaviours, saying that Hal is in Richard II's 'line' (line 85); this suggests that he will be deposed as Richard was, but it also strangely doubles his paternity, and restores some imaginary legitimacy to Hal. Henry also argues that Hal has only 'the shadow of succession' (line 99) in comparison to Hotspur's merits, but such a shadow may be made into imaginative reality, as it so often is in Shakespeare.[17] As Falstaff gnomically says in *Part 2*, 'the son of the female is the shadow of the male. It is often so indeed, but much of the father's substance' (III. ii. 129–31); even if one is only a shadow of one's father, one can still attain one's father's substance, for if one gets his possessions one might as well be said to own his essence too. The king's speech comes close to disowning his son, but Hal does not seem upset by his father's shame. Interjecting, Hal can only promise to 'Be more myself' (*Part 1*, III. ii. 93) without much sense that such selfhood is paternally derived; he gives no direct response to his father's sense of hurt, his self-reliance not allowing him at this point to accept anything from his father, with whom he has no emotional connection. In rescuing the king at the battle of

Shrewsbury (V. iv), Hal *proves* that he has not desired his father's death, but the deed is more a proof of his own inherent honour than of any emotional relationship between them. In sending out doubles to represent him on the battlefield, in fact, it is the king rather than Hal who fragments paternity in this play.

The strain between the Machiavellian father and son persists into *Henry IV Part 2*. Hal says to Poins only that he '*could* be sad, and sad indeed too' (II. ii. 42–3; emphasis added) at the sickness of his father; Poins thinks this unlikely because he is 'engraff'd' to Falstaff (line 63). The fundamental fear is that Hal has taken Falstaff as an adoptive father; the suggestion that fathers can be chosen indicates that there is no inherent identity conferred by paternity.[18] The possibility of Falstaff's engrafting in the royal family has, however, already been dispelled in the extraordinary scene where Hal and Falstaff in turn play a scene between Hal and his father. Hal here has Falstaff to 'stand for my father' (*Part 1*, II. iv. 376), but Falstaff sentimentalizes (and perhaps therefore essentializes) the role, commencing by saying 'I do not speak to thee in drink, but in tears' (lines 414–15). He uses the paternal role, however, to commend himself (Falstaff), to which Hal responds mockingly 'Dost thou speak like a king?' (line 433), and turns the tables, playing the king much better than Falstaff, and arguably better than his father. His insistence that he will banish plump Jack falsifies Falstaff's hopes. No one will be a father to him. He knows that succession is merely a shadow, but he is better at the shadow-play than anyone.

At the end of *Part 2*, when Hal anticipates his father's death and takes the crown, he is clear about the give-and-take of the father–son relationship:

> Thy due from me
> Is tears and heavy sorrows of the blood,
> Which nature, love, and filial tenderness
> Shall, O dear father, pay thee plenteously.
> My due from thee is this imperial crown,
> Which as immediate from thy place and blood
> Derives itself to me. [*Puts on the crown.*]   (IV. v. 37–43)

He believes in 'This lineal honour' not as essential (line 46), but as part of a system of negotiated honours.[19] It is the first moment that we have been convinced by the charge that Hal wants his father to die, and his father's revival gives him the chance to answer it fully:

PRINCE. I never thought to hear you speak again.
KING. Thy wish was father, Harry, to that thought.   (lines 91–2)

It is hard to know what to make of this most famous paternal pun. Apart from a commonplace metaphor which imagines thoughts as children, there is an underlying sense that the chief wish of a son is to be a father, necessarily displacing the actual father. Without the need for a Freudian reading, we can say that this scene provides, in the royal family, a particularly acute version of a common problem in a society based on primogeniture – the son cannot become himself without the death of his father. Hal's prodigality is in fact the most successful strategy to deal with this. His response to his father's charge that 'thou lov'dst me not' (line 104) is finely calculated, and certainly puts a more positive and emotional spin on his reaction to finding the king apparently dead (if it isn't an outright lie about that reaction). The king seems to recognize this in accepting his son's apology, almost as if he smilingly sees something of himself in Hal's ability to make the best of things:

> God put it in thy mind to take it hence,
> That thou mightst win the more thy father's love,
> Pleading so wisely in excuse of it!   (lines 178–80)

'Wisely' is a fine choice of words: he appreciates his son's skill. To adapt the proverb, it's a wise child that can con his father; they have managed a peculiar kind of negotiated recognition. Hal's wisdom here is an ability to create a relationship with his father at the last, and to get a paternal blessing for it (is there a touch of Jacob and Isaac here, even?). Just as the king advises that friendships cannot be relied upon as essential, but must be managed,[20] paternal relationships are constructed, and the father and son know this. The 'plain and right' possession Hal now takes of the crown (line 222) is based on the scene that he and his father have stage-managed between them.

Shakespeare's model for his Henry IV and V plays provides perhaps a stronger sense of the tensions between fathers and sons than any other play of the period. In *The Famous Victories of Henry V*, it is almost a refrain with the 'young Prince' that if 'the king / My father were dead, we would be all kings' (lines 113–14).[21] His friend John Oldcastle, the partial forerunner of Falstaff (though a very minor character in the anonymous play) agrees that 'we shall never have a mery world til the old king be dead' (lines 534–5).[22] John Cobbler, meanwhile, betraying a lower-class attitude to inheritance, suggests that the prince's 'father will cut him off from the Crowne' (line 140) if he continues to misbehave. This prince is sent to the Fleet prison, promises the position of chief justice to his friend Ned, and wears a coat full of needles to remind himself of his impatience to succeed his father. Unlike Shakespeare's Hal, he does not anticipate his repentance, being converted to good ways instantly and almost magically by the sight and admonition of his father. Shakespeare's presentation of his prodigal-son plot is considerably more artful than the anonymous playwright's, but there are points of considerable interest in the father–son tensions in *The Famous Victories*, particularly in the elements Shakespeare does not pick up on. When the young prince is arrested, the Lord Chief Justice is in a quandary: he thinks that Henry IV might have set the scenario up in order to test the judge's impartiality (lines 288–91); this anticipates the disguised-ruler trope of plays like *Henry V* and *Measure for Measure* (see Chapter 4, below), and indicates a key tension between justice and family that Shakespeare's plays will complicate. The consequent dialogue between prince and judge is indicative, though, of a starker tension that Shakespeare represses; after the prince has boxed the judge's ear, we get the following careful reassertion of dignity:

JUDGE. Well my Lord, I am content to take it at your hands.
HEN. 5. Nay and you be not, you shall have more.
JUDGE. Why I pray you my Lord, who am I?
HEN. 5. You, who knowes not you?
  Why man, you are Lord chiefe Justice of England.
JUDGE. Your Grace hath said truth, therfore in striking me
  in this place, you greatly abuse me, and not me onely,
  but also your father: whose lively person here in this place
  I doo represent. (lines 410–20)

This resembles the anecdote with which we began this book, but its implications are different: the prince has indirectly struck at his father, whose dignity is maintained even as the judge's dignity is preserved by separating himself in two – *he* may be content in his private person, but cannot be so insofar as he represents the king. The prince learns a lesson here in how to divide oneself. He will not only not replace this just man with Ned, but will make this proven judge his regent during his French wars.

This is a key step to defusing the prince's rebelliousness, but it must still go further.[23] When the young prince comes into his father's presence a few scenes later, he does so carrying a dagger (line 613); given all that we have heard about the prince desiring his father's death, we must fear that the iconic English hero is to be made a parricide here. Instead, of course, he uses the dagger as a prop in his performance of penitence, asking his father to kill him as just punishment for his sins (lines 631–51). This prince is not as careful a planner as Hal, and is certainly no Machiavel, so that the shift in this scene cannot seem premeditated; perhaps, then, he really does mean to kill his father when he enters, and is only converted by his father weeping (the key stage directions at lines 621 and 628). These paternal tears have something like essential power – and it is revealing that Shakespeare transfers them to Falstaff. Shakespeare's reconcilement of father and son is based on a later scene in this play (lines 701–82), and he has no real equivalent of the dagger scene in *Henry IV Part 2*, but I think that it haunted him, and prepared the way for Hamlet coming upon the praying Claudius (*Hamlet*, III. iii). The scene of near patricide is perhaps the ultimate limit case for the drama of this time, and it never gets closer than here; yet it may be a paratext in both *Henry IV* and *Hamlet*. Hal may not bring a dagger, Claudius may not be Hamlet's father (officially, at least), but the scene from the earlier play, with its simple presentation of repentance, may lurk in the writer's and even the audience's mind. Only the supernatural intervention of a king's tears can prevent the horrifying possibility of murdering one's father.

The young prince, in offering himself as a sacrifice, may turn the patricidal motif into the more pious Abraham and Isaac motif, but he indicates that father–son tensions need to be brought to such limits before they can be settled. Shakespeare's more knowing father–son pair are able to manage things in a more sophisticated way, but they do so by deflecting rather than settling the tensions set up in the earlier play. As Peter Erickson points out, there is a displacement of patricidal tension when Hal describes the crown as the murderer of his father (IV. v. 166–7),[24] but he does so in order to win his father's blessing, suggesting that they have a common enemy.[25] Yet, despite Hal's need to vindicate his father, even to bear his sins, he is never under the kind of uncertain pressure that Hamlet will feel. The tension, at heart, is more commonplace, and can be managed because these men are so able to divide their private and their public selves. The doubleness of paternity is made more straightforward in history than in tragedy.

Elizabethan society may have seen such tensions between fathers and their heirs at the private level, but in the royal family there was no such issue; Queen Elizabeth had no family at all to compete with her. Perhaps this made the presentation of such plays safer: soon after King James I came to the throne, his son Prince Henry started to become a focus of opposition to his policies, Henry supporting militant protestantism against his father's pacifism. One therefore wonders if it would have been advisable to perform the *Henry IV* plays in James's reign. By a curious inversion (which might be called political evasion), having been concerned with father–son tensions under Elizabeth, Shakespeare's plays turn under James to the problem of not having a son, as we shall see in Chapter 4's discussion of *Macbeth*.

Elizabethan history plays offer many more models for succession than the supposedly normative handover from father to son, partly because such a handover was obviously not going to happen on the death of the present queen. What all such plays have in common, though, is the *idea* of the father. Whatever its relation to Shakespeare's play may be, the anonymous *Troublesome Reign of King John* is more strikingly haunted by the paternal figure of Richard the Lionheart than its probable imitator *King John*. The Bastard Philip Faulconbridge is more fully engaged with imitating and avenging his biological father in *The Troublesome Reign* than he is in *John*, where Shakespeare makes him a radical individualist and improvisor of motivation, a forerunner of Hamlet, Edmund, and Iago.[26] Where Shakespeare's character concludes that he might as well be Richard's son, but that 'I am I, howe'er I was begot' (I. i. 175), Philip in the anonymous play becomes (it seems) possessed by the spirit of his true father, and therefore cannot do as he is required and deny Richard to be his father for a third time; he speaks almost prophetically in Latin of his paternity, as 'fumes of Maiestie' ravish him:

> Me thinkes I heare a hollow Eccho sound,
> That *Philip* is the Sonne vnto a King:
> The whistling leaues vpon the trembling trees,
> Whistle in consort I am *Richards* Sonne:
> The bubling murmur of the waters fall,
> Records *Philippus Regius filius:*
> Birds in their flight make musicke with their wings,
> Filling the ayre with glorie of my birth:
> Birds, bubbles, leaues, and mountaines, Eccho, all
> Ring in mine Eares, that I am *Richards* Sonne.
> Fond man, ah whether art thou carried?   (*Part 1*, i. 246–56)[27]

These powerful lines, which have a Marlovian ecstatic rapture, and some of Kyd's deft use of repetitions, lack Shakespeare's fascination with self-identity, for this Bastard is wholly consumed with his father as a model; having accepted his paternity, with no evidence other than his perhaps magically derived conviction, he goes on to pray 'Graunt heauens that *Philip* once may shew himself / Worthie the honour of *Plantaginet,* / Or basest glorie of a Bastards name' (lines 302–4), and to compare himself to Phaethon (whom Ovid has demanded of his mother the knowledge of his descent from the Sun).[28]

The only evidence he has before his mother's confession is that he does not resemble his brother. Whereas in Shakespeare it is Queen Eleanor who sees the resemblance to her son Richard, in the anonymous play it is

John himself who says 'I neuer saw so liuely counterfet / Of *Richard Cordelion*, as in him' (lines 192–3),[29] and this resemblance is pressed throughout the play as it is not in Shakespeare. Seeing Limoges with his father's spoils, Philip's reaction is vigorous:

> My Fathers foe clad in my Fathers spoyle,
> A thousand furies kindle with revendge,
> This hart that choller keepes a consistorie,
> Searing my inwards with a brand of hate.   (ii. 136–9)

The father here is fully internalized and, though he restrains himself at first, ultimately he is given the chance to take revenge as he is not in Shakespeare, recovering his father's lion-skin as 'The first freehold that *Richard* left his sonne' (iii. 46); his laying this at Blaunch's feet gives her the chance 'T''incourage thee to follow *Richards* fame' (iv. 48); he then challenges Austria to single combat, which is rejected, and kills him in battle. His vindication of his identity is as important to this play as the political plot, allowing him to be the play's hero rather than the more ambiguous figure he is in Shakespeare. He announces 'Thus hath K. *Richards* Sonne performde his vowes', making sacrifices to 'his fathers euerliuing soule'. That father is invoked, with Marlovian bombast, as 'Braue *Cordelion*' (vi. 1–5);[30] such apostrophic speeches invoke the presence of Richard onto the stage more fully than anything in Shakespeare, and allow a stricter comparison between the heroic past and the politically compromised present.

King John himself is not thought of as a son to *his* father: associated with his mother (who supports him more vigorously than in Shakespeare, and whose death seems to catalyse his fall), he is not a very manly figure, though more assertive than in Shakespeare. His brother is the precedent for him, but that precedent, as we have seen, has been appropriated by the Bastard. John is also, significantly, not presented as a father until he is dead. As in Marlowe's *Edward II*, the son emerges as a vindicating figure after his father's fall. The new Henry III tells his 'Unckle' (the Bastard) to tear down Swinstead Abbey in vengeance for John's murder – 'For they haue kilde my Father and my King' (*Part 2*, viii. 162). The possessive here is impressive; he makes it clear that he himself is 'thy soveraigne' (line 159), but his father is king for *him*. The redemptive hope of a new reign is nicely conveyed, as in Marlowe, whereas the prince in Shakespeare is a tearful boy who has to be guided by the Bastard – his 'tears' (*King John*, V. viii. 109), though, may be a proof of paternity, as those of Edward III are in Marlowe's play. The anonymous playwright's greater concern for the assertion of patrilineal identity is a central issue, and may be his *explanation* for John's failure both as a king and as a forerunner of the Reformation.

If he was imitating this play, Shakespeare characteristically blurred this issue. Shakespeare's Bastard, like his Henry V in some respects, is a radically free agent, not tied down by questions of paternity.[31] Though they are fundamentally different characters, they represent a pure national identity which has escaped the excessive need to identify with fathers; the Bastard is one who lives in 'The spirit of the time' (IV. ii. 176), and something similar can be said of Henry V, whose victories are very temporary, not laid at the feet of his larger familial dynasty. Both men speak for 'England' more than for their family (*King John*, IV. iii. 145, V. vii. 112; *Henry V*, III. i. 34). The Bastard's ironic discussion of 'Commodity' (II. i. 574–98) has some similarities to Henry V's sceptical meditation on 'idol Ceremony' (*Henry V*, IV. i. 240–84); not only do both set-piece speeches repeatedly apostrophize an abstraction, but both also demonstrate minds that stand independent of that abstraction while using it to their advantage. This habit of mind is reflected in their attitudes to paternity – it is something to be used, not an idol to be worshipped. Where the Bastard gives away his paternity with a blithe 'I am I' (see above), Henry V prays it away, saying 'Not today, O Lord, / O not today, think not upon the fault / My father made in compassing the crown!' (IV. i. 292–4). Any sin is conveniently displaced onto the father, a trope that becomes increasingly common in later drama.

It is significant that the first answer Henry V gives to Williams's charge that the king is responsible for his soldiers' souls runs as follows: 'So if a son that is by his father sent about merchandise do sinfully miscarry upon the sea, the imputation of his wickedness, by your rule, should be impos'd upon the father that sent him' (IV. i. 147–50); refusing the idea of paternal identification is a major habit for Henry, and it frees him for personal and national success. Henry can use the idea of fathers abstractly in the siege of Harfleur, but there is nothing personal in this: 'On, on, you noblest English, / Whose blood is fet from fathers of war-proof!' (III. i. 17–18). The sons' 'war-proof' here will prove them legitimate sons (lines 22–3). Yet it doesn't matter who one's particular father might be: battle is proof of identity and legitimacy in the abstract.

After Shakespeare's grand cycle, history plays largely go into abeyance, but their attitudes persist in other genres. *Look about You* (Anon., 1600) is a 'Pleasant Commodie' about sons' rebellion against their royal father, loosely based on the 1173–4 rebellion of Henry II's sons. As such, it is rather an anomalous development of the 1590s' vogue for history plays, its genre perhaps reflecting a genuine discomfort about its subject matter. Although the main frame of the plot is Henry the Young King taking power from his father, the body of the play is chiefly occupied by a farcical multiplicity of disguises, robberies, and pursuit, hinting at the chaos and even loss of identity that may be the consequence of filial impiety at the highest level.

Though the younger Henry has taken the throne, it is Prince John (the later Bad King John of myth) who is predictably the leading offender against his father, insisting that the old king should 'Liue at his prayers, haue a sufficient pention by the yere, / Repent his sinnes because his end is neere' (lines 225–6); this is a model of disrespect to age masquerading as concern for the elderly. Prince Richard (the Lionheart), though he has rebelled too, now regrets it and wants them to be more 'respectiue' to their father (line 220). Ultimately his crusade will be undertaken as penance for the rebellion, and as the play develops he lines up with those who have taken the old king's side, particularly Lancaster and Gloucester. The play's good characters are strongly opposed to the usurpation, Lancaster setting the tone early on, blaming Queen Elinor for provoking her sons against the king, 'And not the children of a low-priz'd wretch, / But one whom God on earth hath deified?' (lines 165–6).[32]

Such action would be an offence even among the lower classes, but here it is real impiety. It can only be explained by the bad influence of the queen, and of her Frenchness; it is she who influences young Henry into his most transgressive thoughts, urging him almost satanically to say:

> Pride seaze vppon my heart, wrath fill myne eyes,
> Sit lawfull maiestie vppon my front
> Dutie flie from me, pitty be exild,
> Sences forget that I am Henries child   (lines 1010–13)

The disjunction of majesty and law from natural duty and pity anticipates *Macbeth*, and earns a blessing from his mother. When Richard has converted to his father's side she goes so far as to repudiate him, calling him 'that vile abortiue changling brat' (line 974). Interestingly, the weak old king makes no real complaint against his sons, and certainly does not (as would be easier for him) repudiate them. The mother is a force, the father a mere object of reverence denied.

The play's most shocking moment is its final feast, where the old king is forced to act as his eldest son's cupbearer. Gloucester's reaction to this event (which 'Idolatrie' – line 2552 – he has tried to avoid witnessing) shows its impact: 'Kneele to his childe? O hell! O tortor! / Who would loue life, to see this huge dishonor?' (lines 3051–2). The old king is not exactly blamed here; paternal impotence is more a shame on his sons than on himself, he being rather a cipher or figurehead, even perhaps an idol. Young Henry can use classical precedent to justify the inversion of the proper order: 'Saturne kneel'd to his Sonne, the God was faine / To call young Ioue his ages Soveragine' (lines 3053–4). Yet this merely prefaces a sudden *volte-face*. When Richard reminds everyone of their offences, young Henry repents, in the process repudiating his mother as a devil (line 3122). Only John holds out, staying by Elinor's side and confidently anticipating his notorious future reign.

This anticipation may be a key point of the plot: it acts as a narrative of origin for the reign of a bad king, whose rebellion against his father constitutes a starting-point for further evil. The play ends with the old king's grateful prayer 'That England neuer know more Prince then one' (line 3212), probably reflecting fears that civil war would break out when Elizabeth died. Such fears, along with the reminder of John's reign – presented on stage in both Shakespeare's *King John* and *The Troublesome Reign*, both of which feature two princes in John and his victim Arthur – mean that we have hardly arrived at a happy ending. Young Henry's final speech seems rather to set the tone here:

> Let none call me their Sonne, I am no mans brother,
> My kindred is in heauen, I know no other,
> Farewell, farewell, the world is yours, pray take it,
> Ile leaue vexation, and with ioy forsake it.   (lines 3175–8)

The first line here oddly echoes Richard of Gloucester in *Henry VI Part 3* (V. vi. 80), though this is a repentant rather than an emergent villain. The speech is a kind of inverse repudiation of his father, fashioning his own punishment for his earlier impiety – which not even the father can forgive. Even when the father is genuinely weak and may indeed deserve what he gets, such offences against him put the son beyond the pale, and may curse the nation. If God has deified the king, the king is still limited in his power to forgive.

In some ways *Look about You* anticipates *King Lear*: the three children, one of whom is better than the others but must still be punished; the variations of tone; the disguises the loyal characters must turn to. But a sharp focus on the wronged father does not yet seem possible for the drama, perhaps because any repentance on his part would be unbearable, and needs to be left to his son. A modern audience may be sceptical as to whether Lear is more sinned against than sinning, but the audience of the time might have been struck by a father being able to admit that he was sinning at all. That factor needed to emerge in the apparently serener environment of comedy.

COMEDY

Much late Elizabethan comedy starts off presenting women as a problem to be solved by men, but male solutions often expose deeper problems in the idea of masculinity, particularly in relation to the identity of fathers and their scope for action. Such action, as in history plays, often needs to be left to sons, but fathers feel the effects of this, raising the tensions between the generations in ways that will ultimately be developed in tragedy. Such comedy also fills in (or at least adumbrates) the background of ordinary domestic life – a background that will add emotional depth to tragedy.

Henry Porter's *The Two Angry Women of Abingdon* (pub. 1599, but possibly rather earlier), brilliant play though it is, is deeply antifeminist, its main intention being to present women as the cause of neighbourhood strife (and perhaps by implication all other strife), a problem that can only be solved by quick and efficient male action. This remedial action, however, is not straightforwardly patriarchal: the fathers are in some senses displaced by their sons over the course of the play. Validated as they are by their fathers' approval, the sons Philip Barnes and Francis (Frank) Goursey are the play's leading lights, pushing Maister Barnes and Maister Goursey into the background; fathers may act in this play, but only through the agency of their sons. Their wives' quarrel, which is the central problem of the play, is resolved by the marriage of Frank to Barnes's daughter Mall, and by the fathers' (unarticulated) 'pollicie' (line 2428) of pretending to quarrel themselves;[33] though both schemes are initiated by Barnes Senior, they only come to fruition through the sons. The former plan only works because Philip is more able than Goursey to persuade Frank into marriage. More importantly, as we do not see the latter plan being hatched (and might even misunderstand what's going on), we cannot be sure that the sons are in on it; we are therefore allowed to believe, like the angry wives, that Philip and Frank are the ones who solve the quarrel between their fathers; as they gain voices of authority, it is possible that the sons themselves believe they are acting boldly and independently in crying peace. Philip is concerned that he is guilty of 'presumption' in trying to 'teach where he might learne or be derect' (lines 2780–1), and his humble tone sounds as if he is genuinely presuming on the older men's attention, going on to point out that the fathers' quarrel must be settled by the removal of its cause – the mothers' quarrel, based on Mistress Barnes's capricious allegation of an affair between her husband and Mistress Goursey. In doing so, he is taking charge of his mother, albeit diplomatically, and thus asserting his position as a man rather than a boy. Notably, it is Philip who joins the mothers' hands. The effect of this is not only to sideline the fathers, but to make the sons *seem* more rational than their fathers (who are notionally the source of their own male rationality). When the mothers agree to the marriage, which they have thus far vigorously resisted, Philip is the one to give his blessing on his sister and his friend, saying:

> brother, now your wooings doone:
> The next thing now you doe, is for a sonne:
> I prithe, for I faith I should be glad,
> To haue my selfe called nunckle, and thou Dad,
> Well sister, if that *Francis* play the man,
> My mother must be Grandam and you Mam. (2973–8)

Tactfully, no mention is made of his own father becoming a grandfather, but as he does so he must recede into the background, in dramatic as well as social terms; there are virtually no significant grandfathers on the Elizabethan stage. If Francis is to 'play the man' in becoming a father (of a son), Philip is also playing the man in giving this blessing; though unmarried himself, he has taken over the patriarchal role. We are not reminded of his father's directorial role in this performance (and we are uncertain as to its extent).

The sons' position was very different at the opening of the play, in which they went off to play at bowls, and joked about horses and girls with Francis's boy-servant. Notably, both young men were treated with little respect by their fathers' servants. Goursey's drunken servant Coomes says 'I do not like the humor of these Springals, theil spend all their Fathers good at gamming' (lines 76–7), and Barnes's servant, the prating Nicholas Proverbs, tells Philip 'you may speake when ye are spoken to' (lines 917–18). When Frank threatens to strike Coomes, the latter responds 'Strike me, alas he were better strike his father' (line 1801); these servants' assumption of paternal status is overturned in the play, the sons' rebelliousness in this direction being validated as a necessary assertion of social order. During the comic crisis of confusion, Frank nearly couples the servants with his mother in a curse ('A plague on *Coomes*, a plague vpon the boy, / A plague too, not on my mother for an hundreth pound' – lines 2065–6); though he here pays lip-service to the need to respect his mother, the pairing is significant: the young men's assertion of authority over the servants is allied to their development of power over their mothers.

The play's construction of manliness relies, however, on such restraint in speech, which is contrasted to the women's irrational loquacity. Even Mall, whose marriage to Frank is the solution to the problems the older women cause, is considered wordy and domineering, as well as being potentially unchaste; part of Barnes's reason for wanting to marry his daughter off is the fear that she may turn out like her mother (lines 593–601); and Philip shares worries about her character and chastity (lines 838–41, 1081–1110). A connection between sexual restraint and careful speech is made by Barnes early in the play as he tells his wife:

> Do not deforme the beautie of thy toung,
> With such misshapen answers, rough wrathfull words
> Are bastards got by rashness in the thoughts,
> Faire demeanours, are Vertues nuptiall babes,
> The off-spring, of the well instructed soule.   (lines 529–33)

Only if a wife is restrained in her speech, one might infer, can a husband be secure about his own offspring; the shame a wife can bring is not merely social but sexual – she may undermine his reputation, but can also destroy the paternal position that gives him his identity. When he becomes quarrelsome late in the play, it may be a matter of policy, but imaginatively it suggests infection of his identity, something that can only be reasserted by his son's intervention. The son saves the father, but in doing so, as we have seen, pushes him aside from roles that ought to be his. Patriarchal structures may be self-perpetuating, but the individual patriarch is in a perilous position, dependent on his womenfolk, and ultimately on a son who will displace him.

It is Shakespeare who makes the most striking developments in the comic representation of fathers: like other dramatists he starts off with the idea of the father as a comforting figure, but the father's position is undermined more and more in being used as such. Egeon in *The Comedy of Errors* is one of the most passive fathers imaginable (paralleled perhaps only by Shakespeare's later Cymbeline). Given a conditional sentence of death in the play's first scene, he is told to find 'friends' who will redeem him with money, but he is 'Hopeless and helpless' and only able to 'procrastinate' (I. i. 152, 157–8); he disappears from the action and only returns in the final scene to be saved by the wife and sons he has been seeking. The first 'friend' to whom he turns is the Ephesian Antipholus, who of course does not recognize him – Egeon first conjectures that this is because his sufferings have changed him (V. i. 284–301), then laments when even his voice is not recognized:

> O time's extremity,
> Hast thou so cracked and splitted my poor tongue
> In seven short years, that here my only son
> Knows not my feeble key of untun'd cares?
> Though now this grained face of mine be hid
> In sap-consuming winter's drizzled snow,
> And all the conduits of my blood froze up,
> Yet hath my night of life some memory,
> My wasting lamps some fading glimmer left,
> My dull deaf ears a little use to hear:
> All these old witnesses – I cannot err –
> Tell me thou art my son Antipholus.   (lines 308–19)

Here the idea of the father as a figure of pathetic suffering (through failed recognition) is a development of the tradition of paternal 'cares', which were also emphasized in the play's first scene, where Egeon told his pitiful story.[34] The dramatic irony here is powerful, for though Shakespeare gives full credence to the man's sufferings, we know that they will be cleared away at a stroke.[35] This is one of Shakespeare's finest portrayals of age: full of suffering though it may be, another perspective can wipe away all tears. The son here is not quite guilty of a denial, saying 'I never saw my father in my life' (line 320), and it does not occur to Egeon that this may be the lost son his other son went off to seek. Only the Abbess-Mother Aemilia can resolve what ought to be a simple problem for all the men: maternal speech is necessary to solve the impasse caused by the sufferings of paternity.

Fathers can introduce an element of seriousness, but perhaps more as ideas than as real people. The 'merriment' of *Love's Labour's Lost* is interrupted by news of a father:

> MARCADE. I am sorry, madam, for the news I bring
>   Is heavy in my tongue. The King your father –
> PRINCESS. Dead, for my life!
> MARCADE.   Even so: my tale is told.   (V. ii. 717–20)

The princess's prophetic soul here shows her wit, her recognizing oath hinting at the necessity of the father's death without directly expressing any pleasure at it, as many sons would in other comedies of the period. Yet at the core of this reaction is surely an underlying anxiety about her

father, and therefore a genuine grief, even if it does not cause immediate
lamentations. Incapable of grasping this, King Ferdinand tries to get
round her 'new-sad soul' and press his suit regardless:

> though the mourning brow of progeny
> Forbid the smiling courtesy of love
> The holy suit which fain it would convince,
> Yet since love's argument was first on foot,
> Let not the cloud of sorrow justle it
> From what it purposed; since to wail friends lost
> Is not by much so wholesome-profitable
> As to rejoice at friends but newly found.
> PRINCESS. I understand you not, my griefs are double.   (lines 744–52)

His tactless and self-serving *sententiae* may be in the spirit of comedy,
which prioritizes things new-born over things dying, but his inability to
give any meaning to her life before the play treats her as a mere toy of the
isolated academic lover. As in *The Comedy of Errors*, the fact that ordinary
domestic life has not been represented brings a deeper sense of loss than
any representation could. It is fair to say that this incomprehension
doubles her grief. We may share his sense that the French king is of no
account because we have not met him, and may regard his death as an
intrusion on the play, but there is something outside the text here, even if
we hadn't seen it before. Social (not to speak of emotional) expectations of
daughterly mourning are activated, and the idea of 'wholesome-profitable'
love must be set aside. We may agree that love is wholesome and
profitable as grief is not, but the assertion of those properties in grief's
face makes us question whether profit and wholesomeness are all they're
cracked up to be.

Of course, the primary role of fathers in romantic comedy is to oppose
their children's marriage, but in fact this is not common until the 1590s,
and much more often involves the opposition of a woman's father than a
man's. Fathers of course do generally want to marry their daughters off,
and the only conflict tends to be with the daughter's choice. Shakespeare's
plays of the 1590s make something of a speciality of this tension, though
there is usually some mitigation along the way, as daughters are not
allowed to make very radical breaks with their fathers; if anything, they
have less licence to rebel than sons. The pleasure of such plays tends to
come in the ingenuity with which tension is defused, but the ways in which
fathers are made content become more problematic, even destructive, as the
1590s progress. If a man cannot choose a good son-in-law, his judgement in
a wider sense may be called into question, as may his potency.

In *The Taming of the Shrew*, Baptista's judgement is skewed by his eagerness to get his elder daughter off his hands so that he can arrange a marriage for his more marketable younger daughter. He expresses 'love' for Bianca's suitors, and insists that he will be 'very kind' to his sons-in-law, even that he is 'liberal' to his daughters (I. i. 53, 98), but this is merely a matter of money. He seems only able to deal with other men, only able to express affection homosocially and rather indiscriminately. Katherina insists that he is making her a 'stale' for young men (line 58) – which implies that he is no better than a pimp. Her attitude exposes the essential indignity of the marriage market. In private, he is one of the crueller dramatic fathers, calling her 'thou hilding of a devilish spirit' (II. i. 26). The presentation of privacy here is one of the deprivation of love. Though he does insist that Petruchio win her love, 'for that is all in all' (line 129), such love seems a mystery to him. He ignores everything she says, and only understands the concept of love as part of a business transaction between men. He is a 'merchant', desiring only 'quiet' (lines 326, 330). Allying himself with Hortensio and Gremio, he has no real paternal dignity, and deserves no respect from his daughter. He therefore also deserves to have Bianca taken by Lucio, and can't really object to it in the end. Nonetheless, he is needed at the play's conclusion to offer the validating judgement and recognition that Katherine 'is changed, as she had never been' (V. ii. 115) – though we might understand this to mean 'changed as she has never been changed by me', it seems primarily to mean 'so changed that it seems as if the previous Katherina had never existed'. The fact that he can be so pleased at this is indicative of how little paternal affection there had really been in this play. It is a horribly sour moment rather than a joyful metamorphosis; suggesting the wish to think of an inadequate child as a changeling (see *Henry IV Part 1*, and pp. 71–2 above), it also exhibits the merchant's desire to *exchange* his daughter. The play implies not that it is bad to have daughters – in fact, this idea, common in some cultures, is not often expressed in Elizabethan drama – but that it is emotionally withering for a father only to have homosocial bonds.

Much Ado about Nothing's Leonato is a development of Baptista in that he has one daughter of whom it is (at least initially) no trouble to dispose, and a niece nearly as shrewish as Katherina, but he is affectionate to both, breaking away from his homosocial and political bonds with Don Pedro and Claudio when they slander his daughter Hero. In the play's final scenes he is a hugely impressive (if in some ways ineffective) figure. He says that if Hero were guilty, 'these hands shall tear her' (IV. i. 191), but is prepared for serious vengeance on the men (one of whom is his prince) if not. He then begins the final act with an extraordinary set-piece of paternal grief, delivered to his brother, whose counsels of patience he refuses:

> Give not me counsel;
> Nor let no comforter delight mine ear
> But such a one whose wrongs do suit with mine.
> Bring me a father that so loved his child,
> Whose joy of her is overwhelmed like mine,
> And bid him speak of patience.   (V. i. 5–10)

One may suspect that his grief at this point is excessive, given the plot he has in motion, but that may be the point – he is aggrieved that he has to engage in such underhand stratagems to marry his daughter off when he would rather get vengeance.[36] As is very common, the father is a figure of impotent grief, of patience as suffering, but there is nothing ridiculous about Leonato, whose set-piece speech amounts to a kind of self-recognition. The 'joy' in a daughter is all the more poignant for its evident precariousness, the sense of the uniqueness of his situation expresses a loneliness in the condition of paternity that precludes homosocial bonding, and the childishness of having children – observed by Antonio – is powerfully contrasted to the supposedly deified state of the father. It may feel worse to be a Leonato than a Baptista, but there is no doubt for Shakespeare that it is still better to *be* such a man. This way *King Lear* lies.

The problem was set up at the play's beginning: the fact that Leonato owes Don Pedro 'all duty' (I. i. 156) means that he has no real choice in the matter once the prince supports Claudio's suit. Paternal dignity is clearly put in its place by political power, its private nature being turned to deprivation by the non-paternal prince. A little joke backs this up. Asked if Hero is his daughter, Leonato responds:

> Her mother hath many times told me so.
> BENEDICK. Were you in doubt, sir, that you asked her?
> LEONATO. Signior Benedick, no, for then you were
>   a child.   (lines 105–8)

Leonato's comment is a conventional jest that deflects paternal anxiety even as it expresses it, but Benedick's pressing at the vulnerability thereby revealed is an ungracious assertion of the young men's power. Leonato's response is admirable – it keeps the tone light by persisting with the joke's fiction, but it also quietly reminds Benedick of his superiority in years. When Benedick later goes over to Leonato's side, he signals the moral, if not the political, superiority of private paternal authority.

Sometimes a father gets the backing of political authority, if only temporarily. The earlier *A Midsummer Night's Dream* gives one of the clearest statements of paternal opposition to a daughter's love in the drama of the period, but the effect of this is to remove any sympathy for the father in his ultimate defeat, particularly as he seems to be going against English conventions, which gave daughters some choice of husband. Egeus gets the duke's support by appealing to

> the ancient privilege of Athens:
> As she is mine, I may dispose of her;
> Which shall be either to this gentleman,
> Or to her death, according to our law
> Immediately provided in that case.   (I. i. 41–5)

The need to explain this law is evidently a matter of setting up the play-world's conventions: the private father believes in his privilege. It is no accident, though, that Egeus is named after Duke Theseus' own father: it allies law, authority, and paternity in absolute security, even though paternal authority is ultimately overriden by the duke. The play's other source of authority, the non-paternal Oberon, enables these treble chains to be broken with ease – and without anyone knowing it. Egeus may in the end 'beg the law, the law, upon his [Lysander's] head' (V. i. 155), but this hysterical, Rumplestiltskin-like demand is easily brushed aside – as is Egeus, who does not seem to appear in the celebratory final scene. A father imperils himself by insisting too much on the law, his privilege replaced by deprivation.

Such comic precedents turn quite easily to tragedy. The *locus classicus* of father–daughter tension over the choice of a husband is of course *Romeo and Juliet*,[37] but in some ways Juliet's mother is more significant there. Both fathers are 'rebellious subjects' (I. i. 81) and so lack real authority. Capulet is an affectionate enough father at first, reluctant that his daughter should marry too young, and telling Paris:

> Earth hath swallowed all my hopes but she;
> She's the hopeful lady of my earth.
> But woo her, gentle Paris, get her heart,
> My will to her consent is but a part;
> And she agreed, within her scope of choice
> Lies my consent and fair according voice.   (I. ii. 14–19)

The rhyme here signals sententiousness but should also suggest a harmony that will be sadly lacking due to Capulet's own foolish feud with the Montagues. It is Lady Capulet, rather than her doubtful husband, who is absolute for an early marriage, partly because 'I was your mother much upon these years' (I. iii. 72). The father would probably get the audience's assent: 14 would be very early for marriage in Elizabethan England. It is indicated that Capulet is much older than his wife (I. v. 30–40), and he is at first a phlegmatic character, even persuading Tybalt to be 'patient' at Romeo's presence at the feast (line 71). It is Lady Capulet who demands that Romeo die for killing Tybalt (III. i. 181), the two fathers staying silent at this moment. Shakespeare seems to be keen, then, to blame Lady Capulet more than her husband for the tragedy. Such female insistence might, as in comedies of the period, be dealt with by masculine rationality.

But then Capulet does something rather strange, something that helps to turn what might be comedy into tragedy: for a moment he seems to be putting off Paris on the basis of Juliet's grief for Tybalt (III. iv. 1–7) before suddenly changing his mind and deciding to 'make a desperate tender / Of my child's love' (lines 12–13), setting up the marriage for Wednesday – no, it's already Monday – Thursday then. Why? Are his wits addled because it's 'so very late' at night (line 34)? This sheer caprice in a fundamentally good father is a key force behind the tragedy, and the sudden decision to assert paternal authority is alarming: 'I think she will be ruled / In all respects by me; nay more, I doubt it not' (lines 13–14). Though much of the scene's language fits into a pattern of sunsets and sunrises that structures the play, the late-night setting reminding us of Capulet's age, Shakespeare's simple psychology here is also brilliant: he asserts his authority because he's *tired*. The next scene's paternal ranting and bullying of Juliet then marks the play's decisive turn to tragedy. Nothing could be further from Capulet's early harmonious tones: he is 'mad' (III. v. 176), telling her she can 'hang, beg, starve, die in the streets' (line 192). He has picked up his wife's absurd sense of urgency in the marriage, and his language becomes more and more copious and blustering. Soon he will see its consequences, bursting into her room at daybreak with 'For shame, bring Juliet forth, her lord is come' (IV. v. 22 – referring to Paris, but also surely suggesting his own authority), only to find her apparently dead and to burst into impatiently repetitive grief. The point is clear: having lost paternal patience in asserting his power, he has lost his position as a father. He will suffer again on Juliet's second death – but there he will be more patient, and so more paternal. The irony of this 'glooming peace' (V. iii. 305) does not need to be pressed. The play is crepuscular, sunset and sunrise battling for supremacy: the tragedy is that the father did not accept that the rising sun should take priority.

He has turned a play that might otherwise have been a comedy into a new kind of tragedy, and later representations of fathers tend to introduce the possibility of tragedy to comedy more than they provide the comforting sense that there will be a happy ending.

No one thinks to ask Shylock for the hand of his daughter, so he cannot make a mistake like Capulet's. Though he may seem to equate his daughter and his ducats, he may be less wholly mercantile than Baptista. He is concerned to keep Christian 'shallow fopp'ry' out of his house (II. v. 35), and the loss of his daughter is only the most serious of a whole pattern of losses that (retrospectively) motivate his attempts at revenge: he loses his servant, his daughter with the jewels, whose spending is then described in an aggravating sequence that culminates with his ring – 'it was my turkis, I had it of Leah when I was a bachelor. I would not have given it for a wilderness of monkeys' (III. i. 121–3). We sense a depth of feeling here behind the restraint, and its comic context, with the effect that he is not quite the ridiculous figure Salerio and Solanio make him out to be. His further losses – of his religion and half his estate – leave him to say that he is 'content', but 'not well' (IV. ii. 394, 396). Only removing him from the stage in the final act can in any way remove his awkward presence – but even then anticipation of his death may provoke an uncomfortable reaction in the silent Jessica, 'manna' as it may be to Lorenzo (V. i. 293–4).

The fact is, though, Shylock has not really played the role of obstructive father, so cannot seem, even according to the generic rules of comedy, to have deserved Lorenzo's theft. We enter that part of the plot late, it seems, with the result that we may have more sympathy for Shylock than we would normally have for the father of an eloping daughter. Even Jessica is aware of her sinfulness, and has no real ability to mitigate it:

> Alack, what heinous sin is it in me
> To be ashamed to be my father's child!
> But though I am a daughter to his blood,
> I am not to his manners.   (II. iii. 16–19)

The attempt to push 'blood' out with 'manners' is feeble, failing to make the more persuasive potential claim of religious difference even while implying it. It is clear that the second half of this statement is of less force than the first: even if her father is bad enough to deserve being ashamed of, there's no getting away from the sin of filial disrespect. Somehow, this always seems worse from a daughter than a son: we shall see in the next chapter (in the case of *Eastward Ho!*) that the problem of daughterly disrespect is tainted with a degree of silliness as well as of sinfulness. Her motivations seem capricious, as she almost acknowledges. The simple fact of Shylock being Jewish is not really presented as being enough to override the respect due to him as a father – for, after all, the most commonly cited Biblical texts enjoining filial respect are common to both religions. When Launcelot Gobbo says that Jessica would be better off hoping she were not really Shylock's daughter, she responds, recognizing this situation as an impasse, 'That were a kind of bastard hope indeed' (III. v. 13) – the phrase is almost oxymoronic, and certainly rueful. Such bastard hope, though, may be the only way out of the impasses of filial duty, even if it really doesn't solve any problems.

The real problem with Jessica's motivation is the fact that we only get the lightest sketch of the 'hell' she claims her house to be (line 2).[38] The failure to represent Shylock's domestic life means that we do not have much on which to base a judgement of Jessica. It is possible, though, that Shakespeare is doing something characteristic in his use of Marlowe: in *Richard II*, the king's favouritism is not really represented, and we may have to supply some sense of it from Marlowe's *Edward II*; similarly, in *The Merchant of Venice*, we may have to supply our sense of Jewish family life from Marlowe's *The Jew of Malta*.

Marlowe's Barabas is a much more complex father figure than Shylock. He begins the play saying that he has 'But one sole daughter, whom I hold as dear / As Agamemnon did his Iphigen' (I. i. 136–7);[39] the proleptic irony of this is considerable, as Barabas, like Agamemnon, will sacrifice his daughter, but it is hard to think of Barabas as a regal figure like the Greek king; nor is his sacrifice as necessary to the public good as that of Iphigenia. Barabas, indeed, reminds us that Jews do not become kings (line 128), however rich they may be, and Ferneze emphasizes later that Barabas is a 'private man' reluctant to help out the public good (I. ii. 100). Barabas' private dignity is not allowed to become tragic, however deprived he may be. Yet there is no doubt that he loves Abigail (whose name means 'father's joy'): she is his 'lovely daughter' (line 227), and he claims that he needs his wealth as his 'children's hope' (line 151); of course in the latter case he may be deploying her for rhetorical purposes, and we shall certainly see that he is prepared to *use* her as a resource at least as much as an end in herself, but nothing in the first few acts indicates anything other than mutual affection.

In fact, that mutual affection is probably as touching as any father–child relation in Elizabethan drama: Abigail says she will run to the senate 'And rent their hearts with tearing of my hair, / Till they reduce the wrongs done to my father' (lines 236–7). She is clearly kinder to her father than the other Jews who seem like Job's comforters, and the mutual help they bring each other gives us a picture of domestic life. Abigail may have to 'dissemble' to help her father (lines 289–90) in a 'counterfeit profession' as a nun (line 292), but the act is one of filial piety: she is restoring goods from his unfairly confiscated house. He may use her to do this, but he is also concerned to get her out of the nunnery once she has carried out his scheme (II. i. 51–2), and he refers to her as 'my soul's sole hope', 'the loadstar of my life', 'my joy' (lines 29, 42, 58), surely not just because of her usefulness.

Why, then, does he kill her? Her conversion to Christianity seems an insufficient motive. Ithamore's move into Barabas' affections, becoming his surrogate son and heir, seems important to the process of alienation between father and daughter, as of course does Abigail's love for the Christian Mathias. Once revenge becomes a driving force all fond remembrances of familial affection seem to go out of the window. But there may also be something more private at work, more based in the relationship between Barabas and Abigail themselves. The roots of the killing come not only in the mention of Agamemnon, but also in the moment when Abigail pretends to convert to Christianity: acting his part in their scheme, Barabas says 'Away, accursèd, from thy father's sight' (I. ii. 349). Such a curse cannot be unsaid, it seems: she is doomed from that moment. Though she is loyal to her father even when he plots the death of her beloved Mathias, there seems to be no going back. It is possible that Shylock also curses his daughter in saying 'She is damn'd for it [her elopement]' (III. i. 31); though this may be just a statement recognizing a grim certainty, it may also have power over Jessica, tainting her happy ending. Paternity is treated as an absolute fact, and dramatic plots cannot wish it away; curses are likewise reversible.

When Barabas calls Abigail 'a paltry silly girl' (II. iii. 286), he may be attempting to dupe Mathias, but there seems a real danger in an affectionate father using such terms: such acting, like pulling a face, might become a permanent attitude if, as the saying goes, the wind changes.[40] When he says of Mathias 'He loves my daughter, and she holds him dear: / But I have sworn to frustrate both their hopes' (lines 144–5), the coupling of his daughter's hopes here with those of the blameless young Christian shows how unpaternal he has become. He kills her with a mess of pottage, recalling the meal for which Esau gave away his birthright. Abigail, however, never betrays her father (she does confess her part in his sins, but that's a different matter, not least because she really thinks the confession is confidential).[41] Her hell, or at least the danger of hell, comes in keeping his secret, and in the emotional consequences of her father's sins. Rather than being angry with her father, she concludes her thoughts about his murder of Mathias with the piercing simplicity of 'But I perceive there is no love on earth' (III. iii. 50).

It is perhaps such an absence of love that we are to infer makes Shylock's house such a hell. It is exceedingly hard to represent the absence of an emotion, and Shakespeare does not want to represent the loss of paternal love as Marlowe does, for that would make his play too tragic. Nonetheless, he does find some ways to suggest lovelessness as the major problem with Shylock. *The Merchant of Venice* represents an affectionate, if slightly absurd, scene between a father and a son, which points up the contrast with Jessica and Shylock's relationship. Launcelot Gobbo tricks his blind but 'true-begotten father' into not recognizing him (II. ii. 35) in a scene that anticipates Edgar and Gloucester in *King Lear*.[42] The effect of this is not at all humiliating for the father, whose affection for his son, 'the very staff of my age' (lines 66–7), shines through, and is reciprocated. Launcelot gets his blessing in this strange scene of recognition. Jessica, by contrast, doesn't even get a farewell from her father. Less aggressive to his daughter than Baptista is to Katherine, Shylock is nonetheless very cold to Jessica: pretty much the only thing he says to her in the play is 'Lock up my doors' (II. v. 29) – for all his other speeches to her in this, their only scene together, have exactly the same import: 'shut doors after you' (line 53). That's it for the relationship between father and daughter. So much the miser is he that he omits even to say goodbye. Shylock may only be going out for the evening, but the absence of affectionate parting here is significant: most dramatic representations of parent–child separations, however temporary, involve some formal display of emotion and often even a blessing. Shylock's failure to bless may therefore act as a curse. All he is interested in is locking up his possessions.

Of course, this fits with a standard trope. Urban comedies frequently have young men outwit a miserly father, as in *Englishmen for My Money* (c. 1598, probably by William Haughton), where three Englishmen thwart the desires of a Portuguese father to marry his (half-English) daughters to foreigners. In this, the young men are shown to have clear justification for their activities, in that they are gentlemen, and the foreign father, Pisaro, has mortgages on their land, which they intend to recover through the daughters' dowries. In such cases, where the audience is asked to support youth against age and citizens against foreigners, it is hard to decide which is the more important point of allegiance. However, the subtitle of *Englishmen*, which may have been its original title, and which is certainly the play's most frequently repeated proverb, 'A Woman Will Have Her Will', indicates that we are also invited to assent to the idea of female choice; it is therefore not just the father who is humiliated and brought into line, but men in general, despite the momentary success of the young Englishmen. That idea is less accentuated in the Jessica–Lorenzo plot of *Merchant*, but is clearly brought out in the main plot, as Portia subverts her dead father's will, the masculine world of the court, and finally the homosocial bonds between Antonio and Bassanio.

The primacy of women in such romantic plots, then, means that young men's temporary success may be shaded by the knowledge that they will be fathers themselves, and subject to their womenfolk's wills. It is perhaps for this reason that young men are so insistent that their amorous success results in the begetting of sons rather than daughters. The young men in *Englishmen for My Money* tell the ladies 'Weele make you mothers of sixe goodly Boyes' (line 1906).[43] Ned Walgrave ends the play with a back-handed peace-offering to Pisaro; having slept with Pisaro's daughter (not exactly in wedlock), he tells him 'Father, pray Father, let me haue your blessing, / For I haue blest you with a goodly Sonne; / Tis breeding heere yfayth, a iolly boy' (lines 2660–2). The mixture here of taunting and conciliation – underpinned by the fact that Pisaro has ogled Ned while the latter was in female dress – is remarkable, and a signal instance of the conflict between generations. The young men in this play, as in *Merchant*, are given no fathers of their own, and one might wonder how much displaced hostility there is here. Humiliating a future father-in-law is not far away from humiliating a father.

Only by becoming absurdly selfish can a father of daughters deal with the problem of humiliation. In Marston's *Jacke Drums Entertainment* (1600), Sir Edward Fortune insists that he 'was not borne to be my Cradles drudge' (p. 184),[44] and that he wants his daughters to be pleased at his enjoyment of life. This attitude deals with the problem nicely, if sophistically: thrifty fathers who lay things up for their daughters are considered greedy, whereas his own profligacy is recast as a generosity that will make his daughters love him. The need for emotional connection, particularly with daughters, is developing even in such an ironic context. The problem is finding fathers an emotional role without them seeming selfish. The emotional shut-off of a Shylock is a real peril.

Public status is more important than private emotion when it comes to the relations between fathers and sons. Yet this creates its own problems of paralysis and impasse. Even when fathers of sons are most celebrated their scope for action can be seriously undermined. Thomas Heywood's *The Four Prentices of London* (?1596, pub. 1615) may seem exceedingly silly to a modern audience, but it is clearly attempting a serious celebration of burgherly virtue underpinned by chivalric history, and this is in turn underpinned by dutiful behaviour to one's father. The four titular heroes are apprenticed by their exiled father the earl of Boulogne to four major London livery companies, but rather than pursuing their trades they go on the First Crusade to Jerusalem – whither their father has also gone on pilgrimage. Shipwrecked, they all follow different courses, and as they do not recognize each other when they meet, they all get into fights with each other, mostly over footling matters of honour, including the fact that some of them have fallen in love with the same woman (their disguised sister, of course). Two sons separately get to rescue their father from outlaws in Italy, though only one of them recognizes him. The others must wait to rescue him (again) from captivity in Jerusalem – at which stage they all recognize each other, finally, even acknowledging the absurdity of their inability to recognize one another before. The point here may be that the father is necessary in some abstract way to enable mutual recognition between brothers, and perhaps also that fraternal relations are somehow mediated by the father. This has clear allegorical implications for the relations between the livery companies whose badges they carry and honour: there may be rivalries between them, but a presiding father (God or the monarch) acts as a sacred point of reference which enables them to be friendly in the final analysis. The father here is finally made Patriarch of Jerusalem, and has the ultimate happiness to see his 'sonnes all Kings' (p. 253).[45] The play thus gives an idea of what it would be to achieve perfect patriarchal dignity, yet the father himself does nothing other than go on pilgrimage; indeed, so inactive is he that at one point he is carried about in turn by each of his sons. As we have seen, inactive fathers are a continual issue in Elizabethan drama, but here we can see that the greater the dignity attributed to them the greater the need for dramatic passivity.

Perhaps this problem could be overcome by observing the process of becoming the patriarch? That, after all, would enable activity, even if only temporarily. Chapman's *A Humorous Day's Mirth* (1597) provides a rare instance of someone desperately desiring to become a father, but this only entails absurdity. The play begins by showing the elderly Labervele's anxiety to produce more children by his young second wife who, like most people in this play, needs to be worked out of her humour or obsession before this will be possible. We later learn that he has a son

by his first marriage who is a disappointment to him, describing him as
'the sight which I with griefe and teares daily behold, seeing in him the
end of my poore house' (II. ii. 42–4).[46] This son, Dowsecer, seems
melancholy-mad (or philosophically cynical, depending on one's position). When asked to marry by his father, he replies that having children
is merely a 'trouble', preferring other ways of augmenting his father's
estate:

> if you long to haue some fruite of me,
> See father I will creepe into this stuborne earth
> And mix my flesh with it, and they shall breede grasse,
> To fat oxen, asses and such like.   (lines 168–72)

He believes that joy in children is no longer possible, wealth being the
only real pleasure in life. Though in comic mode, Dowsecer can be seen as
a minor forerunner of Hamlet's melancholy: here, as in Shakespeare's play,
melancholy leads one to reject procreation and to ponder dissolution into
the elements; the sense that paternal pressure might contribute something
to that mood of impasse and paralysis is present in both plays. Chapman's
speech makes it beautifully clear that a son is not a joy *in himself*, but that
he must produce sons in turn, thus making fatherhood a pleasure that
continually vanishes over the horizon; a more cyclical husbandry might be
more rewarding. Paternity may only be part of a process, not a key element
in narrative development. If, as Martin Wiggins argues, humours plays are
characterized by a clearer sense of 'human agency' than earlier comedy,[47]
it is still not the case that this agency applies to fathers or enables them
actively to resolve plots. As in Jonson's *Every Man in his Humour*, where old
Knowell is rather easily subverted by an alliance of son and servant,[48] the
father himself is too weak to resolve plots, even though his presence is
needed for a sense of resolution.

   Fathers can fare even worse when their roles are tied up with other
valued relations. Jonson's early *The Case Is Altered* (?1597) neatly ties up
friendship, paternal feeling, and heterosexual love in a romantic plot that
is uncharacteristic for its author. A father may be at the centre of this, but
he is not in the end the key agent. Count Ferneze's son Paulo is unusually
ready to criticize this authority figure for being 'wayward' and for the
'impatience' that explodes his reason (I. vi. 85–90). We have come a long
way from the staid fathers of early Elizabethan drama to a position in
which the father is not the voice of reason; indeed, this anticipates some of
the more irascible fathers of early Jacobean drama. In this case the father's
passions are directly derived from his paternal situation: he is anxious

about his only son, because he lost another son (Camillo) during a siege twenty years previously; the grief and fear of the paternal condition are emphasized here in a way that will later be exploited by tragedy and tragicomedy.

Of course, the recognition of the lost son is the play's key resolution. That son's friendship with a French prince leads to something like a Damon and Pythias plot, in which one friend proves his honour by returning to redeem the other, thus causing a tyrant's anger to soften; it is significant that the father here, as in Sidney's *Arcadia*, is put in the position of the tyrant (or at least harsh judge) who needs to be mollified by exemplary youthful friendship.[49] Camillo (brought up as Gasper) takes his friend's place as a prisoner, enabling a moment of high irony, in which Ferneze decides to execute Gasper/Camillo 'for my sonne' (V. ix. 5) – he means 'because my son [Paulo] has not been returned', or 'in revenge for the loss of my son [Camillo]', but of course what he is really about to do is hang him *as* his son.

The elegance of the play's exchanges, then, all rounded off by friends marrying each other's sisters, allows a purgation of paternal passions which hint at larger father–son tensions than the play will directly express. Ferneze's grief for his sons is presented as equivalent to his steward's loss of the woman he wanted to marry and to the miser Jaques' obsession with his gold. These three laughable 'constant passions' 'make a iangling consort' (V. xi. 28–9). Ferneze may not exactly lose his authority, but paternal indignity is no longer given the privileged position it once had. Fathers are no longer deities on earth, but men among men.

ROMANCE COMEDY

Towards the end of the sixteenth century, comic drama turns again to romance norms which enable a greater range of emotions in father figures than even humours plays do. Whereas Elizabethan drama began with *Gorboduc*'s presentation of a father as restraint on his sons, it ends the other way around. *The Trial of Chivalry* (c.1600, pub. 1605) is a continuation of an older tradition of chivalric romance, particularly that of Sidney's *Arcadia*, but one that, in its elegant organization and moderately sophisticated wit, looks forward to the development of that tradition by the later Shakespeare and by John Fletcher and his imitators.[50] The centre of the plot is a war between the kings of France and Navarre, which obliquely reflects on the recent French civil wars without being a history;[51] peace is brought about by their sons, each of whom is in love with the other's sister (they call these 'crosse loues' – A4ᵛ).⁵² Some contrivance is needed to get drama out of this initial situation. The sons cannot be in opposition to their fathers, so the obstruction to their loves is introduced by the vicious Rodorick, duke of Orleans and by the duke of Burbon, and also by one princess not loving the right prince (she's in love with his English friend Pembroke). Once those problems are removed, however, there is still a need to bring the 'angry fathers' (H4ᵛ) back to peace: in a lengthy series of final-act skirmishes, it is notable that each prince speaks harshly to *the other*'s father – here is one useful role of friendship to get round the taboo of paternal respect (11ᵛ–12ʳ). These 'friendly sonnes of aduerse parents' (14ᵛ) are then nearly executed for their opposition before being recognized as their helmets are removed for their beheading. As in the *Arcadia*, friendship trumps paternal justice, but without removing paternal dignity; by this stage fathers have come to be seen as more likely to be sources of strife and paralysis than of restraint.

If fathers are to have dignity in comedy, they may only acquire it in strangely roundabout ways, and by plot contrivances and recognitions that enable paternal feeling to emerge almost unconsciously (as we might say in the twenty-first century), or naturally (as would more likely be the Elizabethan way of putting it). Quite a common and neat device is to have a good child address his/her disguised father as 'father' – in such a case the word is a term of respect for the elderly destitute. This charitable usage indicates the child's good nature, without compromising the fundamental bond of paternity, and its ironic usage in such cases enables the father to be a witness of the child's goodness. *The Blind Beggar of Bednall Green* (1600, pub. 1659 as John Day's, but probably by Henry Chettle and William Haughton) gives a particularly good example of this. Lord Momford, falsely accused of treason, returns to England in the titular disguise, and finds his daughter Bess is the only one to be charitable to him (calling him 'good Father' – D1ʳ);⁵³ when she is driven out of her uncle's home she goes onto the Green to kill herself, at which point we get the following exchange, in some ways an anticipation of Edgar and Gloucester's meeting in *King Lear*:

> MOMFORD. [*aside*] My Daughter in dispair, then play thy part,
>   Prevent her ills that did procure her smart,
>   [*aloud*] Alas where am I? how shall I return
>   Unto my homely Cabbin? where's my boy?
>   I prethee do not leave me gentle wag,
>   Take pity of my miserable state.
> BESS. Who talks of pity? now alas good man,

What are you blind?
MOMFORD. Yes blind, and like to die,
  [*aside?*] Not for my own, but for thy misery.
BESS. Father be comforted, I am but poor,
  Yet time has been – *sigh*.
MOMFORD. Oh do not sigh, Girl,
  Grief hath so tyranniz'd upon my heart
  That if you mourn my tears will bear a part.
BESS. You are the man I look for.
MOMFORD. I am indeed,
  [*aside*] And yet thou know'st me not, alas the while
  That blind deceit, should clear ey'd love beguile,
  [*to her*] Whence spring thy sorrows from some private wrong.
BESS. Am I asleep, or do I know his tongue,
  Art blind sayest thou, let me see thy face,
  Oh let me kiss it too, and with my tears
  Wash off these blemishes which cruel time
  Have furrow'd in thy cheeks! Oh could thou see,
  I'de show thine eyes whom thou dost represent.
  I call'd thee father, I thou shalt be my father,
  Nor scorn my proffer, were my father here,
  Hee'd tell thee that his Daughter held him dear:
  But in his absence Father, thou art hee.   (D4^v–E1^r)

The ironic weaving of all this is rather lovely: from her perspective, he looks like her father but, being blind, doesn't know it; from his, she is declaring love of her father in a disinterested way, but is really blind (as he is not) to his identity. Shakespeare would draw on this in Edgar's attempts to comfort his blind and despairing father, and perhaps also in the pathos of the Lear–Cordelia recognition scene. It is a fine instance of the idea of the father as absent presence, allowing the validation of what might otherwise appear to be insincere expressions of feeling. Momford must play a 'part' here, as the Blind Beggar, but in doing so he also truly, if indirectly, plays the proper role of a father, bearing a part of her woes for her, as Lear and Cordelia bear each other's woes when they meet (see Chapter 4, below). As with Lear and Cordelia, recognition involves estrangement, cannot quite be mutual, and has as much sadness as happiness in it.

The presentation of a daughter and a vulnerable father seems to have a natural pathos, whereas father–son relations tend to be cut across by other tensions. *The Wisdom of Doctor Dodypoll* (Anon., 1600) develops generational conflict further than most comedy of the 1590s by giving fathers more scope for action, yet it ultimately heightens the sense of paralysis we have seen in so many late Elizabethan plays. As in numerous plays of the period, there are no mothers around, a fact that puts fathers into the romantic market alongside the younger generation. The prince Albedure and his father Duke Alphonsus are both in love with Hyanthe, daughter of Earl Cassimir, which puts Albedure in a bit of a bind; he tells his beloved:

> for my riuall, (whom I must not wrong)
> (Because he is my father and my Prince)
> Giue thou him honour; but giue me thy loue.

He then insists on being bound in duty to this rival, and that he must be silent about it (B2^v–B3^r).[54] The references to his father may be asides, but if they are addressed to Hyanthe this is a particularly disingenuous instance of paralepsis, pretending to be dutifully silent when he is actually disparaging his father: the lip-service to duty fails to conceal a father–son tension that cannot be suppressed. Albedure is subsequently driven mad by a love potion given him by the ambitious Flores, who wants him to marry his daughter Cornelia; yet we might read this madness as really caused by the tension between desire and duty, as an expression of the psychic impasse that emerges in father–son relationships. The madness operates in part as a solution of the play's crisis, twice prompting Alphonsus to wish for his son's recovery (first from madness, then from apparent suicide) even at the expense of his own love. These moments of fatherly relenting, however, are not sufficient to solve things: on the first occasion he seems to blame Hyanthe for driving his son mad, but is really motivated by a desire to get her into his company; on the second, he immediately reneges on his promise to hand her over if Albedure is alive once the son actually appears. Only the arrival of the duchess to whom he is precontracted and her powerful brother converts him: he seems to fall for that duchess immediately, but it may well be that he is cowed by diplomatic necessity.

The father, then, does not come out well here. He has all the wilfulness, capriciousness, and fundamental weakness of a traditional stage tyrant – he even makes up portents to put off his marriage to the duchess, simultaneously seeming superstitious and untrustworthy. We think that he has been properly chastened when he thinks Albedure dead and says 'My loue is dead in sorrow for his death' (G4^r), but he shows no joy at his recovery. The pronouncement he makes here is of particular interest in its perversions of traditional paternal virtues:

> Neither of both know what is fit for you.
> I loue with iudgement, and vpon cold bloud,
> He with youths furie, without reasons stay.   (H1^r)

This father is only a stay in that he is a hindrance; he is cold-blooded to his son and hot-blooded in his furies and passions; above all, he has no judgement or ability to know what is fit. The play can come to a happy ending, even allowing fathers to marry (Cassimir also marries Cornelia), but the father–son tensions that have been more quietly present in much comedy of the 1590s seem to have nearly reached a breaking-point, which can only be managed by the estranging use of madness. The old pieties seem utterly insufficient, and affection is entirely absent. Only the contrivances of plot enable any connection between father and son, and the arbitrary qualities of such plots suggest the possibility of tragedy.

However problematic the resolutions found for fathers may be in late Elizabethan romance-based drama, paternal recognition still remains central to the affirmation of identity. *The Weakest Goeth to the Wall* (Anon., 1600) contrives its whole plot in order to present a multi-part, extended father–son recognition between Lodowick, duke of Bulloigne, and his son Frederick, whom he lost many years previously during a civil war. Firstly, disguised as a sexton, he is an unwitting witness at his son's wedding; then, once Frederick has distinguished himself in war, he (again unknowingly) knights his own son; giving a knowing – but not knowing enough – aside: 'litle thinkes he tis the Sextons hands / Draws forth a sword to giue him Knight-hood here' (lines 1940–1).[55] There are two levels of irony here, for little does he think that he is making his own son his own knight. There was an earlier irony when as the sexton he commended Frederick/Ferdinand to good behaviour in the wars – unwittingly thereby giving a paternal blessing (line 1603). When the duke of Brabant accuses the boy of eloping with his daughter, assuming that he is a bastard, Lodowick again unwittingly commends his son, saying 'I cannot thinke, / So faire a shape hath had so foule a forge' (lines 1974–5). Frederick had first been half-recognized when Epernon, Lodowick's old friend and comrade-in-arms, saw his valour and resemblance to his father (lines 1840–52). When he is put on trial, Frederick then has the double pleasure of recognizing him first as the sexton and then as his father, before the rest of the family is reunited. What we have here, then, is a belt, braces, and pins approach to recognition; partly, this is for the sheer pleasure of it, but it also surely reflects some deep desire to secure paternity by as many means as possible: the church, friendship, military prowess, physical resemblance, narratives, and physical signs are all invoked to assure Lodowick that his son is his son. The plot tries to unify masculine identity as firmly as possible, yet it only does so through extended doubling.

Such doubling of identity is also central to Shakespeare's most romance-based comedy of the period, *As You Like It*, but here recognition is much more muted and marginalized because feminine, natural emotion is ultimately privileged over masculine proof. Filial piety is at the very essential core of the central lovers in the play, and may be seen as the activating force of their mutual love – but that piety is presented as natural rather than ideologically based. Both Orlando and Rosalind are marked out from the first by a sense of dutiful affection to their fathers, but it is much more tortuous in the case of the young man, whose filial attitudes have to be filtered through the problematic status of a younger son. Orlando begins the play thus: 'As I remember, Adam, it was upon this fashion bequeathed me by will but poor a thousand crowns, and, as thou sayst, charged my brother, on his blessing, to breed me well; and there begins my sadness' (I. i. 1–5); referring to his father in the passive voice enables him to avoid any unfilial criticism, and the reference to the blessing looks forward to its partial withdrawal when Oliver is deprived of his lands by Duke Frederick. Orlando complains that Oliver 'stays' him at home (line 8), glancing at a traditional complaint against fathers as well as their traditional virtuous role, so that Oliver can become a lightning conductor for any resentment. Orlando's rebellion against his elder brother is driven by 'the spirit of my father, which I think is within me' (lines 22–3), and he can therefore refuse to be regarded as a 'prodigal' (line 38). In the end, it is Oliver who is 'unnatural', though he only confesses this when it is no longer 'the thing I am' (IV. iii. 124, 137); he more than his brother is the prodigal restored to paternal grace, sketchy though his plotline is. Oliver finally gives his estate to Orlando (V. ii. 9–12) when he no longer has the right to do so; and, it seems, he gives it only to get it back from the true duke. Whatever the complications of this, the gift shows the spirit of his father and erases his sins, enabling him to fall in love with Celia.

Nonetheless, any earlier criticism by Orlando of his father's eldest son might seem a criticism of the father. In their initial argument, Orlando accuses Oliver of such implicit criticism, but in doing so seems to commit the sin he is railing against: 'I am no villain; I am the youngest son of Sir Rowland de Boys. He was my father, and he is thrice a villain that says such a father begot villains' (I. i. 56–9); the paradoxes of this retort – Orlando is nearly calling Oliver a villain, thus by his own account making himself a villain, and both of them thereby illegitimate – can only be managed by reminding ourselves of Touchstone's much later praise of conditionality as removing the force of insults ('much virtue in If'

(V. iv. 103)). The exchange shows how awkward and precarious patrilineal identity is, but identity can be recovered by an assertion of being a natural son – though not in the other, bastardizing sense. Adam has to talk very carefully about Oliver: 'Your brother – no, no brother, yet the son / (Yet not the son, I will not call him son) / Of him I was about to call his father' (II. iii. 19–21), which comes close to bastardizing the eldest brother. Orlando is banished by Duke Frederick in a speech full of similar paradoxes and paralysed tergiversations:

> I would thou hadst been son to some man else:
> The world esteemed thy father honourable,
> But I did find him still mine enemy.
> Thou shouldst have better pleased me with this deed
> [ie. the wrestling victory]
> Hadst thou descended from another house.
> But fare thee well, thou art a gallant youth.
> I would thou hadst told me of another father.   (I. ii. 224–30)

The contradictions in the bad duke's attitude are clear – he seems aware that each repetition of 'I' is self-incriminating, setting himself against the standard of virtue that Orlando has displayed. Orlando has in some radical sense *proved* his legitimacy, but he is banished for it: proof is not enough. As he says immediately after, responding to Celia's implicit criticism of *her* father:

> I am more proud [with a print pun on 'prov'd?] to be Sir Rowland's son,
> His youngest son, and would not change that calling
> To be adopted heir to Frederick.   (lines 232–4)

His name is turned into a kind of vocation ('calling'), brushing aside any idea – implied by Frederick's last line – that one can choose one's identity.

Orlando is, in Adam's terms (recalling the 'remember' in the play's first line), 'memory / Of old Sir Rowland' (II. iii. 3–4); the servant, acting as proxy father (his name is that of all mankind's father), is able to confirm Orlando's identity, but the pressures of memory and filial proof remain powerful.[56] The best and most natural proof comes when he bears Adam in on his back (II. vii. 167): this iconic moment recalls popular Renaissance emblems of filial piety, deriving from Aeneas carrying his father Anchises in *Aeneid* Book II. As Kiernan Ryan points out, though, it is more than a conventional symbol, for Adam here represents something of common humanity that does away with ideas of social rank.[57] It also redeems the rudeness Orlando exhibited on his first entrance to Duke Senior's rustic court, for that incivility was all in Adam's interests. After this, he can whisper his identity to the duke, proving himself again (lines 191–5) without having to say anything aloud. Paternal identity is proved in instinctive action and appearance, with speech being relegated to whispers unheard by the audience.

Rosalind's attitude to her father, as he is still alive and as she is female, is less fundamental to her identity; it may be firmly dutiful and respectful, but it is mainly natural and emotional. Early on, she says of a knight Touchstone is abusing, 'My father's love is enough to honour him' (I. ii. 83–4),[58] clearly indicating that paternal honour is a non-negotiable source of value. Consequently, she can use this as a basis for loving Orlando – 'My father loved Sir Rowland as his soul' (I. ii. 235) and 'The Duke my father loved his father dearly' (I. iii. 29–30); however much this may be an excuse, it drives the rest of the play, paternal friendship preventing any real difficulties in the central relationship. The homology is further pressed when Celia asks 'is all this [sadness] for your father?', getting the reply 'No, some of it is for my child's father' (lines 10–11). Celia is less fortunate in a father, but her disrespect is prevented in careful hypotheticals, wondering if she would act like her father (I. ii. 231), and asking Rosalind if she will 'change fathers' (I. iii. 91); consequently, she gets Oliver as a husband, whose conversion seems to enable that of Duke Frederick, and thus to cure any filial impiety in her escape from home.

Despite this, Shakespeare extraordinarily forgoes the chance to present a father–daughter recognition scene (as he would again in *The Winter's Tale*). Rosalind breezily mentions meeting her father in her disguise as Ganymede: 'I met the Duke yesterday, and had much question with him. He asked me of what parentage I was. I told him of as good as he, so he laughed and let me go. But what talk we of fathers when there is such a man as Orlando' (III. iv. 35–9). This comes very close to being disrespectful,[59] but it is licensed by the conventions of disguise and its attendant equivocations. Like Orlando's introduction to the duke, it is best not directly presented to the audience, as then it cannot seem that there was ever any doubt about the bond, whereas the equivalent grand recognition in *King Lear* suggests that real doubt had been cast on paternity by daughterly speech; overrepresenting recognition, as in *The Weakest Goeth to the Wall*, can also make it seem too conventional. Instead, we get the slyly comic comments of father and husband, lining the men up together:

DUKE. I do remember in this shepherd boy
    Some lively touches of my daughter's favour.
ORLANDO. My lord, the first time that I ever saw him
    Methought he was a brother to your daughter. (V. iv. 26–9)

There have been several hints that Rosalind's disguise is in some uncanny way semi-transparent, and that natural recognitions have taken place at some level. The father–husband analogy thereby is pressed to such a point that marriage seems as fundamental a bond as paternity, a point that seems hammered home when Rosalind says (first to one, then to the other) 'To you I give myself, for I am yours. / To you I give myself, for I am yours' (lines 116–17). Not only is the sentiment repetitive, but it is quite paradoxical (how can she give herself when she is already his? how can she do so *twice*?). Female speech is shown to be the necessary condition of the whole patriarchal system, a point Rosalind seems keen to emphasize in her dialogue with Orlando about female fidelity (IV. i. 157–76). As she goes on to say 'I'll have no father, if you be not he. / I'll have no husband, if you be not he' (V. iv. 122–3). Hymen may 'bar' the 'confusion' Rosalind adds by an analogous comment to Phoebe (lines 124–5), but the whole sequence shows that there is much virtue in a (female) if, indeed.

Rosalind, 'almost divinized' (in A. D. Nuttall's phrase) by the end of the play,[60] has become the father, the source of meaning, and the guarantor of relationships. In this, of course, she resembles Queen Elizabeth. In a court epilogue to the play (possibly by Shakespeare, possibly by Jonson), the 66-year-old queen is told:

> So most mighty Queen we pray,
> Like the dial day by day,
> You may lead the seasons on
> Making new when old are gone;
> That the babe which now is young
> And hath yet no use of tongue
> Many a Shrovetide here may bow
> To that Empress I doe now,
> That the children of these lords
> Sitting at your council boards
> May be grave and aged seen
> Of her that was their fathers' Queen.[61]

The rather ridiculous wish for eternal life in the queen is the wish for the continuance of the paradoxical woman who guarantees continuity without being fertile. Rosalind is, of course, the most maternal of Shakespeare's romantic heroines, thinking of Orlando from the first as a father; as a timeless mother, she may transcend the queen. Her presence makes for the happiest play of the whole period, and perhaps the absence of such a lovingly unproblematic mother figure is a reason for many of the anxieties of the period's other drama. In a strangely plotless play, Rosalind unifies doubleness much more effectively than any plot could do. A woman has a greater, more agile power than the iconic but inflexible figure of the father.

While comedy of the 1590s is ceaselessly inventive, even turning in its more romantic forms to the possibility of tragedy, tragedy proper is rather more uncertain in this period, perhaps because it is as obsessed with its own generic dignity as with the dignity of fathers.

Locrine (1595; probably perf. some years earlier) is preoccupied with the paternal line, the foundational figure of Brutus acting as a moral beacon throughout, but without preventing the cycles of vengeance that drive the play's rather disjointed plot. Before he dies, Brutus bequeaths a wife to his eponymous son, also handing over power with some formality:

> Then now my sonne thy part is on the stage,
> For thou must beare the person of a King.   (lines 225–6)[62]

The theatrical language here is significant: Brutus is handing over a role, suggesting that his son must copy him as best he can; theatrical parts were thus handed down from actor to actor, the aim being not to innovate but to copy the original as much as possible.[63] Despite apparently coming into an adult and burdensome inheritance here, and despite his (temporary) martial success, Locrine never quite grows up: at the end of the play he is still called 'yoong *Locrine*' (line 2268), as he is buried in his father's tomb. Perhaps this is partly to do with the fact that he has uncles who act as restraints on him (in this, he is in some ways a forerunner of Hamlet). Corineus in particular insists that he obey his father's last will, and stay loyal to his wife Guendoline (Corineus' daughter) – 'are the words of *Brute* so sonne forgot?' he compellingly asks Locrine, who has fallen for another woman, Elstrid (line 1535). Having Corineus killed does Locrine no good, however: part of his youthfulness – his lack of mature, paternal skills in ruling – comes from the fact that he is in love with Elstrid; this provokes Guendoline and her family into rebellion. Crucially, their son Madan joins with his mother, saying:

> Mother, though nature makes me to lament,
> My lucklesse fathers froward lecherie,
> Yet for he wrongs my Ladie mother thus,
> I if I could, my selfe would worke his death.   (lines 1960–3)

Calling his father 'froward' is an inversion of normal paternal rebukes, but he goes no further than this: the transfer of this epithet onto the sin rather than the sinner is significant, for it means that Locrine only calls his father 'luckless'. The 'if' here is also meaningful: it may suggest that Madan is too young to fight, but it may also reflect the impossibility of a son attacking his father. In the next scene, he is listed as entering with his mother and uncle to challenge Locrine, and he may be the 'prettie boy' to whom Locrine refers as armed (line 2028) – but that may rather be Thrasimachus, whom Locrine has insulted as a 'beardlesse boy' (line 1840). In any case, Madan does not take part in the battle that follows (line 2061 SD).

Everyone else is fighting for the sake of either love or paternal honour; Madan cannot be seen to fight his father, so his cause is abortive. In *Selimus*, patricide was acceptable because it was set in a distant world, but as *Locrine* is set in Britain the son can only express conditional disapproval of his father – he cannot be a Mordred, and neither Madan nor Locrine can have the full development of tragic crisis that we saw in Thomas Hughes's *The Misfortunes of Arthur*.[64] The full intensity of tragedy is averted in *Locrine* because the father is too sacred, even though he is a sinner. As Touchstone insists in *As You Like It*, 'Your If is the only peacemaker', and here it prevents the full development of tragic selfhood in the son; later tragedy would continue to acknowledge this limit, and would need to find indirect courses of self-assertion for sons.

Thomas Lodge's *The Wounds of Civil War* (c. 1594) is unusual in presenting a father as its central hero from the first, but it does so partly as Roman patrilineal identity is regarded as more uncompromised than that which obtains in later societies. Marius is presented as an ideal leader, whose personal and political interests are not in conflict – he is merciful in victory, and stoical in defeat. The prominence of his son in the play's plot in no way challenges his authority and dignity as it would in most other Elizabethan drama. The younger Marius appears entirely as an extension and affirmation of his father's identity: he is therefore an example of the unmanageable ideal of perfect patrilineal replication that would cause conflict in most other plays of the period. Only in ancient Rome, we might infer, can this ideal be realized. When Young Marius believes his father's cause to be lost, he is not very emotional, thinking only of the dishonour to the family name, but he is told by Cethegus that this is an *opportunity* to gain honour before his time – 'How fortunate art thou, my lovely lord, / That in thy youth mayst reap the fruits of age' (II. iii. 36–7);[65] yet he expresses no sense of being pushed back into the shadows again when he finds his father, whose 'love' is a sufficient requital for all his 'travels' (III. iv. 99). When Marius returns to power, he sends his son off to war, saying 'Remember, thou are [*sic*] Marius' son, and dream / On naught but honour and a happy death' (IV. i. 232); and after his father's death, the son indeed dies a noble Roman death, committing suicide rather than be defeated: there is no thought here of wanting to preserve the family line – honour, as in *Titus Andronicus*, is all. His dying thoughts are familial, and seem absolutely to identify himself with his father: when he says 'Well, Fortune, since thy fleeting change hath cast / Poor Marius from his hopes and true desires, / My resolution shall exceed thy power' (V. ii. 18–20), it is not clear whether the third-person reference is to himself or to his father, and that is precisely the point. His address to his troops – 'Who loveth Marius now must die with Marius' (V. iii. 58) – works on the same basis, as it may mean 'Whoever loves the older Marius, or the Marian family, or me, must die with me, or the family, or my father'; he has become fully 'manlike' (line 7), and even his enemy Scilla concedes that he was 'his father's son' (V. v. 59). The Roman play may demonstrate the ideal to which English ideas of paternity aspired, but the insistence on patrilineal dignity as opposed to the individual does not make for very successful tragedy.

The idea of proving (and perhaps therefore paradoxically transcending) one's paternity impels revenge drama, a predominantly masculine genre, though it is cut through with anxieties about female sexuality which derive from comedy and domestic tragedy.[66] It is clear that revenge tragedy provided better opportunities for filial self-assertion than British or Roman chronicle tragedy, but its generic origins are rather halting, and fail to create individuality. *Alphonsus, Emperor of Germany* (early to mid 1590s, attributed on publication – 1654 – to Chapman, but probably not his) indeed involves patricide, though that has taken place *before* the play's events. In the stage plot the avenger is the servant Alexander, who is tricked by the Machiavellian title character into assisting at murders of those whom Alphonsus alleges killed his father, whereas, in fact, Alphonsus killed his father himself. Alexander's relish for his task and his resemblance to his father (who instructed Alphonsus in Machiavellian arts) mean that we are not to pity him, even if he is himself capable of virtue. He does, finally, find out the truth and take his revenge on the appropriate villain, but by that stage he is so far gone in sin that he must be hanged. The indirect patterns of this play's plot show how far dramatists must beat around the bush in order to represent filial aggression.

Revenge tragedy's popularity attests to larger cultural anxieties about masculine continuity. To revenge is to remember, bringing a sense of certainty to one's identity, which has been undermined by the uncertainty of paternity.[67] In the act of revenging, one can assert oneself, and one's family, as fundamentally patriarchal, preserving the fiction that paternity is secure.

Whether it influenced *Hamlet* or was influenced by it, Marston's *Antonio's Revenge* presents a rather different vision of fatherhood and patrilineal identity from Shakespeare's masterpiece. This is partly rooted in the ideas of familial vindication found in its predecessor, *Antonio and Mellida*, a play which presents the father as altogether stronger than the son, but in which father and son are able to give each other mutual validation against a tyrant.

Antonio's father Andrugio has been defeated by the Venetian Duke Piero, and displaced from his own dukedom of Genoa. The effect of this on the son is that he is a decidedly directionless hero: he tells Mellida (Piero's daughter) that they cannot elope because 'now I think on't, I have ne'er a home; / No father, friend, no country to embrace / These wretched limbs' (II. i. 281–3).[68] Escaping Venice without her, he succumbs to melancholy and rolls about on the ground until his father discovers him:

> ANDRUGIO. Art thou Antonio?
> ANTONIO.   I think I am.
> ANDRUGIO. Dost thou but think? What, dost not know thyself.
> ANTONIO. He is a fool that thinks he knows himself.
> ANDRUGIO. Upon thy faith to heaven, give thy name.
> ANTONIO. I were not worthy of Andrugio's blood
>   If I denied my name's Antonio.
> ANDRUGIO. I were not worthy to be called thy father
>   If I denied my name, Andrugio.   (IV. i. 95–102)

The mutually supporting nature of their identities draws both out of passionate despair. Philosophically speaking, one may never really know oneself, but by investing one's identity in a son or a father one can have the next best thing. Andrugio is able to stir his son into action, insisting he recover 'thy dauntless heart, / Thy father's spirit' (287–8), and threatening to repudiate him if he does not exhibit valour. Later, when he thinks Antonio dead, Andrugio is only concerned that his son died 'valiantly' (V. iii. 195); indeed, he is glad his son is dead, as he will not have to see his own imminent defeat by Piero. Antonio is only feigning death, however, and his apparently miraculous recovery precipitates a sudden relenting on Piero's part. In earlier Elizabethan plays such as *Damon and Pithias*, the firm exhibition of friendship caused tyrants to convert; here, it is the united front of father and son that does the trick.

Antonio's Revenge makes it clear, however, that Piero's conversion was tactical and hypocritical. As the sequel begins, we find that he has killed Andrugio, and the revenge tragedy that follows is a peculiar one: Antonio, without his father's guidance, reverts to his lackadaisical ways.

The appearance of Andrugio's ghost, then, acts as a licence for the passion that has been repressed. The ghost addresses Antonio with the striking epithets 'Thou vigour of my youth, juice of my love' (III. ii. 44), rather disturbingly indicating the mutual reinvigoration that secure paternity can provide. For this to work, though, Antonio's mother must be beyond reproach: the ghost accordingly appears to her warning her against Piero's suit; unlike Hamlet's mother, then, she does not marry the villain, and the hero's family therefore remains untainted.

Antonio mainly wins his father's posthumous blessing by killing Piero, but his most striking moment of revenge comes earlier, in killing Piero's son Julio. This boy, never mentioned before, emerges rather phantasmically immediately after the ghost's first appearance. Owing to Antonio's love for Mellida, there is a mutual affection between the hero and his victim, and it takes some histrionics to push it aside:

> O that I knew which joint, which side, which limb
> Were father all and had no mother in't,
> That I might rip it vein by vein and carve revenge
> In bleeding rases! But since 'tis mixed together,
> Have at adventure, pell-mell, no reverse!   (III. ii. 164–8)

It is not clear whether Andrugio's ghost really approves of this action: his shout of 'Revenge' from beneath the stage may be either a sign of gratification or an incitement to real revenge on Piero himself (line 174), and it is followed by ambiguous groans. Once Julio is dead, Antonio can say that 'He is all Piero, father all' (line 200), for the boy's own soul has gone to heaven. In killing Julio, Antonio may be killing some softer part of himself, and thus himself becoming 'father all', rather as Hamlet hardens himself in using his father's seal to dispatch Rosencrantz and Guildenstern. The murder certainly seems more important to Antonio's development than as a cause of suffering for Piero. Interestingly, Piero never mentions his son; by the time he is confronted with Julio's body he has had his tongue plucked out, and can only '*seem to condole his son*' (V. iii. 81 SD); the phrasing of the stage direction closely resembles that of *Hamlet's* play within a play, where the poisoner and his attendants in dumb-show '*seem to condole*' with the queen (*Hamlet*, III. ii. 135 SD); the villain is not allowed to verbalize paternal or other forms of grief – that is exclusively the province of good men. Yet another form of paralysis emerges, but even as it does, the range of emotional meanings given to paternity is further expanded.

If paternity is memorial, it also *re-members* in another sense: the filial piety of the son puts the father back together in himself,[69] perhaps even in a morally better form, with the avenging son acting as a moral corrective to his father, like the sons of many other 1590s plays. This is exhibited most obviously in *Hamlet*, where the question of paternity and identity is much more powerful than any supposed Oedipal feeling.[70] A. D. Nuttall argues that as a 'bearer of death' on behalf of his dead father, Hamlet becomes 'cut off . . . from sexuality and procreation';[71] in identifying with his father, Hamlet is prevented from becoming a father himself. Yet he may in a sense be more perfect (or at least more complete) than Old Hamlet, even as he berates himself for being less of a man.[72]

Shakespeare has chosen to alter his sources by giving father and son the same name, thus highlighting both the presumed identity between them and any differences he or we might perceive, most notably the disjunction between their epochs: as Peter Alexander puts it, 'Wittenberg – the University – is face to face with the heroic past'.[73] The contrast between father and son is stronger than any continuities. This contrast suggests that there are other anxieties in play: it is surely the most powerful solution – or 'objective correlative' – to the mystery of Hamlet's delay and uncertainty to suggest that he fears he is not his father's son. Hamlet's obsession with his mother's sexuality may be based on a question he dare not ask: how long has her affair with Claudius gone on?[74] As young Hamlet, like Claudius, is more a man of *words* (untrustworthy as they are) than action, could he be Claudius' son? Even the possibility of this may mean that he cannot kill him, at least until he has proved himself in more abstract and general terms. The play never answers the key question, or that of Gertrude's guilt in more general terms (the 'bad' First Quarto does seem to exonerate her).[75] Even if Gertrude is innocent of both adultery and complicity in murder, however, her remarriage has, rather strangely, undermined certainty about Hamlet's paternity.

The key classical precedent for revenge tragedy,[76] Seneca's *Thyestes*, is driven by Atreus' rage that his brother has stolen his wife. Even though that wife absconded *after* the birth of Atreus' children, doubt enters into their paternity, which the play's plot must prove in its peculiar way. Atreus initially plans to keep his sons innocent of his plot against Thyestes (line 322),[77] but then considers that it will be worth making them guilty if that constitutes proof that they are not really Thyestes' sons; though he changes his mind about involving them, for practical reasons, the general principle remains: 'prolis incertae fides / ex hoc petatur scelere' [from this crime will emerge trust about my presently uncertain offspring] (lines 327–8). Feeding Thyestes' own children to their father leads Atreus to conclude 'liberos nasci mihi nunc credo / castis nunc fidem reddi toris' [now I believe my sons were begotten by me, and that faith returns to my marriage-bed] (lines 1098–9).[78] Revenge not only proves one's sons one's own, but refreshes a wife's fidelity.

Hamlet's task is a similar, if trickier, one: he needs not only to assure himself of his paternal identity, but also to exonerate his mother. When he rails at her in her closet, Hamlet's most insistent point is to compare Old Hamlet and Claudius:

> Look here upon this picture, and on this,
> The counterfeit presentment of two brothers.
> See what a grace was seated on this brow:
> Hyperion's curls, the front of Jove himself,
> An eye like Mars, to threaten and command,
> A station like the herald Mercury
> New lighted on a heaven-kissing hill,
> A combination and a form indeed,
> Where every god did seem to set his seal
> To give the world assurance of a man.
> This was your husband. Look you now what follows:
> Here is your husband, like a mildewed ear,
> Blasting his wholesome brother. Have you eyes?
> Could you on this fair mountain leave to feed,
> And batten on this moor? ha, have you eyes?   (III. iv. 53–67)

The idealization of the father clearly overdetermines Old Hamlet, identifying him with all the classical gods. The pun on 'moor' is significant, as it introduces the concept of miscegenation – the ultimate sign of uncertain paternity (as in *Titus Andronicus* – see Chapter 2, above).[79] If Hamlet really does show her pictures here (rather than just verbal pictures) of the brothers, he is implicitly asking his mother to compare himself (presumably standing between them) with these images.[80] Yet at the same time, he knows these representations to be counterfeit – as the Ghost may be, and as Hamlet himself may be. In a world where a mother is unreliable, the true coin of identity is driven out by the possibility of counterfeiting.

His poetic image of his father is an almost ludicrously hypostasized notion of 'a man', and the ideal of 'a man' seems particularly important to Hamlet – he has earlier remembered his father with the simple terms ''A was a man, take him for all in all, / I shall not look upon his like again' (I. ii. 187–8). Hamlet fears he will not be his father's 'like'; he wants his father's 'seal' and the 'assurance' that he is his son. Hamlet's speech is full of generalizations about what 'a man' might do (e.g. I. i. 85; I. iv. 35; I. v. 121, 130; II. ii. 179, most notably 302–10, etc.), as if it were a term he is wrestling to define. He even concludes, in saving Horatio from suicide, by adjuring him 'As th' art a man' (V. ii. 342) to tell his story; perhaps friendship with Horatio has enabled him to become a man on his own terms, but the shadow of paternity has overborne his identity for most of the play.[81] In fact, his first really decisive act, in having Rosencrantz and Guildenstern killed, is carried out by the use of his father's seal. Claudius, by comparison, can only be all that is bad, all that undermines certainty of identity. For Hamlet, not to be his father's son is not to be a man – hence his sense of the femininity of his inaction, calling himself 'a whore' (II. ii. 585); the image of the whore is that which unsettles all male identity – a fact that is accentuated when Claudius, shortly afterwards, thinks of himself as like a harlot (III. i. 51).[82] The 'bastard shame' that Shakespeare associates with the Dark Lady in Sonnet 127 (line 4) seems to hang over both Hamlet and Claudius. Neither man is an adequate substitute for the dead king.

Yet even the Ghost cannot make an adequate judgement on Gertrude, telling Hamlet to 'leave her to heaven' (I. v. 86). Whether this means he thinks her guilty and wants her to go to heaven in any case or that he wants her to be judged by heaven is very much a moot point. Hamlet takes the negative instruction and makes it active, trying to purify his mother so that she can be sent to heaven. In Beaumont and Fletcher's *Cupid's Revenge*, the hero Leucippus, when his lustful stepmother is arraigned, tries to be better than Hamlet in insisting that they 'Leave her to heaven' (V. iv. 150), but it does him no good. His conclusion is also Hamletian, asking 'what is a man? / Or who would be one, when he sees a poore / Weake woman can in an instant make him none' (lines 200–2). The woman's power to undermine masculine identity and patrilineal loyalties is rarely so strikingly expressed. Old Hamlet implies that only heaven can make a proper judgement on a woman's fidelity, and therefore only heaven can really know a man's identity. A woman can make him into nothing so easily that any attempt to define manliness seems absurd. Hamlet cannot redeem his mother and refresh his identity as easily as Atreus in Seneca's play.

Hamlet's manliness is undermined in other ways. Whether or not Hamlet really is driven by his ambition for the throne, the most galling thing for him is clearly being put into a position of sonhood by his uncle; his sense that his uncle is 'more than kin' (I. ii. 65), in addition to its expression of Hamlet's disgust at what he and his society would think incest, also reflects his resentment of being given a new father just at the point where he ought to be coming into his own manhood, that is, as he punningly says, 'too much in the sun' (line 67).[83] This is further rubbed in when Claudius says that Hamlet's grief is 'unmanly' (line 94) – his survivor's guilt is made more acute by the fact that the very man who is unmanning him is calling him unmanly. This public scene is humiliating, and Hamlet needs to find himself and his manhood more fully in the domestic world, in the places and processes of ordinary life; the play's famous delay, in fact, is mostly a matter of establishing the processes of domesticity away from the urgencies of his tragic plot. Wandering the hall, talking to Polonius and others,[84] entering Claudius' chamber and his mother's drawing-room – all this is Hamlet's searching out of family life, finding his place.

At the moment when he most doubts that his father's ghost is really a devil that 'Abuses me to damn me', Hamlet makes a splendid and resonant pun: he insists he will 'have grounds / More relative than this' (II. ii. 603–4); just as Claudius, his 'uncle-father' (line 376), is 'more than kin', he needs evidence from one who is more his relative than his father; he is thinking of the play as providing more reliable evidence, but he is also thinking of his mother, who is the most relative ground of identity available. A father is always more than and less than a relative ground for identity. Hence, the play's tragic pattern is the most acute example of paralysis in the period, but suggestively offers ways out of that paralysis for later tragic drama.

Lust's Dominion (pub. 1657, perf. 1600, probably by Dekker) reflects some of the central issues in *Hamlet* in more explicit, even obvious forms: the proper heir of Spain, Prince Philip, is driven from his rights by a stepfather, Eleazar the Moor. Philip's identity and right to succeed are subverted by his mother's lasciviousness and her claims that he is a bastard. As in *Hamlet*, there may be some oblique glances at James VI of Scotland here: however good the prince may be, his position is undermined by doubts about his mother's marital fidelity; whereas *Hamlet's* Gertrude is offered the benefit of considerable doubts, the queen mother in *Lust's Dominion*, like Mary Queen of Scots, is presented as a model of infidelity and even murderousness (this is perhaps a reason for the play not being published until the 1650s interregnum). If the play preceded Shakespeare's, its influence may be mildly felt in Hamlet referring to Claudius as a moor.[85] Of course, it may actually be preferable for one's mother to be unfaithful to one's father with a Moor: at least there seems less likelihood of him being a white man's father. However, according to the sexual standards of the time, one present infidelity on a woman's part may create doubts about other infidelities in the past.

Eleazar rather than Philip is the play's star turn; he is a moderately vigorous sub-Marlovian figure,[86] bent on revenge for his father's defeat by the old King Philip of Spain. He has been brought up as a captive in Spain, and despite his good treatment, he hates that nation, saying 'He that can loose a kingdom and not rave, / He's a tame jade' (I. i. 160–1),[87] words that may reflect on his father. It is quite common for avenging sons to be rather more impressive than the father they are vindicating, making their assertion of patrilineal identity into an ironic transcendence rather than an imitation (as with the prince in *Edward II*); it is unusual, however, for the son to *express* his superiority. In the case of Hamlet, the difference is found rather in a more complex sense of manly inferiority, mitigated by a touch of moral superiority.

Eleazar's revenge is much more masculine than Hamlet's: first of all he seduces (and abuses) King Philip's queen. Prince Philip insists that this has led to his father's early death. The effect of the seduction is that even in Eleazar's own view the queen's offspring may be called 'bastards' (I. i. 66). Despite these sins, on his succession the king's elder son Ferdinand initially tolerates Eleazar, largely because the Moor is prepared to pander his own (Spanish) wife Maria to him. Nonetheless, when he catches Maria with Ferdinand, Eleazar kills him and takes the throne, having previously persuaded the queen mother to declare Philip a bastard. Philip's rage at this is understandable, but the terms in which he expresses it are very instructive; he says of his mother's marriage to Eleazar:

> This will confirm the worlds opinion
> That I am base born, and the damned *Moor*
> Had interest in my birth, this wrong alone
> Gives new fire to the cinders of my rage:
> I may well be transformed from what I am,
> When a black divel is husband to my dam.   (IV. i. 19–24)

This could be a gloss on Hamlet's unspoken fears. It is not as if Philip seriously believes that Eleazar is his father, nor that the 'world' will believe it either (the claim, later made, is that Cardinal Mendoza is the man responsible); rather, his fear is of Eleazar's rather vaguely stated 'interest', which will somehow retrospectively undermine his identity. Such, I think, is Hamlet's key problem, and it impels a whole new attitude to uncertain individuality in tragedy, setting the genre free to develop fully.

In killing the Moor at the end, Philip vindicates his father and asserts his own identity; he is even able at this point to forgive his mother. Perhaps – though this is not stated – he needs her to survive so that she can retract her earlier slanders on his parentage. The play can conclude with 'Comick joy to end a Tragedie' (V. iii. 181) because the father who died at the beginning of the play has been avenged, the Moor's father being unavenged. The only casualties have been Eleazar's wife and Ferdinand. The latter is more significant: the throne must pass to the younger son because the elder was bad. Not only was he lustful, which led directly to his death, but he was forgetful of his father's memory: in order to retain Eleazar (and his wife) at court, Ferdinand dared – in the younger Philip's words – 'to break their fathers will' (II. i. 34). Such filial impiety forfeits one's birthright in the world of this play – a hint, perhaps, as to why Hamlet cannot survive and succeed.

Hamlet may be morally better than his father, but he is certainly less of a man. His moral scruples have endeared him to audiences for centuries, but of course those scruples actually cause more trouble than they prevent.[88] How much blame Old Hamlet should have for this is very much an open question, but to some extent, at least, Prince Hamlet needs to become his father in order to be an avenger. Even the most capricious of his schemes, to put on an 'antic disposition' (I. v. 172), may contribute to the process of filial identification: punning on 'antique', Hamlet harks back to an ancient, simpler world (one in which even Horatio could be like an 'antique Roman' – V. ii. 341), where father–son identification could be taken for granted, or could at least be actively recovered, as it is by Seneca's Atreus.

Yet this identification is impossible in the modern world. Hamlet's meeting with his father is one of the strangest examples of recognition in the period, not least because his father is a ghost. In front of Horatio and Marcellus the Ghost is silent, only beckoning to the prince; it is not a figure to excite automatic reverence, Marcellus even saying ''Tis not fit thus to obey him' (I. iv. 88). When the Ghost does speak in private to Hamlet, he directs the way his son should respond to him: he must 'Mark' him, but must not 'Pity' him (I. v. 2, 5); significantly, when the Ghost reappears later Hamlet fears that the Ghost's 'piteous action' might move him to tears rather than vengeance (III. iv. 128). No affection passes in the first encounter, except perhaps in this weirdly conditional exchange:

GHOST. If thou didst ever thy dear father love –
HAMLET. O God! (I. v. 24–5)

Not only is this conditional, it is in the past tense; the word 'dear' is strangely loaded, expressing the cost of the presumed love for the father and the father's own self-valuation as father and king as much as it does any real emotion on Hamlet's part; Hamlet's response may anticipate the mention of the murder, but it may also express the assumption that one *must* love one's father, along with a sense that such love may always be inadequate when it is so assumed. Hamlet may be responding to the testing of his love with a sense, like Cordelia's, that one should love and be silent. Yet he is also appealing to higher paternal authority, the ultimate *idea* of the father. Relying on such an ideal paternal authority, though, involves a rejection of all earthly things: he shortly after (once the physical form of the ghost has departed) insists that his mind will be emptied only to contain the idea of his father, 'Unmix'd with baser matter' (line 104); the pun on *mater* (Latin 'mother') here is clear, suggesting that he wants to be purely related to the ideal of paternity. In comparison to that ideal, anything else in the world is worthless (Polonius, Ophelia, his mother). Even the idea of kingship is rejected. When Hamlet refers to Claudius as 'a king of shreds and patches' (III. iv. 102), he seems also to refer to his father, whose ghost enters eerily at that moment – entering his wife's chamber, the ghost here may exist in his private rather than his public aspect, alienated from the role of armed king he sustained in his earlier appearance. Kingship is then further undermined in the following exchange with Rosencrantz and Guildenstern:

> HAMLET. The body [ie. Polonius'] is with the King, but the King
>   is not with the body. The King is a thing –
> GUILDENSTERN. A thing, my lord?
> HAMLET. Of nothing.   (IV. ii. 27–30)

Alluding to the doctrine of the King's Two Bodies, Hamlet dissociates the body of the king from the idea, but then goes on to insist that kingship is a kind of nothing too. All things, all embodiments, are brushed away as the son identifies himself with the purely notional father. Hamlet begins the play wishing that 'this too too sullied flesh would melt, / Thaw, and resolve itself into a dew!' (I. ii. 129–30); as Simon Palfrey argues, 'Hamlet concentrates himself – literally – into this image',[89] wanting a perfectly purified and atomistic identity. Yet this identity, involving identification with the father, is punningly undermined a short time later when Hamlet's odd phrase 'a dew' is echoed in the Ghost's 'Adieu, adieu, adieu! remember me' (I. v. 91); the language of farewells and dissolution replaces the language of resolution. To engage so excessively with the idea of paternity is to reject the world, destroying everyone around one, and leaving only a story to be told by Horatio. Such excessive filial piety is the limit case of a son proving himself, because such proof is a form of self-erasure. At the turn of the century Shakespeare demonstrates, with remarkable and subtle force, that identification between son and father is inhumanly destructive, bringing nothingness rather than unification of identity. The next decade's drama finds a way out of this trap, finding virtue in less drastic self-diminution.

We have seen that excessive attention to paternity in 1590s history plays develops, paradoxically, into a desire to escape its pressures; this desire then finds its way into comedy, where paternal identity remains an important shaping factor or limit, but one which is pushed against harder and harder as the decade goes on, room being found for the father to be presented as sinful; in turn, this attitude filters into tragedy and becomes the enabling condition of more individualistic character representation in that genre. This would then enable tragedy to come into its own in the following decade.[90] By developing the emotional range of fathers, late Elizabethan drama had not only made them into sharper focal points for the crystallization of identity: it had also made them more vulnerable.

CHAPTER 4

Limiting the father in the 1600s: the wake of Hamlet and King Lear

Hamlet's intense preoccupation with an individual finding and losing himself through his deeply ambivalent relation with his father was hugely influential in the coming decade, and plays of all genres responded to its challenges, implicating the possibility of tragic selfhood into comedy and thus enabling the emergence of the hybrid genre of tragicomedy, which attempts to resolve *Hamlet*-posed questions; unsurprisingly, it is Shakespeare himself who responds to those problems most strikingly, first in intensifying familial-dynastic tragedy further in *King Lear* and *Macbeth*, and then in producing the most powerful versions of tragicomic acceptance of human limitation in *The Winter's Tale* and *The Tempest*.

Throughout the decade, one of the major themes of drama will be the attempt to remove the authority of the father, to exorcise the ghost of Hamlet. Yet it is still not acceptable for fathers to be deposed; as a displacement of this impulse, we encounter various attempts by fathers to abdicate; but this then comes to a further limit: for fathers cannot fundamentally deny their paternity. In the end, all they can do is accept its limitations. In doing so, however, they become the centres of some crucial new generic developments, which enrich the dramatic repertoire and do away with the simpler generic distinctions of the Elizabethan period.

This chapter will deal with the dominant genres of early Jacobean drama: revenge tragedy, political drama (particularly plays focussing on the succession to the throne), prodigal-son comedy, and tragicomedy, all of which seek ways of limiting paternal power. The play that fuses all these generic strands, *King Lear*, will be at the centre of this discussion, for only by making the problems involved in fatherhood most acute can ways be found of solving them. Tragicomedy emerges at around the time of *King Lear*, and can be seen as a response to its horrific end, offering more promising images of resolution by limiting the father's power for good (in both senses of the phrase). In almost all of these genres, we see attempts to separate out the doubleness of fathers, the private/emotional and the public/sacral elements being gradually and painfully disentangled.

REVENGE TRAGEDY AGAIN

Hamlet provoked many imitations,[1] not just in a rush to cash in on its evident popularity, but in various ways attempting to find answers to the problems it sets. Most of the solutions involve reductions in the power of filial and paternal feeling. Henry Chettle's *The Tragedy of Hoffman* (1602–3, pub. 1631) is both a homage to and a parody of Shakespeare's play, but it does away with any real seriousness in the idea of paternal pressure on the individual; here it is simply *assumed* that revenge for a father is a reasonable cause for action. The titular hero has already undergone his period of delay when the play begins, so that the plot can focus on his various rather fortuitous revenges. As he is not commanded by any ghost, his father's presence in the play is in the form of an anatomized corpse that Hoffman has stolen from the gallows and hung up in his house as 'the dead remembrance of my liuing father' (line 8);[2] this may suggest that in remembering he keeps his father alive, but the adjectives seem the wrong way around, and the awkward phrasing may hint at the disorder inherent in the idea of 'A Reuenge for a Father' (the play's subtitle); it also subjects the body of the father to an indignity, and that will be a major trope of Jacobean drama.[3]

Ironically, it is the discovery of the spectacle of the father's body, hanging together with the body of Hoffman's first victim, that helps bring about the protagonist's downfall. The father is therefore both spur to action and the partial instrument of the son's nemesis. This perhaps reflects the fact that Hoffman in no way brings his father back to life during his period of success, not even in the abstract sense of remembrance (see Chapter 3, above): his first victim is Otho, son of the duke of Luningberg, one of those who executed his father; in subsequently taking Otho's identity he both loses himself and temporarily supplies Otho's family with an heir.[4] Otho's uncle, Ferdinand of Prussia, is cursed with an idiot son, Jerom (fond of writing poems about tooth-picks), whom the disguised Hoffman displaces from the line of succession; this may help Hoffman's plots, but it also cures Ferdinand's 'shame' and unhappiness with the fool (remarkably expressed at lines 279–90). Ferdinand is therefore able, in a roundabout way, to repudiate his own paternity by promoting Hoffman-Otho over his own son.

Hoffman's revenges take rather an odd course, as he kills people rather whimsically and with no real plan; no one family is wiped out. When the

arrival of Otho's mother threatens to expose Hoffman, he is able to
persuade her that he tried to save her son and that he should continue
to replace him; she adopts him and rechristens him (line 1895), but he
lusts after his 'new made mother' (1909), and this lust becomes the
principal cause of his defeat. This may realize a perceived Oedipal strain
in *Hamlet,* but it more importantly enables the transformation of a
mother into an avenger, thus casting some doubt on the efficacy of
patrilineal vengeance. If a woman can, out of sheer sentiment, choose
who her son is, the whole basis of identity is subtly challenged. In the end,
Hoffman is left lamenting his love, and is only able to be like his father in
dying in the same way (line 2610). The life-force is on the side of the
mother. She took pity on him before the play's action and enabled him to
escape execution with his father, but now she takes away the life she gave
him. Masculine notions of mastery are therefore ironized:[5] the roots of
vengeance lie with women.

   In Middleton and Dekker's *The Bloody Banquet* (c. 1609) paternal and
filial feeling are surprisingly attenuated, despite the deposition of a father
and the murder of a son. The play ends with the titular meal, at which the
disguised rightful king watches his son being eaten; his reaction to this –
'O me, my son Tymethes!' (V. i. 187) – seems rather restrained, and he is
more concerned that he no longer has an heir than emotionally involved
in the horror of this; perhaps one can only develop a visceral response to
the cannibalism of a son if one is eating him oneself, in the manner of
Thyestes and *Titus Andronicus'* Tamora.

   Another reason for the relatively muted response may be that Tymethes
has, over the course of the play, proved himself to be a worthless individual, though his father makes no comment on this. When Zenarchus urges
that Tymethes be merry, the latter responds that he is as joyful 'As your
son and heir at his father's funeral' (I. iv. 2) – on the face of it, this seems
designed as a proverbial statement of his misery, but it would take little
imagination to see that an inheriting son's feelings might have at least an
admixture of joy.[6] The play's ambivalent attitude to filial and paternal
feeling is nicely encapsulated here. After the old king's exile, even the
usurping Tyrant calls Tymethes 'base boy' for abandoning his father and
staying at court (I. i. 98). Tymethes has remained because of his friendship for the Tyrant's son Zenarchus, which might seem a laudable
instance of idealized youthful friendship, but, at least initially, it is used
to put a good 'gloss' (line 99) on the usurpation. The friendship of
Tymethes and Zenarchus is clearly paralleled with the Biblical David
and Jonathan, for Zenarchus, like Jonathan, promises to abrogate his

ultimate right to the throne for his friend's sake. This plan comes to nothing, however, as Tymethes cannot remain loyal: though engaged to his friend's sister, he is easily seduced by the Tyrant's queen (Zenarchus' step-mother), who kills him when she fears their affair is going to be revealed. As a result, when the old king returns to claim his right he must find another heir, abandoning excessive feelings about paternity. It is easy to see that the cannibalistic banquet is rather a good thing for him, a displacement of his own need to get rid of a bad son, without him having to participate.

Fortunately, his wife has managed to preserve another son, the infant Manophes. At first, the king only believes that he has got his kingdom and wife back, but he is soon put right:

> Our joys were perfect, stood Tymethes there.
> We *are* old; this kingdom wants a hopeful heir.
> OLD QUEEN. Your joys are perfect, though he stand not there,
> And your wish blessed: behold a hopeful heir!
> Stand not amazed: 'tis Manophes.
> KING. How just the gods are, who in their due time
> Return what they took from us. (V. i. 234–40)

Manophes is able to be much more 'hopeful' because he is an infant and therefore lacks the personal desires that have led Tymethes astray. The happy ending is predicated on getting rid of a troublesome son. Revenge tragedy gives way to tragicomedy here as paternal feeling is purged.

The play's parallels between the good father with a bad son and the bad father with a good son are quite well developed, and help to get rid of the excess that now seems essential and necessary to father–son relations. The Tyrant is also pleased to lose a son who has priorities that do not entirely mesh with his own. Early in the play he is almost dissuaded from his usurpation by his son's pleas: Zenarchus and Tymethes kneel to him, and urge that kingdoms should be lawfully held, prompting the aside 'The boy hath almost changed us' (I. i. 42); though he is restored to his tyrannous nature by the support of his favourite, this indicates the way in which a son can alter a man's chosen destiny, while also hinting at a plot in which friendship might defeat tyranny. Paternal tyranny here, however, wins hands down over the limited friendship of the sons. Although the Tyrant does not himself kill either of them, his tyranny is clearly the cause of their death and that of his daughter (who kills herself and Zenarchus). His initial reaction to his children's death, which is accompanied by thunder, lightning, and a blazing star, is fearful, and he interprets the signs as the influence of the

heavens' 'malice', considering that 'malignant powers have envied' his children, 'And both in haste, struck with their envies, died. / 'Tis ominous' (V. 1.
115–18). We might wonder how much envy *he* has had for his children, and
how far he is himself associated with the malignant powers that have
destroyed them: in any case, he is only concerned for the ominousness of
this event to his own fate. Once the bodies have been carried off, he is able to
console himself:

> Yes, and we safe; our death we need less fear.
> Usurper's issue oft proves dangerous:
> We depose others, and they poison us.
> I have found it on records; 'tis better thus.   (lines 121–4)

His proverbial–historical wisdom here masks both his lack of feeling and
his lack of concern to have an heir, who would be more the people's safety
than his own. This anticipates Macbeth's need to get rid of Banquo's
issue, which he frames thus: 'To be thus is nothing, / But to be safely thus'
(III. i. 47–8). The only way a tyrant can be safe is to do away with
successors, but that may destroy the people's hopes, a central issue in
The Bloody Banquet. The play is bracketed by two cries of '*Speranza!*' (i.e.
'hope!' – I. i. 1; V. i. 206): the first, when the Tyrant takes the throne, is
purely personal hope, but the last comes from Lapyrus, who is taking the
throne back for his uncle. The latter cry is altruistic, coming from a
repentant traitor; the former comes from one who never thinks of his
son as a hope, either for the kingdom or himself. In a true kingdom rather
than a tyranny, the hopes of an heir are more public property than private.

Cyril Tourneur's *Atheist's Tragedy* (pub. 1611) by contrast presents
an extreme version of the identification of the private individual with
the paternal line, driven by an excessive ideology of primogeniture.
D'Amville, perhaps *because* he is a younger son, has an absurdly strong
desire to identify with his own elder son. He also argues that it is having
sons that makes one ambitious:

> Had not my body spread itself
> Into posterity perhaps I should
> Desire no more increase of substance than
> Would hold proportion with mine own dimensions.   (I. i. 42–5)[7]

He also believes that 'from my substance they receive the sap / Whereby
they live and flourish' (lines 57–8). There is considerable complexity of
paternal feeling here, despite its being exhibited within a seemingly simple
main idea: the feeling that sons (who are considered 'accidents' compared
to the substance of the self – lines 50–1) may rob a man of his substance

suggests that paternity is a zero-sum game, for whatever a son gains, a father must lose. Yet at the same time a father's sense of his own growth is in the form of sons, so that he both gains and loses substance. D'Amville wants to put all his genetic and financial eggs in the basket of his elder son Rousard, but that son turns out to be impotent; this is an 'accident' if ever there was one, but D'Amville refuses to continue his line through the insurance policy of his lusty younger son Sebastian. Although D'Amville is himself a younger son (and treacherous to his elder brother), he cannot see his own affinity with Sebastian. D'Amville takes his identification with his eldest son to the extreme of plotting to sleep with Rousard's wife, but all his plans come to nothing and both his sons die. As with Old Hamlet and Leontes (as we shall see below) excessive identification with a son is fatal.

The Atheist's Tragedy is, in the end, a tragicomedy. D'Amville is providentially if ridiculously killed when he attempts to behead Charlemont (the 'honest man' of the play's subtitle). This obviates the need for the play's virtuous characters to take revenge, but it also results in a sense of a higher power that can deal with problems of familial loyalty. Virtue and paternity are subtly but decisively detached as revenge tragedy develops. Private desires are sidelined as the wild justice of revenge becomes less valid. The identification of private and public interests which so pressurized Hamlet is gradually untangled.

POLITICAL DRAMA AND THE SUCCESSION

The need for such purgation of private family feeling may have its roots in what initially seemed a more optimistic form of political drama, which replaced chronicle history after 1600. Like Shakespeare's history plays, these plays are able to turn to both tragedy and comedy, while keeping a focus on the idea of political succession. In doing so, they raise questions about the limits of paternal authority in the public sphere: without the violent passions that need purging in private revenge tragedy, fathers in these plays struggle to find their place in the political universe.

The accession of a male monarch for the first time in fifty years (and therefore for the first time in all the dramatists' lifetimes) clearly refigured the idea of paternity, particularly given the insistent patriarchal ideology presented by James I himself. The political drama of the period sets up a series of important questions: was this a new world of masculine validation and licence, or was it one of stern authority? When the ruler is not just a man but the father of sons, does this augment or undermine his authority? Is a king-father more secure or more vulnerable than a queen or a private father? The varied genres of political drama in the new reign constitute formal devices for stating (and sometimes solving) these problems, exploring the double roles of royal fathers.

Thomas Middleton's *The Phoenix* (1603) is a satirical comedy about succession to power, written immediately after James I had come to the throne of England. Its hero, the heir to the dukedom of Ferrara, is sent abroad to learn about the world, but chooses instead to remain at home in disguise, probing into various abuses in his future realm. In doing so, he exposes the weakness and blindness of his father's rule and shows that he will manage the state more insightfully in the future. The play obviously reflects hopes that James would be a better ruler than Elizabeth had been in her last years. The way in which the transition of power is presented, however, hints at certain imaginative problems in managing the idea of a son's succession. Clearly, having the protagonist be the duke's only son and undisputed heir makes the accession less uncertain than James's accession to England had been, but the introduction of a paternal line of succession creates problems of its own. The duke begins the play announcing that he will die soon:

> 'twill not be long
> Before I show that kings have mortal bodies
> As well as subjects. Therefore, to my comfort,
> And your successful hopes, I have a son
> Whom I dare boast of –   (i. 12–16)

The reference to 'mortal' bodies reminds us of the doctrine of the King's Two Bodies to which the play's title refers, the Phoenix being a popular figuration of the immortality of the royal body. The curious use of 'therefore' here suggests that the son is a second body for the king: he is a comfort to his father because he is identified with him. Pairing the concept of comfort with that of hope here brings together the two key words used of offspring, particularly sons, but 'hopes' are here transferred onto the people rather than the father himself. The transferred epithet involved in 'successful hopes', meaning 'hopes of succession', but implying that such hopes must be fulfilled, antici-pates an unproblematic transition of power to such an extent that it hardly seems a transition: in a sense the heir might as well already be the king. Such overidentification on the father's part and certainty of success on the son's are key problems for the paternal line: they may allow smooth transitions, but they also blur boundaries and create tensions between individuals, emphasiz-ing the strange doubleness of paternity even as they enable hope for the future.

The son's decision to roam his father's kingdom in disguise may therefore involve some attempt to resolve these tensions. Going out among the people, like Prince Hal in Shakespeare's *Henry IV* plays, is not just a way of learning lessons, but also a way of getting out from beneath one's father's feet without being a threat to him by becoming a focus for opposition. Yet the overall effect here is different. The fact that Middleton's prince is, unlike Hal, much admired by the courtiers makes him more of a danger rather than less; it may even threaten any authority the duke has over him: as Infesto says 'His judgement is a father to his youth' (i. 18), suggesting that he doesn't need an actual father. Anticipating his succession, he is referred to as being already 'the duke' (viii. 287), and it is notable that in other plays of the time which present a disguised royal investigating the state of the nation, such as Marston's *Malcontent* and Shakespeare's *Measure for Measure*, that investigator is (or ought to be in the former case) already the legitimate ruler.[8] The sense that the prince is coming prematurely to power is most fully accentuated at the end of the play when the old duke abdicates rather than waiting to die: the prince's proof of his judgement in his disguise makes his father irrelevant. The essentially comic mode of the play seems to license the defeat of age by youth, however gracefully and willingly this occurs. In a sense the prince becomes himself as the play goes on, and in becoming himself through his disguise he becomes his father or *the* Phoenix, thus reversing the duke's initial identification of them. The confusion over the prince's name may reflect this: although the speech-headings suggest that Phoenix is his name, he is not addressed as such *in propria persona*; but he is twice addressed as 'Phoenix' by Proditor (xii. 1; xv. 1), who most definitely does not know who he is. Phoenix may therefore be both the name of his disguise and the name by which he comes to the throne, supplanting his father, who may himself have been a Phoenix – after all, the father, like Elizabeth I, who identified herself with the Phoenix, has ruled for forty-five years (i. 7).

Given the play's essentially comic genre and its concern with succession, it is surprising that the prince has no love-interest plot. This may be the result of Middleton's desire to make his hero seem completely disinterested, but this disinterest means that there is no secured line of future succession for the dukedom. Phoenix may praise 'Reverend and honourable matrimony // . . . that mak'st the bed / Both pleasant and legitimately fruitful' (viii. 166–9), but he does not do anything to arrive at this state. One reason for this may be that for the prince to promise children would not only make him a threat to his father, but hint at a threat to himself.

It is the treacherous villain Proditor who promises Phoenix to 'bless thy loins with freedom, wealth and honour' (xv. 26), offering him 'a foot-clothed posterity' (28) in return for his planned murder of the prince. The idea of prosperous offspring is therefore associated with treason. Proditor's obvious treachery enables him to act as a lightning-conductor or scapegoat for treasonous feelings that may be inherent in a prince succeeding to his father, just as the alleged treasons of a Ralegh or even of an Essex may have acted as distractions from suspicions that James had plotted against Elizabeth. The fact that *The Phoenix* was played by a boys' company may have helped make its problems with the idea of succession seem less threatening, as the upshot is that one interchangeable boy succeeds to another, but this, like the play's other repressions of problems, tends only to highlight the evasive thinking required when a son replaces his father and when the royal body is transferred.

A play produced by the new Prince Henry's Company, Samuel Rowley's *When You See Me, You Know Me* (1604), is also concerned with producing an attractive image of a king and his male heir. Henry VIII is made into a merry and humanly appealing figure, and his son Prince Edward into a promising, pious, and scholarly youth (as indeed he was): clearly both figures are meant to flatter the new regime, King James and his son Henry, and to help the audience get used to the return of male power. Despite its fundamentally contented tone, the play initiates the idea that a male heir might be a useful focus of opposition to any excesses on the part of the king: Prince Edward is more protestant than his father – as Prince Henry would be – and he manages to dissuade King Henry from executing Catherine Parr (who is, with historical accuracy unusual for this play, subject to catholic calumny). A son, then, is shown as securing the nation's protestant future: Prince Edward's early death can be forgotten because of the hopes residing in Prince Henry (ironically, given Henry's own early death eight years later).

For this reason, the birth of Edward is presented as an event of major significance in the play's first scenes, and some quite powerful drama is built out of this. Henry's delight in his pregnant wife is perhaps the strongest such statement in the drama of the time:

> Thou art now a right woman, goodly, chiefe of thy sex;
> Me thinkes thou art a Queene superlatiue,
> Mother, a God this is a womans glorie,
> Like good September Vines loden with fruite.   (lines 169–72)[9]

This celebration of womanhood's perfection might implicitly criticize Queen Elizabeth for never having arrived at such a state; or it might allegorically celebrate her as the supposed mother of the new masculine regime – in this way, she realizes all her promise, lives up to the superlative praises she has been given throughout her reign. In either case, the irony is that such perfection of womanhood is also final, for it entails her death: Jane Seymour's death in childbirth is made heroic in the next scenes. Informed of his wife's danger, Henry is prepared to sacrifice his son for her sake: after wavering for a moment in despair at losing 'the hope of this great Monarchy' (line 386), he decides to 'let the Childe die' so that the mother may live (line 391), consoling himself with the thought that this is God's will:

> Perhaps he did mould forth a Sonne for me,
> And seeing (that sees all) in his creation,
> To be some impotent and coward spirit,
> Vnlike the figure of his Royall Father:
> Has thus decrede, least he should blurre our fame,
> As Whylome did the sixt king of my name
> Loose all, his Father (the fift[10] Henrie) wonne.
> Ile thanke the Heauens for taking such a Sonne.   (lines 391–407)

The extraordinarily pious final sentiment may be a kind of apotropaic magic, but its basis hints at certain fears about paternity, particularly in royal lines, and resonates with Bacon's sense that one's reputation might be best secured by having no offspring (see Chapter 2, above). In any case, the queen, we are told, insists on dying so that Henry can have a son: his grief for her makes it clear that, the harder-won a son may be, the more worthy he is to rule in future. This too may hint at the long wait for a male ruler being worth it, as if the reign of Elizabeth had been one long gestation. At the very moment of the smooth succession of the new King James, dramatists are also looking to the future and pondering the potential problems of the next succession. In all of this, we are made aware of the human sacrifices that secure paternalistic power entails.

If Henry VIII can be refigured as the ideal father, a pope has to be the opposite. Barnabe Barnes's *The Devil's Charter* (c. 1606) centres on one of the most vicious fathers in the period's drama, the Borgia Pope Alexander VI. Of course, the Pope – despite his paternal title – ought not to be a father, but this initial problem is taken for granted, so that the play can focus on his vices: incest with his daughter (Lucretia), multiple murders, including that of the aforementioned daughter, complicity after the fact in the murder of one son, encouraging the other son to incest with his sister (Lucretia again), general rapacity/avarice, and some of the most fully developed sodomy in the period's drama. All this is enabled by his

Faustian pact with the devil, but unlike Faustus Alexander is not wholly self-centred; his repeatedly stated main motive is to raise his sons up. It is fair to say that the play is distinctly anti-papal; but is anti-paternal?

As well as being clearly presented on stage, many of Alexander's major sins are charged against him by his son Caesar (lines 2079–114).[11] But this son is not a virtuous or reforming hero: he merely makes the case in order to excuse his own murder of his brother, suggesting that he was only following his father's example. Having initially accused Caesar of being a second Cain (lines 2044–59), Alexander realizes that he is no Adamic figure of paternal authority, and has to cover up his son's crime. The play's most virtuous figure is the Duchess Katherine, who is prepared to see her (initially unwilling) sons die rather than yield her city; but she is captured by Caesar, so that maternal virtue (with hinted allusions to Queen Elizabeth) can hardly be said to trump paternal vice here.

Alexander's motive in his 'misty machinations' with the devil is 'for the glorious sunne-shine of my sonnes' (lines 365–7); he seems to think that this is a plea in mitigation for his actions, but ultimately his pride in his remaining son will be his moment of tragic *hubris* (lines 3159–65). He is a perverse paternal-papal figure, presenting himself as a surrogate father to the young Prince Astor, on whom he has sodomitical designs (lines 1277, 1325); in thus twisting the proper paternalistic role he perhaps invalidates his concern for his son(s). However, a dimension is added to the imitation of Marlowe's *Doctor Faustus* in the final scene by presenting his concern for his son:

> if I may not reach that happinesse,
> Since for my sonnes sake I my selfe inthral'd,
> Tell me shall *Caesar* die this death with me?   (lines 3505–7)

The devil replies that Caesar will survive for a while, but will die soon. This adds a surprising element of pathos to the end of the play: as in the same year's *Macbeth*, the tragic villain garners some sympathy because of the failure of his line. Paternity still resonates as an emotional-political value, even in the worst of men.

The play demonstrates, then, that even the worst villain also gains some pathos from the failure of his paternal desires. In *Macbeth*, the last of Shakespeare's plays concerned with the succession to the throne, the hero 'has no children' (IV. iii. 216), and, despite L. C. Knights's famous essay warning against discussion of the subject,[12] this matters immensely. Lady Macbeth has 'given suck', she tells us (and, otiosely, her husband – I. vii. 54), but the inference we are to draw is that the couple's children have died; no direct explanation of this fact is necessary, so common was infant mortality in this period. We may perhaps suppose that the Macbeths might in future have more children, and thus gain some hope for their permanent possession of the throne, but this possibility is imaginatively cut off in two ways: Lady Macbeth's self-unsexing (I. v. 40–54) and her declaration that she would have 'dash'd the brains out' of her own babe if she had sworn to do so (I. vii. 58) both seem to make her barren to our minds;[13] also, the increasing distance between Macbeth and his wife as they step further into guilt makes us sceptical that they could breed again (the murder of Macduff's children also has an important effect). Banquo's line, by contrast, will 'stretch out to th' crack of doom' (IV. i. 117), including James I (and, despite many by-ways, it is still going now). The clear implication is that a throne is not worth having unless one can be sure one's son will succeed to it. Macbeth's gnomic comment that he has 'only / Vaulting ambition, which o'erleaps itself, / And falls on th' other' (I. vii. 26–8) may reflect this; we are to imagine a horseman leaping too enthusiastically into the saddle and falling off on the other side: he never gets to sit in the throne (or even in his chair at the banquet); certainly, it is hard to think of him as ever being King Macbeth, and this is more than partly because he has no son.

Macbeth's initial conception of the murder of Duncan 'unfix[es] his hair' (I. iii. 135). This is an odd image; it is not quite the same thing as Hamlet's hair standing on end like porcupine quills; we feel if anything that Macbeth's hair falls out. This only makes sense, I think, if we see a pun on *heir*, and the murder as paradoxically preventing him having any successor. This idea is made more plausible by a similar pun later in the play: Old Siward says, on being told of his son's death in battle, 'Had I as many sons as I have hairs, / I would not wish them to a fairer death' (V. ix. 14). This hints that Siward has plenty of (expendable) sons – and his name may even hint an origin for the Stewart dynasty. As Macbeth says 'To be thus is nothing, / But to be safely thus' (III. i. 47–8); only a son can make one safe.[14]

Macduff's status as one not born of woman, 'from his mother's womb / Untimely ripp'd' (V. viii. 15–16), seems to make him in some sense unnatural, something of which his wife accuses him in his absence ('He wants the natural touch' – IV. ii. 9). He is therefore a proper opposite or nemesis to Macbeth, who is (according to *his* wife) 'too full o' the milk of human kindness' (I. v. 17). The caesarean section by which Macduff was delivered would very probably have resulted in the death of his mother; this is a man who is detached from women and natural generativity – we never actually see him with his wife. The murder of his children makes him as unlineal as Macbeth; he can therefore be used to commit the tyrannicide as he has no stake in the future or the succession, thus getting round the problem of the national sin in killing a king. He is as much a tragic scapegoat as Macbeth: as both unnatural men are removed, the naturalness of the succession is secured.[15] The death of Lady Macbeth, accompanied by the cry of women, seems to be the death of femininity itself, and therefore of kindness; it is also a purgation of concern with familial inheritance.[16]

Lady Macbeth may be a symbol of everything that undermines masculinity, yet our sense of her capacity for evil is limited by her statement 'Had he [Duncan] not resembled / My father as he slept, I had done't' (II. ii. 12–13). She is incapable of anything resembling patricide, an act that seems to be regarded as particularly evil in a woman. She partly resembles Tullia in Heywood's *The Rape of Lucrece* (pub. 1609), but is less bad: that wicked woman urges her husband to take the throne in order to make himself 'worthy' of her love, saying 'I am no wife of *Tarquins* if not King' (pp. 166–7),[17] a persuasion that strongly resembles Lady Macbeth's (I. vii). Tarquin accordingly usurps her father Servius and has him killed, but the most striking aspect of this is that Tullia treads on her father's skull and then rides her chariot through his blood. Bad as Lady Macbeth is, she is no parricide. For her, the father is a symbol of pity. Private feeling can still operate in this play, even though the political world tries to make it irrelevant.

Macbeth, on the other hand, may take on the infection of the sin his wife refuses to commit, becoming a parricide of sorts. If kings are fathers, then regicide is a kind of patricide. This accounts for the extraordinary image of pity that Macbeth conjures up when he envisages the murder:

> pity, like a naked new-born babe,
> Striding the blast, or heaven's cherubin, horsed
> Upon the sightless couriers of the air,
> Shall blow the horrid deed in every eye,
> That tears shall drown the wind.   (I. vii. 21–5)

This seems like too much. Our attitude to Duncan cannot be the kind of protective pity that we might have for a baby (particularly one in the precarious position of riding on invisible wind). The language here is full of transferences: the babe, more normally an object of pity, becomes its personification; the horses of the wind are sightless rather than invisible;

the baby, who we might expect to be crying himself, makes others cry. Such transferences are typical of a play in which 'function / Is smothered in surmise, and nothing is / But what is not' (I. iii. 140–2), and they indicate a world of emotional slippage. In such a world, killing a king-father can seem like killing one's own children.

Macbeth's 'single state of man' (I. iii. 140) is shaken by the witches and by his wife. She tells him 'When you durst do it, then you were a man; / And to be more than what you were, you would / Be so much more the man' (I. vii. 49–51), insisting that getting to be king is necessarily to be more of a man; there is a scale of masculinity which must unman anyone but a king, an attitude that Hamlet resisted, but could not confute. At the end of *Macbeth*, a man may get to be a fully realized heroic individual, able to connect thought and action without intervening delay, wholly self-reliant in his ability to make 'the firstlings of my heart . . . the firstlings of my hand' (IV. i. 147–8), dependent only on the conception of his ideas as his perfectly realized children; yet the cost of that independence is sharply delineated. Macbeth tells Donalbain and Malcolm that 'The spring, the head, the fountain of your blood / Is stopped, the very source of it is stopped' (II. iii. 97–8); this overstated image seems to insist that Duncan is a source not only of his sons' being, but of all being. Such a figure, given his baby-like vulnerability, seems to make the world rather a precarious place; to depend on such an over-loaded figure of paternity is dangerous in the extreme. We saw in the previous chapter that identification between fathers and sons tended to become destructive in the drama of the late Elizabethan period; in early Jacobean political drama, the identification of fathers and kings may lose its destructiveness, but becomes decidedly vulnerable. If the strange doubleness of fathers is allowed to give way to the single state of man, that single state is precarious, too easily shaken.

PRODIGAL COMEDY

Perhaps in order to deal with the sense of sacrifice involved in paternal power, an old form of drama, based on the Biblical story of the Prodigal Son (Luke 15) was re-invented in the early Jacobean period.[18] Though these plays are comedies, they also act out a considerable sense of father–son tension and mutual obligation that had been set up so problematically in *Hamlet*. One of the effects of this form of drama is to efface and marginalize fathers while still making use of their sacred status.

The London Prodigal (pub. 1605, falsely attributed to Shakespeare) is an early example of the common Jacobean plot in which the father acts as a monitor on his son's doings (as such, it is a form of 'disguised ruler' play – see above), but it is perhaps the most extreme case. Its moral intention is clearly drawn from the parable of the prodigal son, but, unlike earlier comedies which make use of the trope in order to license youthful wild oats,[19] it presents the son as utterly depraved, ungenerous, and without any feelings of love, friendship, or filial piety. As its protagonist is so lacking in virtue, though the play may formally be a comedy, its tone is decidedly uncomic, pushing the limits of comic father–son tensions onto the verge of tragedy, and suggesting that there are serious problems in this crucial element of the genre.

The play begins with Master Flowerdale's secret return to England from Venice: he has come 'to proue the humours of my sonne' (I. i. 2);[20] his brother tells him of his son's bad courses, but he thinks these are acceptable, arguing that 'If they do not rellish altogether of damnation, his youth may priuilidge his wantonnesse: I my selfe ranne an vnbrideled course till thirtie, nay almost till fortie' (lines 21–5). Where there were hints of paternal overindulgence in *Every Man in His Humour*, which might be taken as in some ways a precedent for prodigal comedy,[21] here it is made explicit that the father has his own vices, and that this may have led him to overindulge his son's. Yet he also has a clear sense of potential regeneration that will ultimately inform the play's redemptive plot: growing up involves getting a new self, but that means that the old self must be utterly banished.

The father is not, however, the key instrument of the son's regeneration. He lets it be thought that he is dead, and becomes an observer and *provocateur*. Disguised, he helps young Flowerdale trick Sir Lancelot Spurcock into marrying his daughter Luce; despite her love for another man, once she is married she is utterly loyal, and this is necessary to bring him to grace (infusing 'another soule' into him – V. i. 322), thus enabling the community to forgive him and restore his reputation. Only Sir Lancelot holds out; he needs the revelation of old Flowerdale's identity to make him relent and accept his son-in-law (whom he had previously tried to divorce from Luce). The play thus lines up the two fathers as validating the marriage of the young, but marriage is shown to be sacred in itself, not breakable by paternal authority.

None of this conclusive happiness wholly dispels what has happened earlier, however. The play's most extraordinary moment comes when the young protagonist repudiates his (supposedly dead) father and his new wife virtually simultaneously:

FATHER [disguised as 'Kester']. Thou hadst a father would haue
    beene a shamed.
FLOWERDALE. My father was an Asse, an old Asse.
FATHER. Thy father? proud, lycentious villaine!
    What, are you at your foyles? ile foyle with you.
LUCE. Good sir, forbear him.
FATHER. Did not this whining woman hang on me,
    Ide teach thee what it was to abuse thy father:
    Goe! hang, beg, starue, dice, game, that when all is gone,
    Thou maist after dispaire and hang thy selfe.
LUCE. O, doe not curse him.
FATHER. I doe not curse him, and to pray for him were vaine;
    It greeues me that he beares his fathers name.   (III. iii. 269–81)

Though the father claims this is not a curse, it seems to have the effect
of one: the son tells his wife to 'turne whore' (line 295), and successively
becomes a destitute gambler, a highway robber, a beggar, and a near-
suicide – only to be saved by the proofs of loyalty from Luce.

The marriage itself had no effect on him, for there was not 'a pin' of
love there (III. ii. 153); the father's private reaction to this comment is
highly significant:

> Ist possible, he hath his second liuing,
> Forsaking God, himselfe to the diuel giuing?
> But that I knew his mother firme and chast,
> My heart would say my bed she had disgrast:
> Else would I sweare he neuer was my sonne,
> But her faire mind so fowle a deed did shun.   (lines 155–60)

The idea that a wife gives a 'second liuing' is powerful: it means not only
that the son has new money to begin again, but that she should provide a
regeneration of the self initially given life by the father – the question is
how? Only proving her 'chastitie and vertue' (V. i. 321) seems sufficient: in
doing so, she can make him as secure in his future paternity as the father is
in the passage above. Yet the near-doubt expressed about paternity there
shows the problem of such patrilineal identity. Ultimately, the *proof*
sought at the beginning of the play comes not from the son himself,
but from his wife. The irony is that she needed to prove her love by being
repudiated by her own father (III. iii. 133, 185). The play, which presents
no mothers, nonetheless affords the recognition that true patrilineal
identity really depends on women.

Heywood's *The Wise Woman of Hogsdon* (probably 1604) is a milder
and more farcical prodigal-son play. The anti-hero here is betrothed to

one woman, tries to marry another secretly, and publicly engages himself
to a third. The contrivances of the first woman, with the unwitting help of
the titular wise woman, mean that he ends up married to her, but not
before he has been humiliated in front of his father. Once he has tried to
blame everyone but himself and has found all these characters springing
out of hiding to deny the charges, and after two of the women have been
taken by other men, leaving him apparently married to a young man,
Chartley's father tells him:

> Well art thou served, to be a general scorn
> To all thy blood. And, if not for our sakes,
> For thy soul's health and credit of the world,
> Have some regard to me, to me thy father.   (V. vi. 167–70)[22]

Chartley knows, however, that he cannot be forgiven – he is 'past grace'
(lines 178–9), and all his father can do is rebuke him. Only his wife
revealing herself allows him to be redeemed. A young man who has, as is
so common in such plays, expressed hopes for his father's death (IV. v. 51–3,
71–4), Chartley cannot be saved by his father, but only by the good offices
of a virtuous woman.

   A more redemptive father to a prodigal is the poet Bellamont in
Dekker's jolly if incoherent *Northward Ho!* (1605): his son keeps getting
in debt because of his affections for the whore, Doll. Irked by his father's
rebukes, Phillip tricks Bellamont into Doll's company with the promise of
a poetic commission, but she falls in love with him, after which Phillip
simply loses interest in her. No theological language is used here, and
the son is rather quietly brought into line, though he does participate in a
plan to have Bellamont committed to a madhouse. The father takes it in
good part, however, saying 'your best Poets indeed are madde for the
most part' (IV. iii. 192–3). A poetic father of this kind is rather unusual,
and his vocation does seem to dilute the respect normally due to a father,
also reducing the tensions and intensities in the father–son bond. Nonetheless, there seems to be a quietly reformative role for the father: it is by
passive action that a father can save his son.

   The twist on the prodigal plot in John Day's *Law Tricks* (1604,
pub. 1608) is that the prince, Polymetes (his name suggests Odyssean
cunning), is at first a world-despising scholar, but, given authority in
his father's absence, he turns to tobacco and costly wenching – with
a supposed courtesan who is really his disguised sister. The (rather
original) use of the witty and virtuous sister Emilia to test the heir's
virtue is independently compounded by the disguised premature return

of the father, and in both cases Polymetes is found wanting. The duke, seeing his son's revels, comments (aside):

> *Ouid* not all thy Metamorphosis
> Can shew such transformation, oh my God!
> It is not possible, is this my sonne?
> A has mistook himselfe, my life a has,
> For the seauen liberall sciences; a reades,
> The seauen black deadly sinnes.   (lines 1332–7)[23]

He does not seem particularly upset by this evidence of change, however: early in the play, he had been rather disappointed by his son's scholarly commitments. Most notably, the duke brings a letter announcing his own death, getting a decidedly cheerful response, as Polymetes looks forward to a life of extravagance. The father is even quite phlegmatic about this, perhaps because such joy has become proverbial and even normative; his only comment is the aside 'i'me glad I haue found you sonne' (line 1359).[24] It seems it is better to know the truth, however bad, about a son. The play then goes on rather bizarrely: on his father's return *in propria persona* Polymetes pretends to be engaged in necromancy, presumably because this is the furthest extension of the studious life (in the manner of Faustus); he claims to be trying in this way to rescue his sister from captivity by the Turks, but of course the fake sister he conjures won't stand up to questioning when his real sister reveals herself; confronted with evidence of his trickery, he can only give the feeble Falstaffian excuse that he knew his sister all along, by 'affinitie' (line 2194).[25] His father, however, does seem (or pretends) to be duped for a while; Emilia has to protest when she is denied: 'good father, send mee to a Iustice, for a pretty woman with a smooth tongue and an Angels voice, can do much with Iustice in this golden age, but thus much afore I go, if Iustice will not prouide me a better father, Ile haue you, or Ile giue the beadle of the ward a fee to cry, a new father a new, as they do oysters at Caliis' (lines 1954–60). This disrespectful moment entails a small humiliation for the father, but at the daughter's hands: if she is not quite a Cordelia, Emilia points the way to daughters being more effective correctives to the problems of patriarchy than sons.

Middleton's *A Mad World, My Masters* (c. 1607) further varies the prodigal plot, to which it clearly alludes in the description of a tapestry on the subject (II. ii. 5–8): the grandson Follywit is a prodigal, but only because his grandfather Sir Bounteous Progress keeps him poor, bespeaking a generational tension ('They cannot abide to see us merry all the while they're above ground, and that makes so many laugh at their fathers' funerals' – I. i. 49–51). Yet the old man is at least as much a prodigal as the young one, whose tricks serve to reform his aged ancestor. Follywit, disguised, manages to enjoy Sir Bounteous's hospitality, to rob the old man (several times), to trick more money from him, and to cure him of his addiction to a courtesan. The action is not all one-way, however: Follywit unknowingly falls for and marries the same courtesan, which delights Sir Bounteous and enables mutual forgiveness of a sort. We are here in the territory of young Wat Ralegh's 'box about', but without the direct tensions of paternity.

Another variation on the prodigal-son theme so common in 1604–7 is the question of what may happen to a sinful daughter, and whether she can be forgiven. In *The Honest Whore Part 2* (Dekker, 1605), the disguised Orlando forgives and tries to help his daughter, the reclaimed whore of the title, but finds his son-in-law Matteo is a prodigal, abusing him and beggaring his daughter. He consequently acts as a 'true Phisicion' (V. ii. 191) in correcting the young man,[26] a role more commonly that of the friend.[27] In Edward Sharpham's *The Fleer* (1607), the father is the deposed duke of Florence who follows his exiled daughters to London, where he discovers they have become whores: he manages to reform them, preventing them committing planned murders, and secures them marriages, including the elder daughter marrying the heir of the man who usurped him. Though the play is rather hastily plotted, it is remarkable that even sins of real sexual incontinence can be redeemed by a father's agency. Father–daughter connections are becoming more important and powerful than father–son identification.

Yet it does not always work so simply. In Middleton's *Michaelmas Term*, a country gentleman, called simply the 'Father', comes to town in search of his abducted daughter, going disguised into her service. She turns out to have cheerfully become a courtesan – though it's not at all clear that he recognizes her. Once he's found out his mistress's profession, despite some initial punning on the way he might 'serve' her (III. i. 46–9), no incestuous plot is ultimately forthcoming. Instead, he condemns her in general terms, calling her a 'fair and wicked creature' (line 292), and coming to see illicit sexuality as undermining the idea of a familial house, saying that 'A country filth is like a house possessed' (line 294). Later, she effectively repudiates her paternity, saying 'we are not always bound to think those our fathers that marry our mothers' (IV. ii. 24–5), to which he responds 'True, corruption may well be generation's first' (line 28). The lack of recognition is therefore appropriate: paternity has been more radically undermined that in any previous drama. No *Honest Whore*-style redemption is available for this girl. Indeed, the Father disappears from the play, leaving his daughter to marry Lethe, the man who corrupted her. His only revenance may be in doubling the part of the Judge who makes things right at the play's end; if this is the case, the play separates the double roles of a father, alienating the personal and the judicial roles while suggesting that ideally they would be unified. The loss of the memory that is essential to paternal relations is therefore strikingly portrayed: to lose memory of one's offspring is one thing, but in some way to lose memory of one's identity may be the more radical consequence.

However, the most imaginatively fruitful presentation of a prodigal daughter, *Eastward Ho!* (Chapman, Jonson, and Marston, 1604–5), does not involve real sexual licentiousness, the bad daughter Gertrude here being, rather, guilty of vanity in her desire to marry a knight (supported by her mother).[28] Her new status leads her to despise her father – in contrast to her dutiful sister Mildred, who rebukes her for believing she can 'right yourself in wronging that which hath made both you and us' (I. ii. 14–16). Her repudiation is remarkably strong, made even harsher by not even being addressed to him: 'He must call me daughter no more now, but "madam"' (III. ii. 70–1). Of course, she gets her come-uppance, because her husband's castle is entirely fictitious; her humiliating return may have influenced (at least inversely) the return of Cordelia:[29]

> MISTRESS TOUCHSTONE. Speak to your father, madam, and
>   kneel down.
> GERTRUDE. Kneel? I hope I am not brought so low yet; though my
>   knight be run away, and has sold my land, I am a lady still.
> TOUCHSTONE. Your ladyship says true, madam, and it is fitter, and
>   a greater decorum, that I should curtsy to you, that are a
>   knight's wife, and a lady, than you be brought o' your knees to
>   me, who am a poor cullion, and your father.
> GERTRUDE. Law! My father knows his duty   (IV. ii. 132–45)

This is only allowable because it is ironic, reflecting on his daughter's invisible castle. Touchstone's humour is of a piece with his rugged outlook throughout, giving him paternal dignity more robust than the merely conventional; such an attitude will allow him to forgive his prodigal daughter in the end, inspired by the pseudo-repentance of his prodigal apprentice. Though the play toys with the prodigal genre's conventions, it is still able to give a firm sense of fatherly authority, separating this from the priggish morality of the good apprentice Golding.

The play does, however, reach a point where serious doubt about paternity is expressed, Gertrude saying 'By this light, I think he is not my legitimate father' (V. i. 147–8). She may be a silly girl in a pet, but this moment cannot quite be erased, for her silliness means that her repentance cannot really be taken seriously:

Dear father, give me your blessing, and forgive me too; I ha' been proud and lascivious, father; and a fool, father; and being raised to the state of a wanton coy thing, called a lady, father, have scorned you, father, and my sister, and my sister's velvet cap, too; and would make a mouth at the city as I rid through it, and stop mine ears at Bow-bell. I have said your beard was a base one, father; and that you looked like Twierpipe, the taborer; and that my mother was but my midwife. (V. v. 172–82)

This brilliantly comic speech, compounding her offences with its lovely additions of foolish detail, spins her actual offence of paternal repudiation against her mother, for that sin is oddly too serious to repent of. Touchstone's response to Gertrude and his wife is simply 'No more repetitions' (line 184); her repetitions of 'father' constitute a desperate attempt to reclaim him, to return him perhaps to the position of essential signifier that his name suggests, but only his simple goodwill can really do this. Here, then, we see the beginnings of a new strain in fatherhood: a wearily cheerful acceptance of its uncertainties. This mode would ultimately triumph in later drama, though in doing so it abandoned the intensities of the paternal bond which drove the drama into its most powerful conflicts.

Bastardy becomes available as a real and expressible anxiety from around 1605, having been an undercurrent of earlier drama, and having been brought to the fore through the development of the prodigal genre. *Hamlet* may also have been a crucial catalyst in the developing representation of such anxieties. A play that combines elements of that play with the prodigal genre, Armin's *The Two Maids of More-Clacke*, may help to show how this operates. *The Two Maids* seems to sum up all that was popular at the time of its writing (around 1606). Central to its plot is the faking of a father's death – for the purposes of watching the wife rather than the son; the wife remarries (to a knight, Sir William) before the father can reveal himself, with near-tragic consequences. Humil fails to recognize his disguised father, prompting the comment:

> How ignorance pleads nonage, in his eie
> He knowes me not, tis not the Lyons kinde,
> Whose nature challenges right property.
> Of perfect being, if it were,
> *Humil* would *Humil* know, that him begot.   (A2ʳ)[30]

Paternity does not, as in myths of perfect recognitions among lions, consist in 'perfect being' – though this may be passed off as a consequence of Humil's youth. Nonetheless, in his self-inflicted loss he feels that he has become a 'round O', a 'Cipher' ($A2^v$–$A3^r$); he has erased himself, and there is no remembrance to be found in his son, who speaks thus in his father's hearing, when asked about his father's love: 'He loued me as a king in a play his seruant' – a sentiment to which his father can only respond 'Haue patience' ($C2^v$–$C3^r$). The wife's recognition of her husband may, however, imply that there is some perfect being in marriage. After a bit of mutual rebuke, the parents reconcile. This prioritizing of the parents' relationship is unusual in a comedy, and in fact their son gets no good out of the play.

He is a kind of cut-price Hamlet, but one loyal to his new stepfather. Largely for selfish reasons, when he finds his mother in bed with the servant James (really his father), Humil alerts Sir William. With some anticipation of Freud, he repeatedly wonders if he has dreamed the primal scene he has witnessed (not of course knowing that it's a legitimate primal scene); he howls, and fears that to speak of this would be to announce his 'shame / in quarter'd scutchin of black obloquie', causing 'Detraction from my blood' ($D4^r$, $E2^r$). As with Hamlet, the great problem is that one's mother's dishonour can create doubts as to one's own paternity. He himself proclaims it, though, because he wants Sir William's daughter; and Sir William is impressed by Humil's apparently disinterested loyalty to him. But Sir William decides to cover up *his* shame, and plots to murder his wife and James. Humil prevents this, guided not by know-ledge, but by the 'prophetique Fairies' of his heart ($G4^r$), drawing on Hamlet's 'prophetic soul'. Yet though he saves his parents, another suitor gets Sir William's daughter. The happiest ending he can get is to reunite his family, removing any shame from it; perhaps that is better than an advantageous marriage in this play's world, as perhaps it might have been in *Hamlet*. The existence of those prophetic fairies perhaps proves the perfect being of his sonhood, but only in a strange, contingent way.

What develops from the prodigal genre involves a greater humiliation of father figures, as prodigal youths manage to save themselves by tricking the older generation. In Lording Barry's *Ram Alley, or Merry Tricks* (1608, pub. 1611), William Smalshankes tricks his father, even to the extent of sleeping with the widow to whom Old Smalshankes is engaged; William also marries his whore off to his lawyer and gets out of debt in the process, before marrying an heiress himself; as a younger brother, his tricks are regarded as the only way he can make good ('If God had not made / Some elder-brothers fooles, how should witty / Yonger brothers be maintained' – $I4^r$). The tricks are seen as proof of the young man's paternity, Old Smalshankes being told 'Your sonne ifaith, your very sonne ifaith, / The villaine boy has one tricke of his sire'; the father may be 'vndone', but he has to accept his son's victory (12^r). As in earlier prodigal plays, the young man is helped out by the woman who truly loves him (Constantia), but in this case it seems a token gesture, as the son is really the driving force of the plot. Having disowned his son, Old Smalshankes can hardly complain that the seduction of the widow is incestuous, and this technicality seems to give licence to what might otherwise be genuinely subversive behaviour. The disowning (called 'cashiering'), which might seem like it undermines William's identity, in practice results in him defeating his father. The prodigal-son plot is turned on its head, but the effect is still that the son must be accepted back. The defeat of the elder brother might also suggest an element of the Jacob and Esau plot, allowing a subversion of patriarchal norms of primogeniture.

Inversions and variations of prodigal-son plots, then, enable what had been a mode that affirmed patriarchal norms to be used as a way of introducing flexibility into father–son relations. The title plot (though really a subplot) of Fletcher's *Monsieur Thomas* (1611) is a simple but highly amusing inversion of a prodigal-son plot, in which the father Sebastian longs for his son Thomas/Tom to prove a proper rascal, but is constantly enraged by the civility that he has learned on his travels. For reasons that are not always spelled out – but that have to do with his attempts to prove his civility to his beloved Mary – Thomas conceals his real, wild character until the end. The best moment in all this comes when Sebastian decides to repudiate Thomas and to marry again, calling in all the kitchen wenches to make a selection; Thomas's patrimony is saved when he admits that he has slept with them all himself, his father concluding 'Ile aske no more, nor thinke no more of marriage, / For o' my conscience I shalbe thy Cuckold' (IV. ii. 169–70). The father–son tensions of the early Jacobean period seem to be dissipating into good-natured acceptance of youth's priority.

Sometimes, then, the prodigal-son plot is turned around to the extent of the father becoming the true prodigal; yet even in this role, he may have some passively redemptive power. Francis Beaumont's *The Knight of the Burning Pestle* (?1607; pub. 1613) presents perhaps the drama's most absurdly comic father figure in Old Merrythought. His son Jasper, the play's romantic hero, is a classic comedic instance of aspiring youth, who is sacked from his apprenticeship for winning the heart of his master's daughter; yet this aspect of the play's plot is not a simple triumph of youth over age, as Jasper's father is much more subversive of convention than his son. Young men are traditionally regarded as improvident in city comedy, though they somehow, by their own good grace and the help of providential agents, usually manage to secure their futures. By contrast, this *old* man is improvident beyond any bounds, as if he somehow exists outside time: his irresponsibility is such that he cares for nothing beyond having enough to eat and drink today, and no concern for his family can correct his behaviour. His tipsy singing of a huge range of songs has a dual effect: it turns him into a choric figure in this highly metatheatrical play, offering a contrast to the commentary of the bourgeois Citizen and his Wife; it also removes him from the urgent concerns of a plot in which he ought to be involved and allows him to invoke some extra-temporal order of grace associated with music. Paradoxically, this removal from the petty concerns of the other characters enables him to resolve his son's difficulties.

Sent away from his position with the merchant Venturewell, Jasper comes guiltily to his mother in order to ask her blessing, piously saying:

> There is no drop of bloud hid in these veines,
> But I remember well belongs to you
> That brought me forth, and would be glad for you
> To rip them all againe, and let it out.   (I. 327–30)

This hyperbolic devotion to his mother leaves little room for any love or duty to his father, who is apparently excluded from any contribution to his identity. Yet his mother feels disgraced by his sacking and disowns him, thinking that he wants to take the money she has saved up for her favoured younger son. Though neither seems to care much for each other, Jasper's father is more helpful, if in a rather limited way: he gives him 10 shillings and says 'Bee a good husband, that is, weare ordinary clothes, eate the best meat, and drinke the best drinke, bee merrie, and give to the poor, and believe me, thou hast no end of thy goods' (lines 388–90). Though Jasper tries to engage him in more rational dialogue, the old man fobs him off with a repetition of his blessing, urging his son to imitate him – 'Thy fathers spirit upon thee' (line 395) – and a song. Ludicrously small as the portion is, this is generous, according to Old Merrythought's lights. He offers a distinct contrast to Ben Jonson's Old Knowell, who urges that young men *not* 'thrust yourself on all societies' (*Every Man in His Humour*, I. i. 69); yet both, of course, are objects of comic critique for their expectation that their sons be exactly like themselves.

We struggle, though, to find Old Merrythought quite as reprehensible as the Citizen and Wife do. Even when he says 'If both my sons were on the gallows, I would sing' (II. 483–4), it is hard to condemn someone who so conscientiously objects to involvement in life's difficulties. He might be called a more honest version of Falstaff. His understandably exasperated wife, who has left him but then lost all her resources, is locked out on her return home; we are intended, I think, to share in his laughter at her misfortunes, particularly when she hypocritically claims to be his 'fellow-feeler'; she further insists, to no effect: 'have I not brought you Children? are they not like you *Charles*? Look upon thine own Image hard-hearted man' (III. 510–13). He refuses to accept shared misery when she has refused in the past to share his enjoyment of life; the younger son whom she has jealously guarded as her own is only presented as being his father's perfect image here because she is down on her luck. Old Merrythought only takes her back at the end because Jasper and his bride Luce appeal on her behalf (V. 208); whether he is inspired here by Luce's appeal in particular (for young women's appeals cannot, chivalrously, be denied) or by the fact that his son is pretending to be a ghost remains in doubt. The father, in the event, reacts very sanguinely, and musically, to Jasper's pretended death and return as a ghost:

> [singing] *what hast thou here brought?*
> BOY. A Coffin, sir, and your dead son *Jasper* in it.
> OLD MERRI-THOUGHT. Dead?
> *Why, fare-well he:*
> *Thou wast a bonny boy, and I did love thee.*
> *Enter Jasper.* [as a ghost]
> OLD MERRI-THOUGHT. *Jaspers* ghost?
> [singing] *Thou are welcome from Stygian lake so soone,*
> *Declare to mee what wondrous things in* Pluto's *court are done.*
> JASPER. By my troth, sir, I nere came there, tis too hot for me sir.
> OLD MERRI-THOUGHT. A merry ghost, a very merry
> ghost.   (lines 175–85)

When the living Luce is taken out of the coffin, Old Merrythought clearly sees through the whole trick without the need of explanation. This contrasts strongly with the more uptight Venturewell's terrified reaction to Jasper's spectral disguise. Venturewell has sent what he thinks is Jasper's corpse to his father, in the malicious hope that this will cause Old Merrythought misery; his punishment for this ill-will to his thriftless neighbour is given by Jasper's 'ghost', who insists he send Old Merrythought money. Jasper's goodwill to his father here is reciprocated (though not transactionally) when Old Merrythought gets Venturewell to bless the union with Luce. A circuit of forgiveness and grace is completed, unusually created by the unspoken but powerful accord between father and son. Neither has asked too much of the other, and the result is much more harmonious than in plays where paternity constitutes a significant pressure on a son. *The Knight of the Burning Pestle*, then, is perhaps the sliest response to *Hamlet*: it is as if Hamlet had responded to his father's ghost by calling it a merry fellow, and the ghost had bucked Hamlet up by scaring Polonius into letting the prince marry Ophelia. A new kind of doubleness is licensed in the father, doing away with his sacred quality in favour of his forgiving humanity – yet that also relies on a new kind of mutuality. The generic form of prodigal comedy relied initially on the father being an external figure, able to guarantee plot outcomes by his non-involvement in the son's world, but as mutuality enters, in plays like *Monsieur Thomas* and *The Knight of the Burning Pestle*, that external judging role is removed, and the formal centre of the genre is eroded. Accepting limits on the father's judging role is the ultimate upshot of prodigal drama, because the father is now firmly in the world of the play.

THE FUSION – 'KING LEAR'

All the issues we have dealt with so far in this chapter come to a head in *King Lear*: questions of vengeance and the excessive identifications involved in father–child relations; a barely repressed sense of the uncertainty of paternity; the need for a father to efface himself or even to abdicate when he has heirs; the possibility of paternal humiliation; and the need for paternal sin to enable mutual forgiveness. Lear himself is a prodigal father. In the Biblical parable, the Prodigal Son is accommodated with 'swine' (Luke 15:16); when Cordelia finds her father she is astonished that he had 'To hovel thee with swine and rogues forlorn' (IV. vii. 38), and her finding him seems to reverse the familial dynamic of the parable. *King Lear*, like the parable, can be seen as a kind of tragicomedy – that is, the genre that tries to resolve the tensions inherent in the age's tragedies and comedies.[31]

Shakespeare's main source, the 1590s anonymous play *King Leir* (pub. 1605), is a chronicle play that anticipates tragicomedy, and its motives are accordingly comic: Leir here uses the love-test in order to make Cordella marry a man of his choice. In such a generic context it is acceptable for him to call her 'bastard imp, no issue of King Leir' (I. i. 113), for such a denial of paternity can be overturned by the happy ending.[32] By contrast, denials of paternity remain conditional or partial in Shakespeare's tragedy: Lear says that he *would* divorce Regan's mother if she were not glad to see him (II. iv 131); Gloucester's comment that 'I never got him' (Edgar) (II. i. 78) only appears in the Quarto text.

The possibility of uncertain paternity is too much for tragedy and can only be managed in a tragicomic way, as we shall see in *The Winter's Tale*, for instance. Nonetheless, the broader comic outlook paradoxically has the potential to make tragedy more extreme.

A daughter is an unnecessary thing, as well as a kind of nothing.[33] The fact that daughters are so unnecessary makes them material for comedy, whereas sons are more apt to be tragic as they are necessary in two senses: a man needs sons to be a full father, with a stake in the future of a patrilineal society, and a son has necessary obligations to his father that cannot be wished away. Daughters, then, even if they are frequently problematic, offer a sense of emotional connection transcending necessity – a sense that there is or need be 'no cause'. King Lear, having only daughters, is therefore in a very different situation from his predecessor in dramatic kingdom-splitting Gorboduc: he has the right to think that he is inhabiting a comic world in which he is free to feel greater love for one daughter than the others. The Gloucester family subplot, however, presents a different kind of masculine intergenerational conflict, one in which everything is more literally taken to tragic extremes; here the role of necessity and brinksmanship is reintroduced, infecting the apparently superfluous world of the royal family with the relentless emotional logic that can make it tragic.

Lear tells us that the basest beggar can be superfluous in the poorest thing, that we should 'reason not the need' (II. iv. 264–5), and the *Lear*-world is full of superfluity, the denial of necessity.[34] Even the lesser patriarch Gloucester knows that Lear has denied Cordelia 'Upon the gad' (I. ii. 26).[35] For that matter, 'Age is unnecessary' (line 155), but once we start thinking like this we may wonder what is *necessary* – love, kindness, even life itself?[36] As Jaques says in *As You Like It*, we end life 'Sans teeth, sans eyes, sans taste, sans everything' (II. vii. 166), yet his sense of the pointlessness of life is immediately subverted by the entry of Orlando, carrying the 'venerable burthen' of old Adam (his father substitute); bearing such a burden gives life meaning, and Lear's mistake is to try to give his own up too early (wanting to be 'Unburthen'd' – I. i. 41). Edgar ends *King Lear* insisting that 'The oldest hath borne most' (V. iii. 326), and probably carries the dead Lear off stage; such a burden may be enough to give meaning to life. 'Love's not Time's fool', but rather 'bears it out even to the edge of doom' (Sonnet 116, lines 9, 12). Bearing things to the edge is all we can manage. But is such a burden necessary or superfluous?[37]

The play is full of tests of just this question – the love test, the unnecessary train of knights, the imaginary anatomizing and trial of Goneril and

Regan, the imaginary cliff scene, the trial by combat, the test of whether Cordelia is still breathing. Almost all the tests meet with some kind of denial, giving the key answer 'nothing'; but that 'nothing' is a complex answer. Life may signify nothing, in Macbeth's words, but in signifying nothing it means that it *is* something; the fact that the test meets with denial merely ridicules the question; things are all the more meaningful for not having a necessary meaning; as if anticipating a Popperian scientific method, the process of proof can only lead to disproof. Yet something is discovered.[38] The superfluities of the play's form work in two ways: the excessive desire to find necessity, to find 'the promised end', is destructive; the unnecessary feelings and kindnesses that we see along the way have a different kind of value – but that value is not redemptive, consoling, creative, or any other kind of teleological form of value. That is the point of being superfluous – it refuses to reduce to any pattern of meaning.

Age is unnecessary in two main senses. Firstly, old people, according to the culture of the time, don't need much (that may just be a way of saying that we don't want to give them much, of course). After eighty years of age, men were treated as 'fit for nothing but to sit in a chair in their chamber'.[39] Prosperous older men generally married if they wanted support rather than relying on their children, but they could enter into contracts for support with their children (or with others) in return for handing over control of their property.[40] Secondly, age is unnecessary in the sense that all of life's aims ought already to be achieved. The culture of the time, perhaps particularly in its sterner protestant form, cannot allow people to sit back and enjoy the fruits of achievement. Such is the problem of living under the aegis of necessity, a condition that seems stronger for Gloucester than for Lear, at least initiallly.

At the beginning of the play Gloucester's bastard son '*must* be acknowledged' (I. i. 24, my emphasis); he is immediately given an order to attend on France and Burgundy; earl though he is, he is clearly not free. The 'good sport' that made Edmund has only led to obligation. This perhaps informs his sense that 'We have seen the best of our time' (I. ii. 112), that seniority is only a matter of being over the hill; this is what Lear is resisting. Yet Gloucester also gets this idea from Edgar's supposed letter to Edmund, which begins 'This policy and reverence of age makes the world bitter to the best of our times' (lines 46–7); youth is unfree for different reasons; and such a complaint seems, according to the norms of comedy, basically legitimate. Is it possible that Edgar did write the letter? Edmund never mentions that he forged it, and though he says that Edgar's 'nature is so far from doing harms / That he suspects none' (lines 180–1), the letter may be harmless enough. It only says, gnomically, 'If our father would sleep till I wak'd him, you should enjoy half his revenue for ever' (lines 52–3). If Edgar has only just realized that he has an illegitimate brother, he may have reason to think less well than formerly of his father: at the end of the play, his condemnation of paternal lasciviousness is clear when he says to Edmund 'The dark and vicious place where he thee got / Cost him his eyes', this being evidence that 'The gods are just' (V. iii. 173–4, 171). I think, on balance, that the letter is forged, but I also think we need to *entertain* the possibility that Edgar is guilty of some prior ill-feeling to his father.

The absence of mothers in *King Lear* may account for the persistently unnatural feeling in that play between father and sons. Edmund's allegations of Edgar's words with regard to Gloucester point at a set of ideas about father–son tensions – the fear that paternal retirement might lead to their children mistreating them:[41] 'I have heard him oft maintain it to be fit that, sons at perfect age and fathers declin'd, the father should be as ward to the son, and the son manage his revenue' (I. ii. 71–4). Gloucester thinks this part of the condition of his times, 'the bond crack'd 'twixt son and father' (lines 108–9). The play as a whole harps on fatherhood, presenting it as a tragic condition. The whole problem of the play rests in the uncertainty of paternal affections: when it is *assumed* that children must be dutiful to their fathers, the duties and affections of fathers are taken to be uncertain and conditional, as the following exchange indicates:

> REGAN. I am glad to see your highness.
> LEAR. Regan, I think you are; I know what reason
>   I have to think so. If thou shouldst not be glad,
>   I would divorce me from thy mother's tomb,
>   Sepulch'ring an adultress.   (II. iv. 128–32)

This gives a hint at the underlying reason for the love-test in the play's first scene – statements of affection are to be taken as proofs of legitimacy. The Fool's comment 'I marvel what kin thou and thy daughters are' (I. iv. 182) is a splendidly gnomic keynote here: it means, primarily, 'It's astonishing how similar you are to Goneril and Regan (and perhaps to Cordelia in stubbornness)', but it also has resonances of genuine uncertainty. In the subplot, Edmund insists on his belief that his father loves him as much as he does Edgar (I. ii. 17–18), but Gloucester has said that this affection is to some extent dependent on the 'sport at his making' (I. i. 23) – a parallel perhaps to maternal affection being dependent on birth-pains and nursing. Edgar's proof of legitimacy and honour to his father comes in a drastically strange form: taking his father to the cliffs and convincing him he is committing suicide is meant to be therapeutic ('Why I do trifle thus with his despair / Is done to cure it' – IV. vi. 33–4), but modern therapists would hardly hand depressed patients an empty pistol and say it is loaded; John Bayley rightly calls this a 'crude experiment'.[42] Edgar *proves* his father in some way here – it is the ultimate trial in a play of trials. Killing Edmund finally proves Edgar, but this is more a question of sibling rivalry than filial piety; we do not, in any case, see the recognition and reconciliation between Gloucester and Edmund. Partly, this is because Shakespeare does not want to undermine the magnificent recognition between Lear and Cordelia by staging a similar scene; but it also reflects the fact that no real accommodation can be found between parents and children in this play. The yawning space of the imaginary cliff divides them. Even the reconciliation of Lear and Cordelia itself is a leap of faith across an unbridgeable metaphysical gap: Cordelia is 'a soul in bliss', Lear tormented hellishly, 'bound upon a wheel of fire' (IV. vii. 45–6). The horrible thing is that at this moment of recognition, the greatest in all literature, they have never been further apart. The play ends with a further sense of the disjunction between the generations, as Edgar (Albany in the Quarto text) says: 'The oldest hath borne most; we that are young / Shall never see so much, nor live so long' (V. iii. 326–7).

Recognition, though, relies on this distance, and the ability to respect it, not only in the recognition between Lear and Cordelia, but also in that between Lear and Gloucester.[43] When Kent says 'To be acknowledg'd ... is o'erpaid' (IV. vii. 4), he subtly argues for the (paradoxical, superfluous) necessity for such overpayment. Cordelia being the first to speak to Lear is 'fittest' (says the Doctor/Gentleman – line 42), even if it is not necessary. This sense of the fitness of overpayment goes along with a denial of causal necessity – 'No cause, no cause' (line 75).[44] There is an element of forgiveness in this,[45] but it is not quite complete forgiveness, as it also constitutes another denial, and may in any case respond to Lear's thoughts about Goneril and Regan in the previous line ('You have some cause, they have not') rather than to those about Cordelia herself.[46] Nonetheless, this is the aesthetic moment that transcends ethical, customary meaning, even the idea of forgiveness; it is the one thing that allows Lear to be 'assur'd / Of [his] condition' (lines 55–6) even as he accepts being 'doubtful' as to Cordelia's identity (and Kent's – line 64). There are none of the Aeschylean signs of recognition here,[47] but just this:

> Do not laugh at me,
> For (as I am a man) I think this lady
> To be my child Cordelia.
> CORDELIA.   And so I am; I am.
> LEAR. Be your tears wet? Yes, faith. I pray weep not.   (lines 67–70)

He finds her, simply, through his condition as a man; and, in a virtuous circle, her presence guarantees that he is a man (such is the neat ambiguity of *as* here).[48] Her tears are proof enough, but they are to be wiped away now that they see face-to-face. This is *enough*; finding what is enough, rather than what is necessary or the adornments of crass superfluity, though, means that one must find too much.[49] Her death both does and doesn't cancel this moment. Lear returns at the end of this recognition scene to the idea of necessity, saying 'You must bear with me' (line 81); even though this carries more than one meaning – she must support him physically, must be patient with him, and must suffer with him – it may in some senses still be a fair thing to ask.[50] What he must bear in her death may not be, partly because such suffering cannot be shared.

Even the recognition is coloured with that unbearable death. The first moment of recognition of Cordelia may come when Lear says (in the Folio) 'where did you dye?' (line 48);[51] this is a decidedly strange way of recognizing someone: it is as if, having banished his daughter from his kingdom, Lear cannot comprehend that there was any place in which she could have died. In *Cymbeline*, Imogen insists that 'There's livers out of England' (III. iv. 140), but Lear struggles to accept that there are diers out of his realm. On the other hand, he may be suggesting that she *must* have died as a result of his curse; if so, the great problem is that he cannot undo the curse; dead as she has once been to her father, she cannot return to life. The recognition is only of mortality.

The play's other recognitions are less profound. The mirroring between Lear and Gloucester, both men being 'ruin'd piece[s] of nature' (IV. vi. 134), is very poignant, but strangely pointless; their suffering is common but not shared, not commensurable. That between Edgar and Gloucester is still stranger, lacking the 'benediction' that Cordelia seems, crucially, to get from her father (IV. vii. 57). According to Helen Small, Gloucester 'lives long enough for Edgar to reveal himself as the true son, and ask his blessing, but not to give that blessing'; Edgar's consolations are trite, and Gloucester undermines them: 'After ripeness, rotting' (though the text puts the rotting first). Small goes on, 'Gloucester knows that in old age there is a limit to resistance, though his son declines to accept it'.[52] I would argue, too, that Lear resists such limits, rebelling against his own taboo status as a king and father, and refusing to be time's fool. Yet in resisting limits he arrives at them.

The death of the child here is apocalyptic (as the death of fathers is not), and brings us to the edge of doom; seeing Lear enter with the dead Cordelia, the courtiers comment, almost in chorus:

KENT.   Is this the promis'd end?
EDGAR. Or image of that horror?
ALBANY.   Fall, and cease.   (V. iii. 264–5)

The death of a child is the perfect image of the end of the world,[53] because the production of children secures continuity and, as it were, puts off any sense of imminent collapse. Macbeth's death may be chilling, but there is also something reassuring in its finality, because he has arrived at a state of self-sufficiency. Better, perhaps, not to have any children born at all than to lose them. The death of a daughter (as opposed to a son) is 'the one disaster for which no consolation is enough' in Cicero's view, as a son (in the case of Priam, for instance) could at least increase one's familial honour by a heroic death.[54] The death of the daughter is the death of all that is unnecessary. And, oddly (given that we can lose things we *need*, like eyes), that's the one thing we cannot bear. The identification of the maternal with the material means that the loss of daughters can be seen as the loss of the material world to which one should not cling, but feminized Nature and its emotions cannot be done away with so easily. Lear, who is both father and mother, is perhaps the fullest self in the drama of the period, able to bear both his private and his public roles up to their limits, but that leaves us with the problem that he is also the one with the most to lose.

TRAGICOMEDY

After this pushing of the limits of human experience, a new dramatic form emerges, providing solutions to the problems that stricter comedy and tragedy could not manage.[55] There are many kinds of mixture between tragedy and comedy, but the commonest defining feature of tragicomedy proper is that things turn out for the best in rather unexpected ways, either through supernatural agency or through the use of semi-sacred figures – fathers being an obvious example. Yet the fathers of tragicomedy, with a strange sense of their double identities, often do not own their sacredness, and often bring about resolutions involuntarily, like the fathers of prodigal-son comedies; in fact, their ability to catalyse happy resolutions often depends on them accepting their own limitations. While the genre blends tragedy and comedy, its representation of fathers painfully unblends the public and the private aspects of fatherhood.

A number of early tragicomedies seem to echo *King Lear*. Heywood and Rowley's *Fortune by Land and Sea* (c. 1609, pub. 1655) proclaims itself a 'Tragi-comedy', but it is an unusual example of the genre, including the death of a son in one plot and the death of a father in the other, while having an essentially comic outcome. At the beginning, Frank Forest ignores his father's advice and goes drinking with the quarrelsome Rainsford; Frank may be a prodigal, but he will not tolerate Rainsford insulting his father, resulting in the following argument:

> RAINSFORD. Of all things under heaven what wouldest
>   thou loathest have me do?
> FRANK. I would not have you wrong my reverent Father,
>   and I hope you will not.
> RAINSFORD. Thy father's an old dotard.
> FRANK. I could not brook this at a Monarch's hands,
>   much lesse at thine.
> RAINSFORD. I boy, then take you that. [*Flings wine in's face.*
> FRANK. I was not born to brook this, oh I am slain.   (p. 4)[56]

He is indeed, so Frank's brother then takes revenge on Rainsford, but is pursued for it by the law, because Rainsford is a well-connected man and the Foresters a poor family. Young Forester is only pardoned after he defeats some notorious pirates, his father being impotent to do anything for him. The father here is no protector to his family, serving only as the object of insults, a sign of familial vulnerability.

The father in the play's other plot is much more powerful: Old Harding disinherits his eldest son Philip for marrying Susan, the poor daughter of Old Forester. Philip's complaint at his father's treatment of him is telling (if respectful), as his father himself has just married a poor woman: 'And Sir, for you, with pardon, I could trace you even in that path in which I stand condemned' (p. 10). This looks immediately like an accusation of hypocrisy, but its phrasing suggests a different motive: he is showing himself an ironically dutiful son in following paternal example. This cuts no ice with his father, and Philip and his wife are forced to become servants to the family, enduring insults from the younger brothers. Philip's filial character is highlighted by his repeatedly saying he cares only for his father's favour, love, and blessing, and not for his inheritance. In fact, disinheritance is a matter of expressed will rather than legal will: the younger brothers John and William repeatedly press their father to change his will so that they will be heirs, even nagging at him when a stroke of financial misfortune pushes him to his death-bed. Their grief on his death is therefore founded on avarice, whereas that of Philip, who does inherit, is founded on love; the play's moral is therefore clear enough, allowing the good son to succeed, yet such an outcome depends on the father's premature death. This plot has faint echoes of *King Lear*, but turns the situation to comedy not in spite of the death of the unfair father, but because of it. Philip's final comment on his father tries to give the situation aphoristic quality, but the effect is of a taboo being broken by the most strait-lacedly virtuous of sons: 'though his life brought sorrow, death content, we cannot but with funeral tears lament' (p. 42). The truest contentment comes in death, however much one ought to lament. The lip-service to filial piety has turned to paradox; tragedy has worked itself out into comedy, even if that comedy relies on the death of the father.

The erasure of the father is almost a keynote of tragicomedy, even if it is usually less drastic than in Heywood's play. William Rowley's *The Birth of Merlin: Or, The Childe hath Found his Father* (pub. 1662 as by Rowley and Shakespeare)[57] has three plots, two of which involve problems of paternity, the third (main) plot involving the rise to power of Uther Pendragon, legendary father of King Arthur. Questions of patrilineal inheritance are to the fore, but without any satisfactory resolutions. As a whole, the play seems indicative of a loss of confidence about patriarchal power.

The strangest plot of the three involves the nobleman Donobert and his daughters Constantia and Modestia; both have paternally approved suitors, but both, due to the involuntary influence of Anselm the Hermit, become nuns rather than marrying. Modestia's suitor Edwin has killed many men as a soldier; he responds to her belief that this should diminish his amorousness by saying 'The more my Conscience tyes mee to repair / The worlds losses in a new succession' (I. i. 34–5),[58] but he will not get the chance to do so. The play's conclusion has a gloomy prognosis, looking to disasters after the future King Arthur rather than to successes in his reign; the failure of personal succession contributes to this gloom. Donobert seeks 'the fruits of Age, Posterity' (III. ii. 98) from his daughters' marriage, but Modestia goes on to convince her initially enthusiastic sister that marriage and motherhood only bring sorrow: 'At best we do but bring forth Heirs to die, / And fill the Coffins of our enemy' (III. ii. 105–10). This is a remarkably apocalyptic sentiment, and the scene ends with an averted crisis of father–child relations, Donobert coming close to Lear-like rage:

> Bewitched Girls, tempt not an old mans fury,
> That hath no strength to uphold his feeble age,
> But what your sights give life to: oh, beware,
> And do not make me curse you.
> MODESTIA.   Dear father,
> Here at your feet we kneel, grant us but this,
> That, in your sight and hearing, the good Hermit
> May plead our Cause; which, if it shall not give
> Such satisfaction as your Age desires,
> We will submit to you.
> CONSTANTIA.   You gave us life;
> Save not our bodies, but our souls, from death.
> DONOBERT. This gives some comfort yet: Rise
> with my blessings.   (lines 144–55)

This exchange encapsulates many of the difficulties we have seen in
paternity: the idea of children (particularly daughters) as a support; the
fear of the paternal curse; kneeling in submission; the sense of debt; a
concern for bodily succession here put in tension with the destiny of the
soul; the idea of comfort; and the blessing. Anselm will accept that it is
not a sin to marry (V. i. 9–10), but the daughters are not convinced.
Donobert ends the play in grim acceptance: hearing the news of Uther's
victory over the Welsh, he says to his once-prospective sons-in-law,
whom he now makes his heirs, 'The joy of this shall banish from my
breast / All thought that I was father to two Children, / Two stubborn
Daughters' (lines 31–3). This is a gloomily shadowed happy ending,
making the best of things with a vow 'by the Honor of my Fathers
House' which has now come to an end (line 35). Tragedy may have been
averted by Donobert's refusal to be a Lear, but in so refusing he ceases to
be a father.

The father comes out no better in the comic title plot, in which the
pregnant mother-to-be of Merlin, Jone Go-too't, goes about accusing
various courtiers of having fathered her child. Even Uther is accused, but
the real father turns out to be an invisible devil. The fiction of the
fathering incubus is quite acutely probed here, being recognized as a
device by which identity can be conferred without tarnishing the gentry
who might all in some way be implicated – as Jone's brother says 'though
there be many fathers without children, yet to have a childe without a
father were most unnatural' (III. i. 100–2). Merlin is born unnaturally (he
is already bearded and literate, though small), but shows some natural
kindness at the end of the play, rescuing his mother from his devil-father,
who accuses him of disobedience:

MERLIN. Obedience is no lesson in your school;
    Nature and kind to her commands my duty;
    The part that you begot was against kinde,
    So all I ow to you is to be unkind.   (V. i. 57–60)

Though this is made acceptable by the father's devilishness, the sentiment, which identifies maternity with nature, and paternity with the unnatural, may resonate more widely, reflecting a sense of the uncertainty, weakness, and insecurity of the father–son relation: there are many fathers without children, as Jone says, many men who think themselves fathers when they are not, in other words; motherhood is more natural, strange, and subversive. In the prophecy at the end of the play '*Merlin's* learned worth' – intellectual and not natural value – is linked with '*Arthur's* glory' by the latter's father. It may be that non-familial success is deemed more valuable. It is better not to be a father.

Yet sometimes drastic measures are required to do away with the possibility of fatherhood. Paranoia about uncertain paternity rears its head to be the centre of Edward Sharpham's splendidly ribald comedy *Cupid's Whirligig* (1607), and it impels an outcome that must in some senses be described as tragicomic. The jealous husband here, Sir Timothy Troublesome, anticipates Leontes in *The Winter's Tale* in that he is mistaken, but is less ridiculous than a standard citizen 'wittol'; his passions are given serious attention, if not legitimacy. However, despite his being given some powerful speeches, his role descends into grotesque absurdity when he decides to have himself castrated in order to prove that his wife is unfaithful. So anxious is he that he believes this radical course will at least provide certainty: 'I will geld my selfe, & then if my wife be with childe, I shal be sure I am a Cuckold, that will do braue y faith, God a mercie braine' (p. 6, lines 8–10).[59] Amusing as this is when proposed, it is rather astonishing when he actually goes through with the plan (with the punning help of a stone-cutter), cutting off his balls to spite his wife, as it were. The play seems a little undecided as to whether he and his wife have already had children: at one point, he demands of her 'hath not thy vnsatiate womb, brought forth the bastardie of lust to call me father? but ile abandon thee, disclaime that, and hate ye both' (p. 10, lines 21–3); later, however, when the disguised Young Lord who wants to seduce Lady Troublesome falsely tells him that she is pregnant (after the gelding), Sir Timothy says 'I wonder much she would not giue me leaue to make my first childe my selfe' (p. 42, lines 3–4). The castration therefore seems to destroy the Troublesome line, as well as ruining any chance he might have of marrying a new wife – as his servant Wages points out, even if

Sir Timothy were to divorce his wife, he has 'cut off al the content of marriage' (p. 51, lines 13–14). In the end, he is tricked into remarrying his old wife, but has no resolution to his anatomical problem. Some of this may be mitigated by the fact that this is a children's company play, so that no real man is presented as castrated, but one can't help seeing this as an uncompromising conclusion to a comedy. Even the invisible deity Cupid – who presides over the play – can do nothing to help. A wife (if not a son) can be restored in *The Winter's Tale*, but some things that are lost can never be found.

The ideas about fatherhood in the play are the more striking for this central plot device. At one moment of renewed trust (before the gelding), Sir Timothy says 'Man was made when nature was but an apprentice, but woman when she was a skilfull Mistresse of her Arte, therefore curssed is he that doth not admire those Paragons, those Moddels of heauen, Angels on earth, Goddesses in shape: by their loues we liue in double breath, euen in our Offspring after death' (p. 23, lines 23–9). Having taken this position of extreme faith in women, he then lurches in the other direction, under the influence of the disguised Young Lord, who tells him that even if his child resembles him, it will be no proof – indeed, it will prove the lady's infidelity: 'doe you not knowe the Philosophers hold the childe is alwaies like the partie which the mother thinkes off in the conception: now she thought moste of you, for feare you should come the whiles, and thats the reason so many Gentlemens sonnes are like your Cittizens, and calles them fathers too' (p. 45, lines 32–7). Absurd as this is (prompting the reaction that he should 'see if it be like me, that I may bee sure tis none of mine' – p. 46, lines 11–12), the idea seriously undermines any certainty of paternity. In a play that also presents the Old Lord as a seriously loving father (see pp. 4, 49), Sir Timothy's loss has to be taken quite seriously.

Other losses are more easily restored. In the seventeenth century's first decade, dramatists turn with an increasingly compulsive eagerness to the imaginative possibilities of the dispossessed paternal ruler and his often tragicomic restoration. The factor that adds the tragic element to these romance plays is the sense that there is something inherently sad about the condition of paternity. Both political and generic factors are in play: the latter being founded on the increasing disrespect for fathers we have seen in early Jacobean drama, the former being more mysterious. The idea of a restored king had an obvious resonance in the late Elizabethan period, when playwrights could fantasize about the return to proper paternalistic rule after the strange interim of female power, but its persistence in the

Jacobean period suggests a compulsive desire for the pleasure of restoration, perhaps founded on disappointment with the actuality of James's rule and therefore on a revisionist nostalgia for the interim. Paternal authority can thereby be accepted as fundamentally valid, but kept in imaginative abeyance.

Though we should not treat dynastic politics as a simple explanation for changing attitudes to patriarchy, it is clear that events on the nation's biggest stage were at least a minor factor in changing representations of fathers on the theatrical stage. It is impossible to pinpoint exactly when disillusionment with the patriarchal image of James I set in, but I think we can see certain key events as marking a clear enough process: the rise of Carr (later Somerset) as favourite in around 1606 coincided with a definite split between James and Queen Anne, and at the same point James seems to have given up public appearances (the plague in 1607–8 being a factor in that); the Overbury scandal of 1613–16 did crucial damage to the king's reputation; the Addled Parliament of 1614 was only worse in degree than earlier parliaments, but seems to have entrenched an alienation between king and country; the rise of Villiers (later Buckingham) as favourite coincided with a growing sense of royal effeminacy in the king's failure to intervene to help his son-in-law and daughter in the Palatinate and Bohemia (1618).[60] Along the way, the deaths of James's children compromised his image as a father: in addition to the crucial death of the heir Prince Henry in 1612, infant daughters died in 1606 and 1607, events that must have acted as reminders of the precariousness of paternity. Early in his reign, James could be celebrated for fecundity (and therefore dynastic security), and in 1606 he briefly had five children; yet by 1613, after the departure of Princess Elizabeth to the Palatinate, only one child, the 13-year-old Charles, remained in the country, and Charles's health was never entirely secure; if his robust brother could die, so could he.

John Day's *Humour out of Breath* (1608) may be taken as an absolutely typical instance of a restoration plot: a schematic play, heavily influenced by Marston's *Antonio and Mellida*, it lacks the gloomy overtones of its prototype, but still demonstrates the impotency of fathers. The rightful duke of Mantua Antonio gets his throne back remarkably easily. No Prospero-like 'potent art' is used to restore Antonio: he simply sits about despairing for a while until his people rebel against the usurper Octavio's deputy in Mantua. The plot focusses much more on the loves of Antonio's and Octavio's children which entrench the restoration, but do not actually cause it. Neat as this is, a few tensions arise on the way. The fact that Antonio has to confess himself 'new create[d]' (p. 327) by his people does offer a potentially subversive endorsement of the idea that rulers owe their legitimacy to the will of the people.[61] This idea fits with the passive role that is ultimately assigned to Octavio and Antonio by the dominance of their children's loves. In the middle of the play, Octavio, who has disguised himself to follow his sons on their courtship journey, forbids their marriage, calling them 'bastards' (p. 295) if they disobey; but when the girls turn out to be princesses, his objections lose their force. His 'father's wakeful providence' (p. 285) is ruled out of court. By the end of the play, his daughter Florida may wish for his presence to validate love, but without much real respect, saying 'O that the old graybeard, my father, were here!' (p. 331). Probably, we should take this as a fitting response to her father's minimal affection for her: not only does he fear for her actions (where he only doubts his sons'), he even tells her at the play's beginning 'Thou art mine own, I must think well of thee, / Yet Florimella, many do excel thee' (p. 277). Familial affections are necessary, but hardly the cause of great passions here. Antonio's son Aspero may want to avenge his father, but he does so mainly for abstract honour's sake, and his desires are easily distracted once he has fallen for his enemy's daughter. Love has a privilege here which leads to the marginalization of political and paternal authority. Yet they do remain on the margins, as markers of the limits of action. Octavio's admiration for Aspero's 'true moulded honour', even though it is directed against himself, indicates that all will be well, but this admiration also entails an ultimate concession that the father must give way to the younger generation.

A form of tragicomedy (and sometimes of tragedy) that becomes increasingly popular emphasizes the weaknesses involved in being the father of daughters. As such, it chimes with Shakespeare's preoccupation with daughters in his late plays. Dekker's *Match Me in London* (?1610, pub. 1631) presents fathers of daughters as vulnerable and apt to use their daughters' sexuality for their own ends. It may be 'Braue phrase to say my Sonne in Law the King' (III. i. 110), but the position of father-in-law to the lustful tyrant of Spain only puts Valasco in danger, as he is threatened by the king, nearly murdered by the king's brother, and is helpless as the king puts his daughter aside in favour of Tormiella and tries to have her killed. The deprivation of the private father is clear. Meanwhile, Malevento, the citizen father of Tormiella, has to accept his daughter eloping with a man other than the one he has promised her to, and ultimately accepts the position of Vice Admiral as a pay-off for the king's planned affair with his daughter. Malevento may be 'As kind an old man … as euer drunk mull'd Sack' (II. i. 83), but he is powerless, and even tries to get his son-in-law to 'wincke at small faults' in being cuckolded (IV. i. 39). He and Valasco are only saved in the end by the fact that their daughters are virtuous: the queen is too virtuous for Gazetto (Tormiella's original fiancé) to murder; and Tormiella resists all the king's blandishments. Valasco is restored to his original position of honour, but Malevento loses his position at court. The converted king moralizes on the 'prostitutions' that enable rising at court (V. v. 49); as in Dekker's other play of roughly the same year, *If This Be Not a Good Play, the Devil Is in It,* the presentation of a corrupt court may reflect obliquely on the court of Henry VIII, and thereby very indirectly on James I's: advancement of a family by the means of a young woman's attractions had been a problem eighty years previously, but it was more likely to be achieved by means of a young man's charms at James's court. By reflecting on the humiliations a father might undergo in getting courtly advancement, *Match Me in London* plays on the anxieties of a masculine identity's dependence on women in ways that would become increasingly common in the second decade of James's reign. The play solves all its problems, though, because the ideal of the virtuous daughter still remains potent.

The idea of a father being tempted to use his daughter to win the favour of a tyrant is taken much further in *The Second Maiden's Tragedy* (1611, probably by Middleton, whose Oxford editors have renamed it *The Lady's [or Ladies'] Tragedy*). Here the heroine's father Helvetius tries to persuade her to marry the Tyrant or, failing that, to be his mistress. The Tyrant calls him 'Happier than a king / And far above him, for she kneels to thee / Whom we have kneeled to, richer in one smile / That came from her, than she in all thy blessings' (I. i. 16–19), setting up an economy in which Helvetius thinks of her as needing to repay his blessings by prostituting herself to the king (lines 158–9). She, though still accepting the need to kneel to her father, does not accept this exchange, as she is betrothed to the legitimate king, Govianus. Helvetius is instructed to 'play the father' in wooing for the Tyrant (line 226) – a phrase that indicates such immoral fathering is only roleplay. He calls his daughter 'base-spirited' in refusing to 'make a latter spring' for him (II. i. 17, 21), hinting at but not quite developing a repudiation of paternity on the basis of her failure to renew his age unnaturally. She admits, Cordelia-like, that she owes her father 'A debt which both begins and ends with life, / Never till then discharged' (lines 50–1), but sees his proposals as so unnatural as to cast doubt on whether her father is really speaking (lines 94–100).

Fortunately for the authority of fathers, Helvetius is soon converted to virtuous courses by Govianus firing a blank pistol at him: he then becomes again 'my most worthy father' (line 162), and is duly imprisoned by the Tyrant for his defiance of the evil commands. That is the end of him in the version of the play that was performed, though he comes on at the end of the original text.[62] In neither version does he play a role in the key action of the plot, however. As his daughter is about to be abducted for the Tyrant's wicked purposes, she demands that Govianus kill her, thus setting up a parallel with Virginia (of *Apius and Virginia*) while casting the fiancé in the father's role (he isn't up to it, and his fainting forces her to do herself in). Taking the father out of play here indicates the point of his role: he was needed to exert pressure on the Lady, but his presence would only compromise our sense of her moral determination. She is the play's central focus, and her moral determination even continues beyond the grave, as her ghost impels Govianus to prevent the Tyrant's necrophilic designs on her corpse. The fact of her father's absence, along with her status as betrothed rather than wife, makes her a free agent in all this, dependent on no man. She, rather than the father, is the one who is doubled here, her character simultaneously appearing as a corpse and a ghost. Govianus gets his kingdom back and gets his revenge, but this depends on her support. Her choice is everything: in the first scene, her father tells her to kiss the king, and she kisses Govianus; in doing so, she manages an equivocal response that validates the true king's identity and that indicates her proper obedience to the true ruler, the true lover, and the true idea of her father's authority. The father himself, less perfect than the ideal, is not necessary for this. Restoration of the idea of the father can in fact make the father more alien than familiar; recognition becomes still stranger. The lady's own ghost now has an authority that supersedes that of the father.

Both the idea of restoration and the increasing authority of daughters are pivotal to Shakespeare's later plays. Though these are more focussed on the kinds of forgiveness and acceptance we have found in tragicomedy, they retain the tragic sense – most acutely felt in *King Lear* – that there is an epistemological gap between the old and the young, a gap that cannot simply be bridged by good nature. *The Tempest* presents the father as superhuman magus, beyond simple fatherly affection.[63] The mother is absent again, and is mentioned, as in *King Lear*, only in order to assert legitimate paternity – which of course brings up the possibility of wifely infidelity. When Prospero puzzles her by mentioning her father as duke of Milan, Miranda asks, quite reasonably, 'Sir, are not you my father?', to which Prospero benignly replies, 'Thy mother was a piece of virtue, and / She said thou wast my daughter' (I. ii. 55–7). Of course, this is affectionate and playful, but the metre of Prospero's lines does betray an element of hesitancy at making the joke: the flimsy 'and' which ends the line suggests an effort to bind the idea of the wife's virtue and her statement of Miranda's legitimacy together syllogistically (the *and* should be stressed, but it would be absurd to do so). Underlying the joke is the sense that paternity can *never* be certain, relying as it does on maternal speech.[64] The fact that Prospero is only now conferring full identity on Miranda by giving his narrative and that he is thus only fully acknowledging paternity at this late stage suggests a need for long trial in fatherly affection.

Like *King Lear*, *The Tempest* is a play about giving way to the younger generation; the greater benignity here does not hide the estranging distance that this process interposes between the generations. There may be a hint that Prospero's feelings are possessive to the verge of being incestuous, that Caliban's desire for Miranda is an externalization of the 'darkness' that subsists in the duke's feelings for his daughter;[65] that darkness may also reflect a sense of the dark uncertainties of the womb, but the darkness he acknowledges in Caliban is perhaps mostly a sense of his own mortality – a mortality which poignantly grasps at the nearest thing he has to a son; Caliban is most truly 'a lump bred up in darkness', as Hieronimo has it, but he must be accepted, rebellious and vicious as he is.[66] In abandoning his magic and acknowledging his mortality, Prospero is shuffling off the sacred element of his paternity, leaving himself with the full pathos of his position as a private – and deprived – father. When Prospero sympathizes with Alonso on the supposed death of Ferdinand, there is a great truth spoken in the fiction: he tells him 'I / Have lost my daughter'(V. i. 147–8); what he means by this irony is that he has lost his daughter in marriage to Ferdinand, but the 'I' hanging at the end of the line, and the slight catch in the breath required to begin the next line with an 'h', hint at real grief.[67] Prospero effects a sea-change in their common loss by revealing the couple, but it is only to ameliorate an underlying sadness in the condition of paternity.[68] The play's greatest grace is in its acceptance of this.[69]

A different kind of acceptance is required, however, of Ferdinand. *The Tempest* deploys the relatively common comic trope of a son and heir thinking that his father is dead, but his reaction is not the common one of scarcely suppressed joy. When he hears Ariel's song announcing that 'Full fadom five thy father lies', Ferdinand speaks truer than he knows in saying 'This is no mortal business' (I. ii. 397, 407), for there is no death here; perhaps a son – particularly a royal one – can unconsciously intuit that his father is alive. Yet he does boast, albeit mildly, of his new status once he meets Miranda: 'I am the best of them that speak this speech, / Were I but where 'tis spoken' (lines 430–1). Prospero ironically rebukes

him for this boast, gaining an extraordinary response that is almost a
self-recognition, seeing his father in himself:

> PROSPERO. What wert thou, if the King of Naples heard thee?
> FERDINAND. A single thing, as I am now, that wonders
> To hear thee speak of Naples. He does hear me,
> And that he does I weep. Myself am Naples,
> Who with mine eyes (never since at ebb) beheld
> The King my father wrack'd.   (lines 432–7)

Ferdinand is alone, and therefore a mere thing, even though he is (or thinks
he is) king; having become his father, he weeps for his father. This confirms
the 'sea-change / Into something rich and strange' (lines 401–2) that Ariel
claims has transformed the king-father. Ferdinand undergoes here a self-
estrangement that is at the same time a self-realization. Yet it is an illusion.
When we return to reality, Ferdinand gets 'all the blessings / Of a glad
father' (V. i. 179–80), but the highly valued idea of the paternal blessing
here is a bit of a damp squib. Only the fresh perspective of Miranda
('O wonder!' – line 181) as she acquires a second father can give power to
this recognition. Self-recognitions and the recognitions of grief are stronger.

No one really dies in *The Tempest*, it seems, but there is a hint of one death:
Ferdinand mentions 'the brave son' of the duke of Milan (Antonio) as one of
those shipwrecked (I. ii. 439); this trace character is not saved, but whether
Shakespeare forgot him, or whether he intended him to die does not matter
too much,[70] for such a son must be got out of the way so that the marriage will
unite kingdoms. Something similar happens in *The Winter's Tale*, whose more
fully tragic plot realizes the anxieties of paternity more explicitly. The play gets
rid of a much more fully realized son so that a daughter may join kingdoms.
Leontes' jealousy results in the death of his son, Mamillius, who is emphatically
praised in the preamble scene of the play between Camillo and Archidamus:

> You have an unspeakable comfort of your young prince
> Mamillius: it is a gentleman of the greatest promise that ever came
>   into my note.
> CAMILLO. I very well agree with you in the hopes of him; it is a
>   gallant child; one that, indeed, physics the subject, makes old
>   hearts fresh. They that went on crutches ere he was born desire
>   yet their life to see him a man.
> ARCHIDAMUS. Would they be else content to die?
> CAMILLO. Yes; if there were no other excuse why they should desire
>   to live.
> ARCHIDAMUS. If the King had no son, they would desire to live on
>   crutches till he had one.   (I. i. 34–46)

Hopes for the future generation, perhaps paradoxically, cause people to want to live longer; Archidamus may be joking, suggesting that, whatever the condition of things, people would find some reason for wanting to go on with life. Yet there is also a tragically proleptic irony here in that the king will soon have no son, and will only get one after a very long wait when his daughter finally marries Florizel. One hopes that the old men live to see it.

As soon as Leontes' jealousy of Hermione and Polixenes emerges, he turns to Mamillius in order to calm himself, asking:

> Art thou my boy?
> MAMILLIUS. Ay, my good lord.
> LEONTES. I' fecks!
> Why, that's my bawcock. What? hast smutch'd thy nose?
> They say it is a copy out of mine. (I. i. 120–2)

The reassurance he is seeking here hardly needs comment. Whatever the basis for his jealousy, Leontes *knows* that Mamillius cannot be the product of a liaison between Hermione and Polixenes (who has only been a recent visitor), but of course jealousy is apt to spread, acting retroactively and without a sense of temporal logic. He seeks further reassurance from looking at his son, presumably and inevitably seeing more difference between them the more he looks:

> Thou want'st a rough pash and the shoots that I have
> To be full like me; yet they say we are
> Almost as like as eggs; women say so –
> That will say anything. (lines 128–31)

Leontes seems crazily to suggest that Mamillius will be a cuckold like his father, with the horns that attend on cuckoldry.[71] The identification and recognition of his son is eerie, involving a strange homosocial acknowledgement of common masculinity and its peril; accordingly, there is ambiguity in Leontes' 'we' here: he might be likening himself to Polixenes as much as to Mamillius – after all, there has been talk of the friends as having been 'twinn'd lambs' (line 65) – and therefore the signs of recognition only bring doubt. The fact that women are proverbially 'false' (line 131) means that no words about paternity can be trusted; the similarity of eggs is no reassurance – for two unrelated eggs would look as alike as related ones. That which ought to reassure becomes a cause of further doubt. The radical undermining of identity here is not *specific*, then, to Leontes' character, but is something that implicitly underlies all paternity. In *Cymbeline*, whose ending recovers sons as well as daughters, Posthumus says 'We are all bastards' (II. v. 2); as McCabe points out, it takes 'the President of the Immortals' Jupiter to assure us that this is not the case.[72] Only the voice of the highest father can wholly validate paternity; without divine intervention, the sense that the basis of identity is fundamentally insecure must persist.

The bond between Leontes and Mamillius is unusually strong for a father and son in Renaissance drama. Leontes oddly asks Polixenes, 'Are you as fond of your young prince as we / Do seem to be of ours' (lines 164–5) – in this, he is perhaps simply talking of the impression that Polixenes gets, but there is a strange element of *wonder* at his own feeling in it. Perhaps much of Leontes' jealousy can be accounted for by an unbearable and surprising feeling for his son. Hermione is not exactly affectionate to Mamillius: 'Take the boy to you; he so troubles me, / 'Tis past enduring' (II. i. 1–2). Of course she is heavily pregnant with a second child, and we perhaps have been watching a bit of straightforward humane realism (more applicable to common than royal families), with Mamillius for the first time being driven into his father's attention due to his mother's pregnancy. Could one say that Mamillius' incipient sibling jealousy has infected his father? Despite his greater attachment to his father, Mamillius becomes sick when his mother is maltreated; the cause, however, does not seem to be direct affection for her (though Paulina interprets it thus – III. ii. 195–8), but, at least as Leontes puts it, an identification with his father:

> To see his nobleness,
> Conceiving the dishonour of his mother!
> He straight declin'd, droop'd, took it deeply,
> Fasten'd and fix'd the shame on't in himself,
> Threw off his spirit, his appetite, his sleep,
> And downright languish'd.   (II. iii. 12–17)

Leontes may be projecting his feelings onto his son, but such is the resemblance between them that the projection really does kill Mamillius. Mamillius is made into a father, begetting his own death. In the end Leontes will recover a wife past childbearing age, but will only get a son through his daughter's marriage to his former friend's son.[73] The death of Mamillius is taken as heaven's righteous punishment for Leontes' 'injustice' (III. ii. 147) – to lose one's son is the truest of all punishments, it is implied.

His recovery of a daughter is only given in the narrative of a court gentleman:

Our king, being ready to leap out of himself for joy of his found daughter, as if that joy were now become a loss, cries, 'O, thy mother, thy mother!'; then asks Bohemia forgiveness; then embraces his son-in-law; then again worries he his daughter with clipping her. (V. ii. 49–54)

The daughter is here associated with her mother rather than her father, for whom she shows no evident affection. This same gentleman describes her reception of the story of her mother's death as 'One of the prettiest touches of all' in the scene (line 82), aestheticizing grief; Leontes tells this tale, and 'attentiveness wounded his daughter' (lines 86–7). She has natural feeling for her mother, and wants to see her statue (which she, in a manner, revives); but no feeling for her father. This is not unreasonable, given her mother's treatment, and her love for Florizel (which puts her in a position akin to Cordelia's, incapable of loving her father all), but it means that the happy ending is very muted. The losses of paternity are not balanced by the gains, even though they are seemingly miraculous.

Cymbeline is printed in the Folio as the last of the tragedies, but it hardly counts as such given that the only people to die are the wicked stepmother queen and the vicious idiot Cloten; nonetheless, the generic categorization suggests some deep seriousness in the play, and this clearly has to do with the dignity of the titular character.[74] Yet Cymbeline himself is one of the most bizarrely inactive characters in Shakespeare's oeuvre, his dignity being in some ways dependent on his inaction. This is an odd form of dignity: on his first entrance, rather than reverence, he is met with Posthumus' 'Alack, the King!' (I. i. 124), and he is a rather impotently irascible father to a daughter who has married without his consent, heaping terms of abuse on Imogen, but without much sense of being able to control her. He has all the weaknesses of Lear but without the 'darker purpose' of love that made Lear at least fascinating. He simply seems like a bumbling old man, content to let Cloten and the queen deal with both Imogen and the Roman emissaries (when he does talk to the emissaries, it is in pointless terms of reminiscence, his only defiance being to observe the precedent of other states in rebellion against Roman rule – III. i. 68–76). Even in dismissing the emissaries, Cymbeline seems subject to his subjects, saying:

> Our subjects, sir,
> Will not endure his [the emperor's] yoke; and for ourself
> To show less sovereignty than they, must needs
> Appear unkinglike. (III. v. 4–7)

The apologetic concern for appearance is self-undermining: no other Shakespearean king ever appears more unkinglike than this. It is possible that this blurred leader constitutes a mild satire on James I, but he may also be considered a wise fool; after all, we might consider the above speech a clever bit of diplomacy, designed to avoid or mitigate war.

Sir Anthony Weldon's famous description of James in fact acts as a condemnation: 'A very wise man was wont to say that he beleeved him the wisest foole in Christendome, meaning him wise in small things, but a foole in weighty affaires.'[75] What I want to suggest is that Shakespeare configures the idea of a wise fool differently, and more approvingly, as someone who acts foolishly, but whose actions turn out for the best, or even as someone who is wiser than he appears (after all, one of James's model rulers, the Biblical Solomon, was a wise fool).

After his initial rage, Cymbeline's reactions to the main plot – his daughter's marriage – are so gnomic that we barely notice him. Told that Imogen's doors are locked and no one has seen her, he says 'Grant, heavens, that which I fear / Prove false!' (III. v. 52–3); does he fear that she has killed herself, run off, been murdered? We cannot know, as he immediately exits, characteristically leaving the stage to others. We next see him worrying about the queen (who is pining in Cloten's absence), and about the Roman invasion. With some understatement, he says 'The time is troublesome' (IV. iii. 21) – this is valetudinarian whingeing, yet it also enables a certain wise passivity:

> Let's withdraw,
> And meet the time as it seeks us. We fear not
> What can from Italy annoy us, but
> We grieve at chances here. Away! (lines 32–5)

A great exiter (this is perhaps a symbol of his patience), Cymbeline has attitudes that might have helped Lear to accept the burden of age. At the beginning of the play, he told Imogen – in a rare example of coherent speech to her – that she who 'shouldst repair my youth, thou heap'st / A year's age on me' (I. i. 132–3). The absence of hyperbole here (just one year of age) is quite striking; one gets the impression that this is a very old man who knows the exact weight of his burden. This is a different kind of dignity from Lear's, but it is perhaps better attuned to the spirit of the play, where patience is essential: as Jupiter tells Posthumus (or more precisely, tells the ghosts of Posthumus' family, including his father):

> Be not with mortal accidents oppress'd,
> No care of yours it is, you know 'tis ours.
> Whom best I love, I cross; to make my gift,
> The more delay'd, delighted. (V. iv. 99–102)

Novy nicely calls this moment 'an epiphany of continuing parental care',[76] but the very grand entrances here contrast strongly with the exits of the king, and the active clarity of Jupiter is very different from the passive and muffled figure Cymbeline plays.

The almost absurdly extended unravelling of *Cymbeline*'s plot sees its titular king acting almost as a chorus, hearing more and more wonders. Yet he is not truly at the centre: the recognitions are validated by him, but are not really about him. The father–daughter recognition may not be as muted as in *As You Like It*, but the recognition between Posthumus and Imogen is clearly more important. Cymbeline can only comment 'If this be so, the gods do mean to strike me / To death with mortal joy' (V. v. 235–6) – this is a very different kind of mortal joy from that which may kill Lear when he (possibly) thinks Cordelia alive at the end of his play, and of course it does not really kill Cymbeline. However, we feel that he is on his way out, only able to witness the denouement of his family's romance with a certain baffled wonder. Rather than validating his manhood, though, his conclusion turns him rather hermaphroditic; informed of the safety of his sons, he says 'O, what, am I / A mother to the birth of three? Ne'er mother / Rejoic'd deliverance more' (lines 368–70). The whole progress of the play has been a labour, after which the only solution is tranquillity, with all being pardoned, including the Romans, to whom Cymbeline submits despite his victory. Such passivity is the truest wisdom.

Like Imogen at the end of *Cymbeline*, who is glad that she has lost a throne because that loss releases her to love Posthumus, Arbaces in Beaumont and Fletcher's *A King and No King* (1611) offers 'Loud thankes for me, that I am prov'd no King' (V. iv. 353) because the discovery enables him to marry the woman he had thought was his sister. The play's denouement not only gains Arbaces a wife, though, but also, and almost as importantly, a father.

The play's point seems to be that the acquisition of a father, though an odd idea, may diminish an individual, but may do so in morally edifying ways. Arbaces is intially an overly proud king, criticized by the good counsellor Mardonius for his vaunting about military success. Such hubris might lead to tragedy, particularly as Arbaces' passionate nature means he will not listen for long to Mardonius, despite calling him 'more then friend in armes, / My Father, and my Tutor' (I. i. 329–30). What he really needs is a real father rather than such a father substitute, but this seems impossible, given that the old king is dead. The play's seemingly tragic trajectory develops as Arbaces falls in love with his sister Panthæa, a passion which might seem like punishment for pride. The turn to tragi-comedy comes very late in the play, when Arbaces decides to kill his other good counsellor Gobrius, whose letters to him have primed his incestuous desires. Gobrius is, it turns out, Arbaces' real father: the moment of potential patricide, which might be the worst of tragic crimes, ironically becomes the catalyst for a happy ending.

Arbaces' identity may be unsettled by the revelation, and for a moment it leads him deeper into sin. He initially responds to Gobrius' statement that he's his father by assuming that the older man has committed adultery with the old queen; considering himself the off-spring of a lustful, illegitimate union, he decides this must be the reason for his own wildly lustful and beastly nature (V. iv. 124–8, 171–5). He is almost dehumanized by this thought; law and legitimacy seem not just a support for status, but a bedrock of the most basic sense of identity. The simpler truth – that he was Gobrius' legitimate son, smuggled into the queen's bedchamber when she faked a pregnancy for the sake of getting an heir to the throne – does not entirely do away with this sense of radical uncertainty: rather than repeat the story to Mardonius, Arbaces says 'the whole storie / Would be a wildernesse to loose thy selfe / For ever' (lines 286–8). Establishing the truth is less important than fixing the emotional and dutiful relations of the family: Arbaces' arrogance is removed not only by the fact that he is no longer king, but by the presence of a father whom he must revere. The father solves a problem by forcing a diminution of selfhood here; yet Panthæa is also needed to prop Arbaces up again, for only by marrying her can he gain back some status. As so often in prodigal-son plays, the father reduces the son, and a wife lifts him up again. Arbaces has lost his public father, but has gained dignity in his private life.

The role of a daughter, as we saw in the cases of *King Lear* and *The Tempest*, is still more complex, allowing diminution and moral edification in exquisitely balanced measure. Shakespeare's late romances all deal with the problems of paternity, but the play which most clearly allegorizes the difficulty of becoming a father is *Pericles*, the first of these plays by some years. Here, the key emphasis seems to be on the fact that patriarchal masculinity should not be taken as a simple given, but is a state whose achievement requires true suffering. As such, the play is as much a happier counterpart to *Lear* as it is an anticipation of *Cymbeline*, *The Winter's Tale*, and *The Tempest*. If the condition of maternity requires labour and suffering, the play suggests, paternity can be emotionally validated by an equivalently laborious passion.

Pericles' self-confessed weakness at the opening of the play is striking: he may be king of Tyre, but when he discovers Antiochus' incestuous secret he becomes melancholic, saying:

> the passions of the mind,
> That have their first conception by misdread,
> Have after-nourishment and life by care;
> And what was first but fear what might be done
> Grows elder now, and cares it be not done.
> And so with me. The great Antiochus,
> 'Gainst whom I am too little to contend,
> Since he's so great can make his will his act,
> Will think me speaking though I swear to silence.
> Nor boots it me to say I honour him
> If he suspect I may dishonour him.   (I. ii. 11–21)[77]

Though these lines are almost certainly by Shakespeare's collaborator George Wilkins, they resemble the initial conception of the murder in *Macbeth* and that of jealousy in *The Winter's Tale*; what is different here is that the clotted conception of a passion is so fearful. Suzanne Gossett, the Arden editor, argues that lines 17–18's 'statement of inadequacy is strongly Oedipal, suggesting male fear of the castrating father', but it may also be fear of becoming a father. Pericles says that he went to Antioch to seek the king's daughter 'From whence an issue I might propagate' (line 71), but Antiochus has demonstrated the potential monstrosity of propagation. Antiochus' transparent riddle says that '*He's father, son, and husband mild*' (I. i. 69): the second term is confusing, but simply means that he is his own son-in-law; Pericles cannot become a father until he accepts a proper position of son, and such a role is not available at Antioch. Rather, Pericles seems to fear that Antiochus' sin will infect him, saying 'vice repeated is like the wandering wind / Blows dust in others' eyes to spread itself' (lines 97–8). Even to speak of the incest would be in a sense to repeat it, but the effect of Pericles' silence is that he is displaced from his own kingdom. The double bind here blocks the achievement of paternal masculinity. He has to be a 'better prince' (II. Chorus. 3) than Antiochus, but in order to do so he must suffer.

Act II of the play, however, seems to make the achievement of masculinity easy: Pericles can dress up in his father's rusty armour and win Thaisa with the full approval – indeed, the active desire – of her father. The allegorical significance of the paternal armour is clear enough (it resembles the battered armour of George at the opening of *The Faerie Queene*), but it is not a spear: paternal identity is at best defensive and passive, not aggressive; Pericles will be rather passive as Thaisa (and her father Simonides) woo him. Indeed, he will be passive throughout the play. Even with Simonides, he seems cowed:

> Yon king's to me like to my father's picture,
> Which tells me in that glory once he was,
> Had princes sit like stars about his throne,
> And he the sun for them to reverence.
> None that beheld him, but like lesser lights
> Did vail their crowns to his supremacy;
> Where now his son's like a glow-worm in the night,
> The which hath fire in darkness, none in light.
> Whereby I see that time's the king of men,
> He's both their parent and he is their grave,
> And gives them what he will, not what they crave. (II. ii. 36–46)

Like Hamlet, Pericles is evidently a lesser king than his father was, but this is not a revenge play in which he will vindicate his father's inheritance by fighting or conquest. Instead, he has to accept his own limitations in order to achieve anything. He will remain a glow-worm, with no need to become a sun. This seems the new condition of patriarchal identity at which we have arrived in the wake of *King Lear*.

As Terence Cave points out, 'the paradoxical metonym with which Pericles addresses Marina at the climax ("O, come hither, / Thou that begett'st him that did thee beget") recalls the reversals of the order of generation in the opening incest riddle',[78] and reinforces our sense of Pericles' passivity. Even in the conception of Marina, he is not presented as very active: 'Hymen hath brought the bride to bed, / Where by the loss of maidenhead / A babe is moulded' (III. Chorus. 9–11). On the death of Thaisa, the nurse Lychorida has to say 'Be manly and take comfort' (III. i. 22) before Pericles will receive his new-born daughter, and what follows indicates that he cannot look after his daughter, only hoping that her life be 'mild' (line 27); the word echoes the odd description of Antiochus as '*husband mild*' to his daughter, and suggests a persistent link between the two men. Pericles' acceptance as a son by Simonides has not yet made him complete.

His vow after the apparent death of Thaisa (and after handing over Marina to be raised by Dionyza) is crucial in a number of senses, not least in being the play's most famous textual crux: he swears that until Marina marry

> By bright Diana whom we honour all,
> Unscissored shall this hair of mine remain,
> Though I show ill in't.   (III. iii. 29–31)

The Quarto reads as follows:

> by bright *Diana*, whom we honour,
> All unsistered shall this heyre of mine remayne,
> Though I shew will in't.

Suzanne Gossett is quite right to suggest that the Quarto reading makes sense on its own terms,[79] yet it is a very peculiar sense: why would he presume that any child he might beget would be a *sister* to Marina? (Perhaps he thinks himself not manly enough to get a son?) And if the vow gives him a loophole to have a son, wouldn't that prevent Marina remaining his heir? (Perhaps he has given up the impulse to patrilineal self-duplication.) On the other hand, the word 'will' runs through the texture of the play, frequently attached to the paternal impulse: for instance, when Pericles recovers his armour from the sea, he says 'My shipwreck now's no ill, / Since I have here my father gave in his will' (II. i. 129–30); Time, as we have seen, is parent and king of men, giving what 'he will' (II. ii. 46). The human will, particularly the paternal will, has to give way to larger patterns, for it has to become more passive and patient.

That patience will emerge in the recognition scene with Marina, just at the point where patience in the normal sense of the word is no longer needed. Yet another kind of patience – a word etymologically linked to passion and passivity, all rooted in the Latin word for suffering – is required, as the recognition is stretched out in a kind of sweet agony (as well as being repeated in the later recognition of Thaisa). In a way, the scene is a recapitulation of the recognition between Lear and Cordelia: both fathers worry that they are being mocked (*Lear*, IV. vii. 58; *Pericles*, V. i. 133); on the one hand, this means that they fear a cruel trick, but on the other there may be the suggestion that a daughter is a *mock* version of the father, rather than the proper imitation a son might be. Yet such mockery turns out to be more kind than cruel, the daughter more natural than a son. She, more properly than a son, can enjoin 'Patience' (V. i. 135) and, with her feminine tears, heal the divisions of the play.

Marina not only begets her own father (line 185), but delivers him, in delivering her tale (he says he is 'great with woe, and shall deliver weeping' (line 97); she has a tale which her nurse 'Delivered weeping' (line 151)). The framing of that tale is as powerful a moment as *Lear*'s balancing of emotions between father and daughter, Pericles saying:

> Tell thy story.
> If thine considered prove the thousand part
> Of my endurance, thou art a man, and I

> Have suffered like a girl. Yet thou dost look
> Like Patience gazing on kings' graves and smiling
> Extremity out of act.   (lines 125–30)

The exchange of identities here is one of the most powerful acceptances of paternal limitation in the drama of the period, but it does not radically fracture and unsettle the relation of father and daughter as *Lear*'s climax does. Where *Lear* tries to compare the suffering of the old and the young and therefore takes us to unbearable, extreme loss, the conditional mood of *Pericles*' recognition finesses away competition in suffering. Marina's patience makes such extreme accounting irrelevant. Cordelia may forgive her father in saying 'no cause', but her forgiveness is in some sense an evasion, just as her apparent survival in the final scene is a falsehood which makes her father die in erroneous happiness. Cordelia does have some cause to be angry with her father, but Marina does not; therefore she can smile, and that smiling patience is more active than Cordelia's denial of her suffering. If Pericles *has* suffered like a girl, that may not be a diminution: he becomes more fully a man in accepting her feminine patience. He has realized something more than his own paternal will.

As we have seen in this chapter, though, the idea of the patriarch is very much a mixed blessing: it validates certain kinds of emotional bond and thus holds together the imagined community of a play, allowing a sense of meaningful recognition to emerge; yet such meaningful recognitions are often very strange, and are recognitions as much of the limitations of human connectedness as they are of its strength. Politics alone cannot account for such a shift in representations of fathers: the drama of the period sets its own problems, the generic system gradually erodes its own keystone in the interests of a greater human truth. The consequences of accepting that truth, of recognizing that the father cannot be indubitably sacred, will be the subject of the next chapter. Once the clear analogy between fathers' authority and their emotional roles has been broken down, new systems and principles of order need to emerge.

CHAPTER 5

After The Tempest

We have seen that many of the problems of paternal authority were resolved by a hard-won acceptance of paternal limitation in the first decade of Jacobean drama, often involving a separation of public power and private emotion. But new problems emerged, despite (or perhaps because of) that acceptance. Later Jacobean drama, in its 'higher' forms, shows an ambivalent obsession with matters of familial honour and virtue, but in its 'lower' forms – particularly city comedy – that obsession is shown to be ill-placed, resulting in an increasing scepticism about masculine authority of all kinds, not just about patriarchal power. This chapter starts by dealing with the end of Shakespeare's career, where he returns to the paternal preoccupations of history in *Henry VIII*, but with a stronger sense of the contigency of patrilineal history. The contingency of paternal authority is based on an increasingly authoritative role being given to women, and this is the subject of the chapter's next section, where paternal limitation leaves a power vacuum which is filled by more and more confident feminine speech. Perhaps in reaction to that, men start to search for new sources of masculine authority: turning to an insistence on ideas of abstract honour or virtue and tying up their identities with religious and political commitments, particularly after the commencement of what would become the Thirty Years War. Later Jacobean drama is characterized by a search for new moral centres now that the limitations of paternal power have been accepted. As a result, the drama of this period often seems to be searching in vain for adequate individual motivation, in love, friendship, religious or political commitment, or in more abstract notions of honour and virtue. But ideas of honour cannot, in the end, be detached from the problems associated with fathers and with masculine identity. Those problems need to be confronted and accepted for any kind of resolution to emerge. Running through all of this, though, is an increasing acceptance of the uncertainty of paternity, which is the subject of the chapter's final section: in the lower classes this enables happy resolutions, but in the upper classes it returns us to tragedy of the most acute kind, as fathers again become insistent on proving themselves to be the centre of the culture.

'HENRY VIII' – CONTINGENT HISTORY

As we have seen, being a father in Shakespeare's histories, tragedies, and late romances is a precarious condition. Only in the comedies is paternity seen as something hopeful, but that is achieved not so much through present fathers as through figures who will be fathers, such as Orlando. Even in the comedies, procreation is not so much an internal goal as a final, extra-textual, validating end: 'the world must be peopled', as Benedick says with a sigh of ironic acceptance in *Much Ado about Nothing* (II. iii. 242). One of the few babies born in a Shakespeare play is Queen Elizabeth herself in *Henry VIII*, and the atmosphere around the birth here hovers between comedic hope and tragic precariousness.[1] Elizabeth's birth is a subject of considerable ambiguity, possibly caused by the co-authorship of the play with Fletcher, but also by the difficulty of celebrating the birth of someone who was dead at the time of writing. Suffolk, contemplating Anne Bullen (*sic*), says:

> She is a gallant creature, and complete
> In mind and feature. I persuade me, from her
> Will fall some blessing to this land, which shall
> In it be memoriz'd.   (III. ii. 49–52)

As well as the sense that the future queen will only be remembered, not that she will achieve much, the lines have an unfortunate jingle ('creature', 'feature'), and there's something rather coarse or even ominous about the blessing *falling* from the dubious figure of Anne, who had earlier said 'By my troth and maidenhead, / I would not be a queen' (II. iii. 23–4); despite her pious pity for Queen Katherine, we may detect some dramatic irony in her oath, given Anne's dubious reputation. Katherine is a contrasting figure of genuine pathos, and her speech about her daughter rather undermines our valuation of Anne's offspring. She has:

> commended to [the King's] goodness
> The model of our chaste loves his young daughter –
> The dews of heaven fall thick in blessings on her!   (IV. ii. 131–3)

She asks her followers to 'strew me over / With maiden flowers, that all the world may know / I was a chaste wife to my grave' (lines 168–70). This emphasis on Katherine's chastity is important; as Anne was later convicted of adultery, and Elizabeth declared illegitimate, these lines remind us of the doubtful origins of the child whom the play seems to hold up as a figure of hope. This reminder is further accentuated in the king's exchange with the old woman who has attended Elizabeth's birth:

KING.   Is the Queen deliver'd?
    Say ay, and of a boy.
OLD LADY.   Ay, ay my liege,
    And of a lovely boy. The God of heav'n
    Both now and ever bless her! 'tis a girl
    Promises boys hereafter.   (V. i. 162–6)

This is a bizarre moment, and one that seems for a moment to subvert history in favour of Henry's paternal will. The Old Lady also says, with some absurdity, ''Tis as like you / As cherry is to cherry' (lines 168–9), but then undermines that statement when she isn't paid enough: 'Said I for this, the girl was like to him? / I'll have more, or else unsay't' (lines 174–5). The contingencies of paternity are as sharp here as anywhere in the drama.[2] Cranmer's negotiation of these contingencies, prophesying the indirect heir James I, prompts Henry to say 'Thou hast made me now a man!' (line 64); others' speech is necessary to found paternal masculinity. As a peculiar resurgence of an outmoded genre, *Henry VIII* might have been expected to re-entrench teleological models of providential patrilineality, but – perhaps responding to the death of King James's older son – it rather demonstrates the contingent nature of patriarchy in the manner of the dominant tragicomic mode of the time.

THE INCREASING AUTHORITY OF WOMEN

If fathers are downgraded by this, the corollary might be an increasingly authoritative and often confusing role for women. Yet that emerges in very diverse ways, and often through considerable confusion. The idea that mothers might encourage their sons to disrespect their fathers seems to have been nearly proverbial, as Henry Peacham suggests in *The Compleat Gentleman*:

a great blame and imputation (how justly I know not) is commonly laid upon the Mother; not onely for her over tendernesse, but in winking at their lewd courses; yea, more in seconding, and giving them encouragement to doe wrong, though it were, as *Terence* saith, against their owne Fathers.

I dare not say it was long of the Mother, that the son told his father, he was a better man, and better descended then he.[3]

Maternally derived identity becomes more important in later Jacobean drama. *Beggar's Bush* (?1618, by Fletcher possibly in collaboration with Beaumont, possibly revised by Massinger)[4] begins its final scene with a powerful father–son recognition which is cut across by several currents of feeling: even as he reveals himself, the father Gerrard asserts his authority in insisting that his son Florez not marry his commoner fiancée now that he knows himself to be a prince; yet, at the same time, Gerrard has to kneel to his son, who is the true ruler, because the son's political authority is derived from his late mother.

However, the tension between familial authority and political status derived from a woman is not all that is in play here. Gerrard's authority derives as much from a promise of obedience Florez made to him when he was in disguise as a beggar and loaned him money as it does from filial duty; Florez's beloved turns out in any case to be a princess; and last but not least, it is not clear that Gerrard really is Florez's father. The play's *Dramatis Personae* states that he is his 'Father in Law' – i.e. his stepfather – yet within the play that is not mentioned; he is always called his father, and Florez behaves as if he were, even reacting to Gerrard's kneeling with horror

> Kneele to me?
> May mountaines first fall down beneath their valleys,
> And fire no more mount upwards, when I suffer
> An act in nature so preposterous.   (V. ii. 17–20)

The reference to nature here surely rules out the idea that Gerrard is his stepfather, but the confusion may have arisen from Massinger's revisions to the play, of which this sequence is probably an example. There are few stranger examples of the doubleness of fathers than this: like Wittgenstein's duck-rabbit, Gerrard is both a private father and a public subject, but cannot be both at once. At the beginning of the play we are clearly told that Gerrard is 'but a Gentleman' (I. i. 27), that being why he couldn't fight for the realm himself. Though he does become King of the Beggars during the course of the play, he only gets this position due to Florez's help, and there are persistent reminders of Florez's superiority in status. It is as if a Hamlet were being helped out by a Claudius. When Gerrard is in disguise and helps his son out of a financial jam, there's much punning on this being a *blessing* (IV. i. 39–55), the term referring to the main thing a son needed from his father, yet the whole process of the play's plot – and above all the doubts about the father–son relation here – serve to diminish the importance of paternity. Here we find doubts about paternity based not on the character of a wife/mother, but on the fact of a matrilineal descent, and on textual confusion.

Confusions caused by women also drive the plot of Fletcher's *The Pilgrim* (c. 1621), which presents a fine set of humiliations for an irascible father, culminating in his confinement in a madhouse, which serves to work him out of his angry humour, in a comic version, perhaps, of *King Lear*. Alphonso's initial humiliations are mostly caused by his daughter's servant Juletta, during his ill-tempered hunt for his runaway daughter Alinda. Juletta tells him from the first, 'You are my master, but ye owne an anger / Becomes a School-boy, that hath lost his apples' (I. i. 74–5); she later gets him locked up because 'He's in love with a boy, there lies his melancholy' (IV. iii. 133 – this works as Alphonso is seeking Alinda in her boy's disguise). Displacing these insults to masculinity onto the servant pulls their sting a bit, even while making it objectively clear that such anger is unmanly; yet Alinda herself does trick him on at least one occasion, convincing him that she is an imbecile or natural fool:

> gaffer, here's a Crow-flower, and a Dazie;
> I have some pie in my pocket too.
> ALPHONSO.   This is an arrant foole,
>   An ignorant thing.
> ALINDA.   Believe so, and I am happy.
> ALPHONSO. Dost thou dwell in *Sigovia*, foole?
> ALINDA. No no, I dwell in Heaven.
>   And I have a fine little house, made of Marmalad.   (IV. i. 30–5)

Alinda is not quite a 'soul in bliss' as Lear imagines Cordelia, but there is a similarly eerie alienation; such exchanges indicate a comic turn to the whole proceedings, effected through the locales of the forest and the madhouse. She displaces him from authoritative paternity into the old age of being a grandfather. The play began with Alphonso's forceful model of precedence between the sexes, in which 'She is malliable; shee'l endure the hammer' (I. i. 32); but it ends with graceful acceptance of the daughter's will:

> I have no title in her,
> Pray take her, and dispatch her, and commend me to her,
> And let me go home, and hope I am sober:
> Kisse, kisse, it must be thus: stand up *Alinda*,
> I am the more Childe, and more need of blessing.   (V. vi. 88–92)

This scene clearly echoes *King Lear*, reflecting the fact that Alinda had played both Cordelia and fool here, yet the father is much more prepared to let his daughter go for good.

Daughters like Alinda can more powerfully yet acceptably undermine
their fathers than sons can, a fact perhaps connected to King James's
humiliations and vacillations in foreign policy matters related to his
daughter.[5] Middleton and Rowley's *A Fair Quarrel* (c. 1616) begins with
a striking statement about the difference between fathering sons and
daughters, Russell saying that all his love and care must be in his daughter:

> Had I been left
> In a son behind me, while I had been here
> He should have shifted as I did before him,
> Lived on the freeborn portion of his wit.
> But a daughter, and that an only one, O,
> We cannot be or too careful o'er, too tender;
> 'Tis such a brittle niceness, a mere cupboard of glasses,
> The least shake breaks or cracks'em.   (I. i. 2–9)

The idea that one lives *in* a son is not repeated (except by elliptic
implication) with regard to a daughter, but there is a sense of greater
emotional investment needed with girls. Yet what he really plans to do is
to marry her to a wealthy fool, Chough; he justifies this not in terms of
mastery, however, but in terms of parental care, arguing that 'fools are the
fathers / To many wise children' (lines 405–6), and telling Jane herself
that Chough will be easy to control, and that 'domination is a woman's
heaven' (II. ii. 197). Jane is already betrothed (*per verba de praesenti*) to –
and pregnant by – the bankrupt Fitzallen. She therefore has a rather more
acute case of Desdemona's 'divided duty':

> O my hard fate! But my more hard father,
> That father of my fate. A father, said I?
> What a strange paradox I run into:
> I must accuse two fathers of my fate
> And fault, a reciprocal generation.   (lines 56–60)

The sacred name of father here is put into strikingly ambiguous play:
Russell is the father given her by fate, who has brought about (fathering in
the sense of 'being responsible') her fate (in the sense of doom); Fitzallen
meanwhile is the cause (father) of her fault, and the father of her child
which represents that fault. Fatherhood is here identified with responsibility – largely for crime – and each father seems responsible not only for
his own sins and Jane's, but for the other's too. This bravura decon-
struction of the doubleness of male authority is easily enough undone in
the play's resolution, where Russell discovers his daughter's pregnancy
and palms her off as damaged goods to Fitzallen, giving him a bigger

dowry than planned. Yet neither Fitzallen nor Russell is exactly responsible here; it is Jane's braving of the consequences of her fault which
enables all this, showing that she is the one most able to take responsibility
for her fate and fault. It may depend on both men loving her, but her
bravery is central and even authoritative as neither father is. As is increasingly typical in later Jacobean drama, daughters are not the fragile vessels
their fathers make them out to be.

Indeed, they can be robustly wicked. The unnamed Father in Fletcher's
The Captain (c. 1609–12, pub. 1647) has about as big a problem as that
encountered by any dramatic father: not only is his widowed daughter
Lelia a whore, but she also falls for him (initially when he is disguised, but
his self-revelation doesn't turn her off). Such lusty widows are normally
no one's responsibility but their own – as such they posed a problem
to the patriarchal system, being anomalously authoritative women. Yet
here her father is around and is prepared to take responsibility for her,
despite him being aged and poor. Their key dialogues are lengthy and
emotionally powerful, typical of Fletcher in their overwrought but rather
compelling tensions between natural desires and social conventions. In
their first big scene, Lelia repudiates her father with breathtaking articu-
lacy, throwing over all the norms of daughterly reverence. She tells him:

> I grant you are my father; am I therefore
> Bound to consume my selfe and be a begger
> Still in relieving you? I doe not feele
> Any such mad compulsion yet within me.   (I. iii. 57–60)

What she calls 'mad compulsion' is the supposedly natural feeling to a
parent whose embers he had hoped would make 'all new againe' 'like
another nature' (lines 33, 32). The truth is that she cannot be so remade.
When he pushes his appeal to her, asking 'Did I beget this woman', she
replies with a stinging repudiation of any natural filial debt to a father:

> Nay, I know not:
> And 'till I know, I will not thanke you for't;
> How ever, he that got me had the pleasure,
> And that me thinkes, is a reward sufficient.   (lines 97–100)

The worst fears of a patriarchal system are here expressed, though in the
mouth of an outcast. Here we see the beginning of the articulate bad
woman who would dominate the later Jacobean stage. Such women may
be contained within narratives of punishment and repentance, but their
ideas are never really blotted out.

Lelia, indeed, proposes her own test of what is really *natural*. Once her father has revealed himself to avoid her seduction (and the hell to which he thinks it will lead), she mutters 'never let me live / If my lust do abate' (IV. iv. 157–8), and sets about arguing against his aghast refusal to do the deed:

> 'tis not against nature
> For us to lye together; if you have
> An arrow of the same tree with your bow,
> Is't more unnaturall to shoot it there
> Then in another?   (lines 185–9)

Of course we are meant to treat this as sophistry, but it has an appealing logic to it, based on notions of natural sympathy. Her attitude here is mainly to be taken as proof that she is beyond the pale, even the devil that her father sometimes thinks she may be; yet it also points to an only partly fearful fantasy of the absolutely free woman – this, we may infer, is what would happen if the fictions of patriarchy collapsed.

The Father can tie her up – with the aid of one of her shocked lovers who has witnessed the seduction scene – and can force her into semi-respectable marriage to one of the play's gulls; but he can have no real *answer* to her. Patriarchal authority is not really natural at all: even when tested by the incest taboo, which ought to be its tragic limit, its testing can only be resolved by comic goodwill. As such, Lelia's marriage is 'slubberd up' (V. v. 32) in a manner that is strictly equivalent to the play's other, more obviously comic marriages.[6] The play may even ask us to contemplate the idea that the titular Captain Jacamo's drunkenness, misogyny, and violence are in some ways equivalent to Lelia's sexual conduct; both are pardonable, it seems, according to generic norms. Her repentance is only really marked by her restoration of her wealth to her father's control, not by any grand speeches; the only real authority is the practical authority of wealth. The Father may be a restorative figure, but this is not due to any Prospero-like magical powers: it is clear that it is due to the generic conventions – which are more obviously fictional versions of social and material norms.

Women, in fact, have come to be more redemptively powerful than fathers. Heywood's *The Captives* (c. 1624) is a late example of a play in the mode of Shakespearean romance, in which long-lost daughters are found by their fathers. All the usual material of such plots is present: when Ashburne rescues two girls, one of them (who later turns out to be his daughter) tells him that they come to him as as a father, and he says he'll protect them 'as weare you myne owne children' (lines 1540–1).[7] But when he brings the girls home to his wife, she thinks them his whores, forcing him to insist that he is only motivated by pity and 'charity / in the remembrance off our longe lost child' (lines 2069–70). His fisherman servant then finds a chest with the proof of his daughter's identity, prompting the response:

> I that so many yeares have bin despoyld
> neclected skattered, am made vpp againe.
> repaired, and new Created.   (lines 2239–41)

This new creation and restoration of his identity is then reinforced by his brother coming to Marseilles and telling him that he is no longer in debt in England, enabling his return from exile – and the other rescued girl turns out to be this brother's daughter. Commonplace and predictable as such a plot may be, Ashburne's phrasing, in the recovery of a scattered identity, is particularly telling – he is 'made up' into wholeness by fatherhood as he can be in no other manner. It is surely significant that a *daughter* seems more able to effect this recovery of self than a son. Something in the essence of such plots seems to need daughters rather than sons. Women, it seems, can now be the grounds of one's identity, and can bring one to wholeness. If they once threatened identity – particularly in the cases of Hamlet's mother and Lear's daughters – the very recognition of their power involved in such plays may have enabled them to become a force for real good.

HONOUR AND VIRTUE

Questions of honour are increasingly central to the drama of the 1610s, yet ideas of honour are becoming more detached from any particular allegiance. An emphasis on honour at this time may suggest an effort to re-entrench the idea of the family due to anxieties about the decline of the aristocracy, based on increasing social mobility.[8] It may also relate to a sense that, in the absence of war, there was little chance of individuals gaining martial honour as an earlier generation had done. These problems naturally impinge on attitudes to paternity, as people become deeply ambivalent about deriving their sense of honour from their fathers. In Massinger and Field's *The Fatal Dowry* (c. 1618), for example, Charalois comes to court to request the burial of his father who died when imprisoned for debts incurred in military service; rather than demanding his father's body be released as of right (a line taken by his friend

Romont), he asks to be imprisoned himself for his father's debts. His motive here is not so much affection for his father, or even a strongly held sense of duty, but rather a desire to seem honourable: when the judges agree to imprison him, he says 'They haue in it confirm'd on me such glory, / As no time can take from me' (lines 252–3). Though he does express considerable grief for his father, the prime element of the emotion is a sense of injustice that his father's public services have had no reward, whereas corrupt arrivistes are thriving; much admired as he is for his 'natural' duties, these have no really personal character. Charalois' conduct so impresses the good judge Rochfort that he pays off his debts and marries him to his daughter; however, the fact that this daughter is then unfaithful makes the reward a poisoned chalice, undermining the idea of filial honour getting its due.

Rochfort, unfortunately for his son-in-law, is a doting father as much as he is an objective judge of goodness. When presented with his daughter Beaumelle's infidelity he initially gives a classic account of the unforgivable nature of wifely misconduct, saying that Charalois has given her in trust:

> All hee receiu'd from his braue Ancestors,
> Or he could leaue to his posterity? –
> His Honour, wicked woman, in whose safety
> All this lifes ioyes, and comforts were locked vp,
> Which thy lust, like a theefe hath now stolne from him.   (IV. iv. 127–31)

This prompts Charalois to kill her, but Rochfort then expresses the other side of himself, the father rather than 'Iudge onely, and friend to iustice' (line 158), insisting on her feminine weakness and the fact that she was 'my ages comfort' (line 169). His affection for his daughter (which always seems greater in plays of the period than that for sons) prevails, as Charalois says, above his 'vertue' (lines 175–6); but he also appeals to Charalois's gratitude – a sense of individual obligation that he thinks ought to compromise familial honour. Rochfort will ultimately forgive Charalois, but that does no good, for the latter is killed in vengeance for slaying Beaumelle's beau. The play must end tragically, for a man's honour is thoroughly lost in a wife's infidelity and cannot be redeemed by revenge. It is important that this honour continues to be conceived as a patrilineal resource (however abstract it might be). This emerges not only in Rochfort's condemnation of his daughter but in various urgings throughout the play of 'the great spirit of thy father' (as Romont puts it – III. i. 461–9). Charalois even kills his rival with his father's sword (IV. ii. 96). Yet this idea of the father, identified with honour, offers no more real protection than the law can. The ideal father's redemptive power is undermined by the passions associated with women and by their ability to taint one's honour.

Familial and political honour come into conflict increasingly often in later Jacobean drama, staging a debate about the nature of a son's loyalties in such plays as Fletcher's *The Loyal Subject* (c. 1618). Schematic as plays of this kind may be, they often develop and articulate passions that had been implicit in earlier plays, such as *Coriolanus*. They also enable the emergence of very explicit conflicts between fathers and sons. *The Laws of Candy* (c. 1619, almost certainly by John Ford) is premised on the most formalized of conflicts between father and son over matters of martial honour: the basic idea is that both Cassilane and his son Antinous have done well in battle, but only one can claim the triumph. The workings out of this in the first act are remarkably elegant, allowing intense conflict while keeping the son fundamentally virtuous. Before the trial to decide who will be awarded the triumph, Antinous kneels to his father because he is sensitive to 'the piety / Of filiall duty' (I. ii. 5–6), but Cassilane responds 'What, so low? canst thou finde joynts, / Yet be an Elephant?' (lines 7–9), and accuses him of ambition. His son stingingly asserts the limits of his sense of duty:

> For proofe that I acknowledge you the Author
> Of giving me my birth, I have discharg'd
> A part of my obedience.   (I. ii. 15–17)[9]

But he insists that if his father, 'Tyrant-like', wants to usurp his 'peculiar honours', which are not 'successary' from the family, he's got another thing coming (lines 20–2), and the son will be a champion for himself. The idea here of partial obedience might momentarily seem a paradox, but Antinous makes his case well by performing his obedience even as he asserts that which is his own. Even at this early point Cassilane is made to seem a little absurd: he is the uncompromising one, and his claim to be grasping thunder like Jupiter (line 14) highlights the absurdity of excessive duty to fathers, without Antinous having to say anything against him.

He goes on to do so, however, in the conditional mood and through transference:

>   as you are
> Great, and well worthy to be stiled great,
> It would betray a povertie of spirit
> In me to obstruct my fortunes, or discent,
> If I should coward-like surrender up
> The interest, which the inheritance of your vertue,
> And mine owne thriftie fate can claime in honour.   (lines 39–45)

At first blush it almost seems as if Antinous here accuses his father of poverty of spirit before he turns this on himself – but of course the identification between their honours on which his argument is based *does* imply that his non-resistance would redound, however ironically, to his father's discredit. His further argument reinforces this point:

> a father
> Heightens his reputation, where his son
> Inherits it, as when you give us life,
> Your life is not diminish'd, but renew'd
> In us, when you are dead, and we are still
> Your living images.   (lines 82–7)

This argument, like the argument about thrift above, seems to echo some sentiments of Shakespeare's *Sonnets* in making paternity not a zero-sum game – in this case even when father and son are in direct competition. The implication, of course, is that the father ought to yield to the son, even as the son honours him.

Antinous seems to redeem his filial piety, however, in a neat reversal at the end of the trial. After he has won, all he demands is that a statue honouring his father be erected in the city. Bizarrely, it may seem, Cassilane takes this as an insult; yet his doing so is indicative of the bind that an excessively honourable father finds himself in: he cannot accept anything from his son. Of course, this is in spite of the fact that he expects his son to be grateful to him. The fundamental asymmetry of this is pointed up by Candy's other law: that ingratitude is to be punished by death. This will be the central point of the play's denouement.

Antinous is unmanned by his father's curses to the point that he can't respond to the wooing of the proud Princess Erota, indicating how fundamentally destructive such curses were taken to be. Given his father's inability to accept a favour, however, it seems impossible for him to win the blessing he needs, and this accounts for his almost literal paralysis in the middle of the play. He even fails in his plans to pay off his father's mortgage. Despite this paralysis, the movement of the play becomes essentially comic. When Antinous makes his first attempt to win his father over by sending a letter, Cassilane's immediate reaction is to think the letter a challenge, comically suggesting that his wish is father to this thought (III. ii. 152–3). Father–son conflict has become automatic, even codified. When Erota reveals that she has paid off the mortgage for Antinous' sake, Cassilane, thinking this an act of ingratitude, wants his son to be executed. What might be a tragic moment, a rare though not

unique dramatic example of a father seeking the life of his son, is comic
from the first owing to the absurdity of the father's case, and stays comic
in its development. Erota calls Cassilane 'old wretch' and 'wretched old
man' (V. i. 74, 138), which matches his attempts to insult Antinous as a
bastard, and makes both seem like unmanly railing. Erota then brings
a legal case against Cassilane for *his* ingratitude, and Antinous brings one
against her too, so that all are subject to the law – all, in fact, declare
themselves guilty, so that the scene is less Mexican stand-off than
attempted mass suicide. Cassilane's daughter then throws in a charge
against the whole senate who are justices here, leaving the only unaccused
person – the Cyprian prince Philander – to sort out the whole mess.

The key point here is that at no stage does this stop being funny.
However much paternal dignity and filial loyalty are at the centre of this,
and however seriously these ideas are taken, they create a situation which
is only comic, even though the language used would in other situations be
fundamentally tragic. At the point when both Antinous and Cassilane
seem likely to be executed, we get this exchange:

> ANTINOUS.   Sir,
>   May I presume to crave a blessing from you
>   Before we part?
> CASSILANE.   Yes, such a one as Parents
>   Bestow on cursed sons.   (lines 240–3)

Both characters are stuck in the posture with which they began the play.
Such intransigence cannot help but be ridiculous. Indeed, it is put
alongside the silly pride of Erota so as to suggest that masculine values
can be as absurd as feminine vanity.[10] Just as they are trapped by the laws
of the land, the men are trapped in the rules of the comic genre, which
will give them a happy ending willy-nilly; their voices therefore lose all
their force: even a father's curse does not work.

Arbitrary laws have come to organize dramatic genres. No longer able
to rely on the sacredness of fathers, dramatic plots have come to hinge
on something more contingent. The central premise of Middleton and
Rowley's *The Old Law* (c. 1618, with some contribution from either
Heywood or Massinger) actually codifies the marginalization of fathers
we have seen in the drama of the 1610s: a law has been passed by which
all men of 80 and women of 60 must die. This delights the bad son
Simonides, but drives the good son Cleanthes to extravagant despair. The
latter's filial piety, indeed, is perhaps the most extreme example of such
virtue in Renaissance drama; only by setting such a supposedly natural

virtue against the law can it be given its fullest expression. Simonides hurries
his father off to death, but Cleanthes manages to hide his father in a
countryside lodge, covering his subterfuge by claiming his father has died
of natural causes. This stratagem prompts a doubly paradoxical scene of
filial joy: in front of the duke (and dressed in unfunereal gaudy) he
proclaims his glee at his father's death, supposedly on the basis that his
father has escaped the rigour of the new law; this glee, we know, is really
caused by saving his father; yet it might also ironize the glee at a father's
death that we have seen becoming a paradoxical proverb in the early 1600s.

Cleanthes is clearly the play's moral centre, and his long speeches leave
us in no doubt of this; his comments on Simonides' corruption of
traditional values are trenchant, and stand as a classic articulation of the
natural duties owed to parents:

> Does the kind root bleed out his livelihood
> In parent distribution to his branches,
> Adorning them with all his glorious fruits,
> Proud that his pride is seen when he's unseen?
> And must not gratitude descend again
> To comfort his old limbs in fruitless winter?   (I. i. 317–22)

If vegetative Nature is thus improvident, man must be a better example:

> Make some a pattern of thy piety,
> Lest all do turn unnaturally against thee,
> And thou be blamed for our oblivions
> And brutish reluctations.   (lines 331–4)

This brilliantly captures the tensions between nature and justice, human
nobility and selfishness that is so central to drama's representations of
fathers. It is also quietly ironic in that Cleanthes will become the pattern
of piety he desires: for the law is a trick, the parents are not being killed,
and the whole thing is designed as a test which only Cleanthes passes, thus
becoming the arbiter over his own generation. In contrast to this elegant
thinking, Cleanthes' later expressions of piety are rather over-egged: his
father is 'all my life's treasure' (IV. ii. 5), and even to be identified with
Christ as a 'man of sorrow' (line 163). He then tries to sacrifice himself
when his father is caught and hauled off to be executed, thus giving the
fullest filial proof imaginable; he later invokes the classic example of
Aeneas carrying Anchises just to hammer home his own exemplary status
(V. i. 181–90). Even when the test is revealed, he sees himself as criminal in
having disobeyed the duke; such virtue starts to go beyond the exemplary
and become an example that no one could reasonably follow.

Nonetheless, Cleanthes' final confession of disobedience to the duke raises the issue of law's tension with nature again. Simonides, acting as an unjust judge on Cleanthes, makes the telling argument that:

> there is none can be
> A good son and a bad subject, for if princes
> Be called the peoples' fathers, then the subjects
> Are all his sons, and he that flouts the prince
> Doth disobey his father; there you're gone. (V. i. 197–201)

The phrase 'be called' here perhaps brings in an element of scepticism about the connection between the two that may also be hinted at in the final revelation that the executioner is called Cratilus; the name invokes Plato's dialogue, which expresses scepticism about the natural connection of words and their referents. It may also remind us of the arbitrary authority exercised by the duke, first in producing the law, then in overturning it.

Be that as it may, it doesn't resolve the tension between the obedience of a son and that of a subject, nor does it resolve the fact that the vast majority of people do want rid of the old men. As the law itself (I. i. 139–63) puts it, the old are no use to the commonwealth, and Cleanthes' joy in his father seems like an attempt to over-protest the value of their persistence. In a proliferation of subplots, meanwhile, we see a wife and a collection of husbands delight in the prospect of doing away with their ageing spouses. This may point up Cleanthes' virtue, but it also blurs the play's focus, while allowing for some very funny satirical moments. So, not only does the play's central premise show disrespect for patriarchs, but its comic or satirical structure dissipates the impact of that disrespect. In the play's twist, the fathers lose their patient dignity (they've been enjoying themselves while pretending to be dead), and all that dignity ends up focussed on Cleanthes. Even the most filial of sons subtly diminishes paternal importance.

In Middleton and Webster's *Anything for a Quiet Life* (1621), Young Cressingham, who has been disinherited at the insistence of his new stepmother, imitates Hamlet's discourse with his mother, and tells his father that he wants 'to turn your eyes into your own bosom' (V. i. 152–3), yet it is his stepmother whom he ultimately converts (rather abruptly and unconvincingly). This means that his father can return to his high-status ways (wearing rich clothing) and has to concede 'I am my son's child, sir; he knows of me / More than I do myself' (V. ii. 239–40). The son, throughout this play, is clearly

the bearer of familial identity: when he expostulates to his father
against selling their lands, he says:

> 'Tis a strange precedent this,
> To see an obedient son labouring good counsel
> To the father! But know, sir, that the spirits
> Of my great-grandfather and your father moves
> At this present in me.   (IV. i. 92–5)

This may be merely a pious formula designed to soften the giving of advice,
yet the language points to a transcendent masculine identity that is not
borne by any one individual. We might expect a plural verb to agree with
spirits, but the singular 'moves' (though not wholly irregular at the time)
fixes a unitary identity. He reminds his father of grandparents' warning him
'On your deathbed' not to waste resources (line 96): the mention of *your*
rather than *their* deathbed reminds us forcibly of the idea that this family
has only one place of life and death, which is at present being alienated to
Cressingham's wife. The paradox of paternity is particularly neatly managed here – one's full being is confirmed by fatherhood, yet that being
resides more in the son than the father himself. However, it is significant
that Young Cressingham still signs away his patrimony, because his father
charges him on his blessing to do so (lines 194–5). The blessing remains the
key bond between father and son – more important than any land or sense
of identity, or anything that the son can speak of.

Abstract notions of honour enable increasing defiance on the part of
sons. The anonymous *The Costly Whore* (c. 1620, pub. 1633) contrives
humiliations for a father which go beyond almost anything seen in tragedy,
but the fact that it is based on some strangely arbitrary premises pushes it
into its declared genre as 'Comicall Historie'. The duke of Saxony, who has
a son and a daughter, comes to inherit Meath (i.e. Metz), where his brother
the archbishop has been eaten by rats; there his son finds a glove, with
which the duke falls in love. The play's other plot involves the love intrigues
of this duke's daughter, but these seem dignified compared to the duke's
own pursuit of the titular whore who owns the glove, and put a peculiar
spin on the father's authority in that main love-plot.

The duke decides to marry the courtesan Valentia, but his son
Frederick firmly opposes this, draws his sword, and leads a rebellion.
Nowhere before in the drama of the period does anyone other than a Muslim
(or Mordred in *The Misfortunes of Arthur*) so firmly oppose his father;
however, he is still guided by a Christian's instinctive scruples, for when he
meets his father in battle, he cannot raise his weapon against him:

FREDERICK. My naturall father in my blood I feele,
    Passion more powerfull then that conquering steele.
DUKE. Why dost thou pause base boy thy Soveraigne's come,
    To inter the life *I* gave thee, in this tombe.
FREDERICK. My father, oh my father: nature be still,
    That I may have my fame or he his will.   (E3^{r-v})[11]

The twin imperatives here are based on the fact that Frederick is fighting for the family honour against the individual who is at present the bearer of that honour; natural instinct, though, is treated as more powerful than Frederick's concern for the family's fame.

The battle continues, without father and son directly fighting, and Frederick captures Valentia. There then ensues one of the most extraordinary scenes in English Renaissance drama: the duke kneels to his son and begs for the return of his wife; he calls himself 'vassaile-like', laying aside his authority, and even his flattering brother tells him 'You do abase your honour to intreate' (F1^r). This, says Frederick 'appals my blood', but he does not relent until his father makes a curious appeal to the fact that the son was the one who found the glove, perhaps suggesting at some level an appeal to their mutual responsibility for action whether good or bad, based on identification, and indicating that the duke's prodigality has been a mere reversal of normative narratives of a prodigal son.

The duke soon reneges on his promised pardon, condemning his son to death. He also condemns his daughter Euphrata, who has married her base-born beloved, on the basis that 'My father married to a Concabine, / Then hee will pardon though *I* marry thee' (E2^v). What really incenses her father is her direct statement that ''Twas base in you to wed a Curtizan.' Her defiance, she says, is proof that she is 'no bastard', as she resembles her brother (F4^r); this suggests that Frederick has taken on the proper role of the father. Nowhere else, not even in *Lear*, is there such a reversal of authority.

Indeed, despite its happy ending, the play does overturn authority: after various tragicomic twists (including Valentia offering herself to Frederick), the youngsters survive their father's murderous intentions. He, of course, as soon as he thinks his children dead, is penitent, saying he is 'a tyrant, doe not call me father' (H1^r), as if the two roles were incompatible; he then turns on Valentia. Yet she, when they turn out to be alive, turns on him, claiming that his harsh words have constituted a divorce. He finds himself having to get his children to appeal to Valentia, and when this does not avail, he gives over 'My selfe my Dukedom, and my crowne' to her (H3^r). The happy ending only leads to a second abasement: Valentia hands the dukedom over to Frederick, and insists that she and her penitent husband must go into monastic orders. The absolute supersession of the father here is powerfully contrived – but one must notice that it is not the son who personally effects it. In the end, the complicated processes of preserving a family's honour need to work *through* the son rather than the father, but must still be mediated, usually through women.

When a father takes it upon himself to preserve the familial honour, it seems that it can only be tragic. The influence of *The Spanish Tragedy* on masculine codes of honour is still being felt in 1625, when William Sampson's *The Vow-Breaker* gives us a scene very reminiscent of Hieronimo finding Horatio's body.[12] The crucial difference here is that the boy, Young Bateman, has committed suicide – his hanging from a tree may therefore prompt lamentation from his father, but not revenge, which he says heaven must take. The suicide is the result of the infidelity of Young Bateman's fiancée Anne Boote, her father having persuaded her to break her troth and marry a wealthier man. From the first, the fathers' conflict is treated as the cause of the problem, Anne justifying her infidelity by saying 'when I saw how disproportionable / Our jarring fathers were! I then began / To alienate all love' (c4^r).[13] She means not only that the fathers didn't get on, but that they were of different, disproportionate social status. This may supply another reason why the lower-status Old Bateman cannot get revenge; he is brought to the humiliating position of bringing legal action for breach of promise, but his relative poverty makes him powerless in this regard too.

Old Bateman's reaction to finding his son's body is less powerful than Hieronimo's, but he nonetheless curses the Boote family: 'Curs'd be thy ground, and curs'd be all trees / That brings forth such abortive fruit as this' (e3^r). The parallel with Hieronimo and his wife is clear (see Chapter 2, above). However, he also says to Anna:

> I will not curse thee, t' was my boyes request
> Such deedes as these sinke not in oblivion,
> The justnes of my cause I leave to Heaven. (e3^v)

He even wishes her to be a happier mother than he has been as a father; and Anne, it turns out, is pregnant by her husband, but she is so haunted by Young Bateman's ghost (which seems a figment of her maddened conscience, as no one else can see it) that she seems likely to lose the child: she says, in words that clearly echo Old Bateman's general curse on her father's ground, 'T'will be abortiue' (g1^v); at this, Old Bateman takes pity and promises her 'comfortable cordialls', causing her to say 'Be you my counsellour, and father too' (G2ʳ). An ironic paternal transposition has taken place, through the agency of the son's ghost – or at least his memory.

Yet this does not avert tragedy. After her child is born, the ghost comes to take Anne away, making good on an earlier promise that he'll have her alive or dead. The child survives, but the primary feeling is grief: Old Boote and Old Bateman both lament their children; the former has his daughter's body to grieve over, whereas the latter has a picture of his son (which he had earlier, Hamlet-like, brought on to stir Anne's conscience even as she was looking at the invisible ghost).[14] The fathers continue to quarrel here – this time over whose grief is the greater, as well as over Old Boote's original act of bad faith. Here, for once, fathers are both initiators of and reactors to tragedy. Some forgiveness – based on a common woe – does emerge: as such, the play's end may resemble that of *Romeo and Juliet*. Yet it does seem even darker than Shakespeare's conclusion, Old Bateman saying:

> Our angers have like tapers spent themselves,
> And onely lighted others, and not us.
> Striving like great men for supremacy!
> We have confounded one anothers goodnes.   (H4ʳ)

The fathers, having confounded one another, now compound as friends, left only to write the tragedy 'Of oure poore children'. Here is the condition of paternity – full men trying to be great make only tragedies for others as in *Macbeth*. Nothing really is learned. Concern for familial status and honour means that one loses one's family.

POLITICS

Other issues also start to attenuate the human, emotional side of drama in the later Jacobean period. Political controversies and religious tensions (not always easy to separate) increasingly undermined reverence for the Jacobean regime in the 1610s, and that undoubtedly had an impact on dramatic representations of fathers. In particular, James's failure to intervene on his daughter's behalf at the beginning of what would become the Thirty Years War raised questions of national honour as well as of the value of his patriarchal power. More generally, other forms of allegiance than the purely familial are brought into play in the drama of the period.

Politics are central to *The Hector of Germany, or The Palsgrave*
(1613, by W. Smith), which curiously weaves a father–son rivalry plot
into its main plot, a political pseudo-history which anticipates later
campaigns for English intervention on behalf of the Elector Palatine.
The play was written in celebration of Princess Elizabeth's marriage,
and imagines the kind of military alliance in favour of European
protestantism that James was to avoid five years later. The main plot
sees Edward III intervene successfully in German wars despite the death
of his son the Black Prince, mention of whom clearly touches on regret
about the death of Prince Henry. Edward can nevertheless console
himself that:

> Though the *Blacke Prince* be dead, so many sonnes
> I haue left to gouerne, which marres their rule.
> *Edward* himselfe has left a hopefull heyre,
> The Princely *Richard* to inherit it.   (E2ᵛ)[15]

Of course James I had only one other surviving son, and Prince Henry
had not lived long enough to produce a son of his own. There may be an
implication that, had the Stuart monarchy felt so dynastically secure, the
king might have been bolder in his foreign policy. Within such a frame-
work the tensions of the father–son comic plot take on extra meanings,
particularly as they can only be resolved by royal intervention.

As is increasingly common in Jacobean comic plots, Old Fitzwaters
and his son both want to marry the same woman, Floramell. Young
Fitzwaters's defiance, however, is more assertive than is usual, founded
on seemingly unshakable principles:

> I as little estimate a Father
> In these Pathaires, as he esteemes my griefe.
> There's no preoritie in loues high Court
> Graunted vnto the Father 'fore the Sonne;
> But like the purest gouernment of all,
> Every mans minde is his owne Monarchy:
> Where reason nere set foote to make a law,
> Shall common sense keepe one, that were absurd.   (B4ᵛ)

Passion is given primacy here ('pathaires' meaning passionate outbursts),
overturning rationality and natural duty (which is perhaps implied
in 'common sense' – the father–son common interest). The father's
position is just as passionately intransigent; he echoes Ben Jonson's
additions to *The Spanish Tragedy* and D'Amville's sentiments in *The
Atheist's Tragedy*.

What is a sonne?
The effect of a sweete minute, he shall dye,
Being my pleasure to effect my pleasure. (B3^{r-v})

The metonymic identification of the son with the father's sexual pleasure goes further than Jonson or Tourneur, however, implying that the bond which had once been taken as the model of consonance between rationality and natural duty is really only the site of uncontrolled passion.

Generic norms, as well as the preference of Floramell, mean that we are clearly intended to side with the son rather than the father here, yet the normal tendency to exonerate the son from any unfilial feelings is laid aside. Young Fitzwaters is quite prepared to kill his father in self-defence, even if he won't strike the first blow. Convention is followed insofar as the son does go into exile at the threat of his father's curse, but once he has accepted this deal he fears that his suffering without his beloved will be such that he will commit suicide: 'And thats a murther worse than paracide' (CI^{v}). The clear implication of this is that the self is to be preferred to the father, and he saves himself by eloping with Floramell anyway. Filial respect is presented as at best an inconvenient superstition, about which Young Fitzwater exhibits few scruples.

In fact, the son has the law on his side, the bishop's witness of his precontract ultimately providing a resolution. Yet this has never been in dispute – it is a fact mentioned several times early in the play. The play's middle teases us with the possibility of a more graceful and romantic solution as the son is exiled and stranded on a rock in the ocean before coming to the king's aid in war; his appeal to the king on the basis of his service, however, is neutralized by similar services on his father's part. The king only intervenes on a strictly legalistic basis, not on the basis of romantic heroism. Law rather than regal grace must overcome the passions of the father–son bond in this play. The effect of this is to detach good kingship from the tangled human emotions involved in fatherhood.

The exact political implications of this are not quite clear, but the basic thrust is: James must act as a good king entirely on the basis of rationality; he is not being appealed to as a father. Emotional arguments are laid aside, and James is asked to take a bolder policy, as Edward does in support of the titular Palsgrave, on the basis of the goodness of that individual. It is as if James, like Edward, is not quite so complete a father after the death of his elder son. If this is the case, we can see a key reason for the idea of paternity losing some of its combined political and emotional force after Prince Henry's death.

Sons take on redemptive roles in such contexts. *The Noble Spanish Soldier* (c. 1622, pub. 1634, probably by Dekker)[16] focuses on a murderous father, the king of Spain: though precontracted to the noblewoman Onælia, he has illegitimately married a Florentine princess, and therefore decides to do away with his true wife and their son. His motive for wanting rid of his son, despite having no children by his supposed queen, is a clear statement of the selfishness inherent in a desiring father: 'that Cocke / Will have (I feare) sharpe spurres, if he crow after / Him that trod for him' (I. i. 39–41). Rivalry with a son is almost taken for granted.

A faction builds to protect Onælia and her son Sebastian, including her uncle Medina and Baltazar, the titular noble soldier; they even bind the son into this group, though it would seem to entail filial rebellion, a problem that is then neatly negotiated, Medina asking Sebastian:

> what will you doe to him
> That hurts your mother?
> SEBASTIAN. The King my father shall kill him I trow.
> DÆNIA. But, sweet Coosen, the King loves not your mother.
> SEBASTIAN. I'le make him love her when I am a King.   (III. ii. 119–27)

The young boy's blend of precocity and naivety means that he is not wholly rebellious, but of course what he is saying is at least passively so – for him to be a king he would have to usurp his father; yet the boy's confusion of identities, not clearly seeing that king and father are the same thing, is founded on the king's own self-alienation, for what the boy can't conceive is that his mother's enemy and his father are the same man. The tension is thus displaced onto the king, who is acting tyrannically, and therefore rebelling against himself (an idea that gathered force in resistance theory, particularly during the civil wars).

After the king's various plots to kill his son and Onælia are thwarted – though the king at least thinks Sebastian dead – the king is killed, ironically at the hands of his new pseudo-queen. Yet this tragic death is made redemptive by Baltazar bringing Sebastian on in a friar's costume, bringing this splendid recognition scene as the king dies of poison:

> SEBASTIAN.   Haile my good Sonne
>   I come to be thy ghostly Father.
> KING.   Ha?
>   My child! 'tis my *Sebastian*, or some spirit
>   Sent in his shape to fright me.
> BALTAZAR. 'Tis no goblin, Sir, feele; your owne fleshe and blood,
>   and much younger than you tho he be bald, and cals you son;
>   had I bin as ready to ha cut his sheeps throat, as you were to

send him to the shambles, he had bleated no more; there's lesse
chalke upon your score of sinnes by these round o'es.
KING. O my dul soule looke up, thou art somewhat lighter.
Noble *Medina*, see *Sebastian* lives;
Onælia cease to weepe, *Sebastian* lives;
Fetch me my Crowne: my sweetest pretty Fryer,
Can my hands doo't, I'le raise thee one step higher:
Th' ast beene in heavens house all this while sweet boy?   (V. iv. 95–109)

The idea of son as father is very powerfully handled here: when the father
is not himself, the son becomes the father, a figuration that expresses the
paradoxical way in which fatherhood can and perhaps must be alienated
from the father himself. The light allusion to the story of Abraham and
Isaac makes this incident into a redemptive rather than a tragic moment,
and it is significant that no one else dies, not even the wicked queen;[17] a
new covenant seems to be made, but the father must be sacrificed to it.

However, in the following year's *The Welsh Embassador* (also in large
part at least by Dekker), a very similar situation has a much happier
outcome. Here, in a play that is almost a companion piece to *The Noble
Spanish Soldier*, we see King Athelstane try to put away his contracted
bride Armante (who has also had a son by him) in favour of a new love,
Carintha, wife of the supposedly dead Penda. Carintha herself is reluctant
to marry the king, but temporizes with him in order to redeem him.
Though she and various other virtuous characters are crucial to enabling
the play's happy comedic ending, it is the king's son who is crucial to
redeeming him, this time without the father having to die.

From his first appearance the precocious young prince has complete
confidence in the paternal bond, saying 'My father? / What brauer wings
can ore an eaglett spred / Then the old eagles?' (III. i. 75–6). This confidence
that his father will not hurt him turns out to be well founded. The prince
comes to beg a blessing from his father, after his mother has apparently
withdrawn her claims by going into a nunnery; this is successful, but then
Carintha (who is in on the plot to reform the king) insists that the boy must
be removed, prompting an extraordinary scene of paternal/filial testing. The
prince is unafraid when he is called to his father's side, and says:

> Ile stand you like a little harmelesse lambe,
> I will not cry out neither.
> KING.   It has beene tould mee,
> That thou art like mee boy.
> PRINCE.   My grand sir swore
> My chin and nose weare yours, and my good mother

Said I was but your picture.
KING.   She was deceaud,
   For thou art fairer far.
PRINCE.   Thats cause I am
   But yett a child, and if you doe not lay mee
   In some vntimely pitt hole ere I grow
   To mans estate, I shalbee as you are.
KING. A kinge thou meanest?
PRINCE.   Noe I meane a man
   That shalbee iust like you.
KING. Lett me looke on thee.
PRINCE.   Praye doe.
KING.   Heeres a white forehead
   Of inocence whose allabaster sweetnes
   Rebates my cruelties.   (V. i. 136–49)

The dialogue is worthy of Shakespeare: again delicately alluding to
Abraham and Isaac, Dekker manages to pull off the most redemptive
father–son recognition in the canon of Renaissance drama, in which the
boy is allowed to judge his father. The Christian connotations here are
clear: the son is to redeem all. The play can end more happily than *The
Noble Spanish Soldier* because a new dispensation is in place.

In no pair of plays, then, can we so clearly see an articulated difference
between tragic and comic modes. But what makes that difference? It may
simply be the fact that *The Welsh Embassador* takes place in England: it
may be a pre-protestant England, but there may still be a nationalistic
sense that England's religious and therefore moral dispensation is different
from catholic Spain's.[18] England is not to be the site of tragedy, and
English fathers must not die, however much they may have to be abased
or disrespected as villainous. The political import of the play may be that
King James's son can save his father's honour. As the 1620s go on, then,
there is a sense of a new political hope around the corner: anticipating the
succession of Charles puts patriarchal power into abeyance, making the
king-father something of a lame duck at best.

The premise of the anonymous *Swetnam the Woman Hater* (pub. 1620)
is rather similar to that of Middleton's *Phoenix*, in that the heir to the
throne returns to his father's court in order to observe the *mores* of his
future realm. The later play makes less of this, but like its predecessor it
is a fairly transparent reflection of contemporary English politics. King
Atticus of Sicily, at the beginning of the play, has lost his elder son, just as
James I had lost his; he also has a younger son and a daughter, again like
James, and the play focusses on them. The younger son Lorenzo, who

would now be the heir, is supposed dead or captive (having fought nobly at the battle of Lepanto);[19] clearly, this doesn't reflect anything specific about James's new heir apparent Prince Charles, except in that it flatteringly romanticizes him. The daughter, Leonida, cannot inherit in her own right, but marriage to her, in Lorenzo's default, will bring the throne; this is just as clearly not an exact parallel to the situation of James's daughter Elizabeth, but her plot becomes nonetheless a striking rebuke to James for not intervening on her behalf, and ends with a powerful assertion of the monarch's paternal duties.

Atticus is tricked into having his daughter executed, prompting the queen into a tirade against her husband, whom she calls a tyrant, demanding of him the whereabouts of their children:

> And would to God I were intomb'd with them,
> Emptie of substance. Curse of Soueraigntie,
> That feed'st thy fancie with deluding hopes
> Of fickle shadowes (H4^r)[20]

Her repetitive rebuke seems to suggest that the king's injustice to his daughter has deprived him of his sons – albeit retroactively. The loss of hope, which is turned to mere shadow (one may be reminded of Henry IV's 'shadow of succession'), is an apt punishment for such a king. The play's moral is fairly clear in its implications for James: he has risked the hopes of his dynasty by failing to act on behalf of his daughter and her husband. Fortunately, Atticus is reformable: when presented with a pageant, he repents of his injustice. The import seems to be that James may be similarly persuaded by this play.

And that, of course, is enough, for the play is a tragicomedy: neither Leonida nor her beloved Lisander is really dead. Both, significantly, have been preserved by the disguised Lorenzo. Atticus' reflection on this fact concludes the play happily: 'Was euer Father happier in a Sonne, / Or euer Kingdome had more hopefull Prince?' (L1^r). The implication of this may be that Charles, like Lorenzo, can act to reform his father. Such looking to the next generation for the safety of the protestant cause, of course, marginalizes James even as it rather boldly tries to criticize him into action. If there is to be any credit for bold action, it will be given to the next generation.

UNCERTAINTY

The examples of *Henry VIII*, plays which give women authority, and plays which centre on familial honour and politics demonstrate that paternity has now become something negotiable, something dependent on speech acts and socially founded systems of meaning, and that it is merely one value among many. Late Jacobean drama, particularly tragicomedy, accepts many of the problems with patriarchal authority, and tries to solve them in a bewildering and highly imaginative variety of ways, using frequently bizarre plots to entrench new codes of meaning. Some of these solutions, as we have seen, involve putting paternity up against royal power, religion, the sexual authority of women, and codes of martial honour. Often, the attempt to shore up paternal dignity has contrary and destructive effects, leading to new ways of accepting paternal limitation. Perhaps underlying all of this we also see real doubt about paternity emerging in ways that had only been expressed in very partial or conditional terms in earlier Jacobean drama. Though we saw some recognition of the uncertainty of paternity in early Jacobean plays, it is only in later drama that people accept it.

The idea that a man might accept another man's children as his own when a wife or mistress is unfaithful, and that he might even be well regarded for doing so, takes a long while to emerge, but becomes increasingly available in later Jacobean drama. Its first occurrence is in a decidedly absurd context: in *The Nice Valour* (c. 1615, printed in the Beaumont and Fletcher Folio of 1647, and now taken as mostly Middleton's), the mad 'Passionate Lord' tells his supposed mistress (really the First Lord, whom he has mistaken for a woman) 'Lady, I'll father it, / Whoe'er begot it; 'tis the course of greatnesse' (I. i. 242–3).[21] Shamont responds with the exclamation 'How virtue groanes at this?' (line 244), but his notion of manly virtue is shown throughout the play to be too 'nice' or pedantic.

In Middleton's *A Chaste Maid in Cheapside* (1613) uncertainty of paternity is rife, but is ultimately treated quite cheerfully. In this play, Allwit is complacent about his family being maintained by Sir Walter Whorehound, who has fathered Allwit's children, soliloquizing with weak self-congratulation:

> I pay for none at all; yet fools think's mine;
> I have the name, and in his gold I shine;
> And where some merchants would in soul kiss hell
> To buy a paradise for their wives, and dye
> Their conscience in the bloods of prodigal heirs
> To deck their night-piece, yet all this being done,
> Eaten with jealousy to the inmost bone –
> As what affliction nature more constrains

> Than feed the wife plump for another's veins? –
> These torments stand I freed of; I am as clear
> From jealousy of a wife as from the charge.   (I. ii. 40–50)

His understanding of jealousy and his vigorous disavowal of the feeling does perhaps imply that his anxiety is merely suppressed for advantage, and he does go on to abuse 'his' sons as 'villain' and 'bastard' (lines 111–12). The proud sense of his false appearance to the world invites us to condemn him or at least find him ridiculous, but in the end he is 'clear', his identity not being fundamentally undermined by being a wittol. His cuckolder Whorehound is the play's true villain, and he is the one who is punished. Whorehound's reliance on an inheritance from the Kixes – who are infertile – as well as on marrying Moll Yellowhammer are hopes in which he has his due come-uppance: the virtuous Touchwood Junior gets to marry Moll (who loves him), and Touchwood Senior hoists Whorehound with his own petard by impregnating Lady Kix. The fact that Whorehound's punishment comes by the same means he has been using himself shows that dubious paternity is not a tragic matter, but one that enables happy resolutions.

Touchwood Senior, meanwhile, is a figure of excessive fertility; he complains to his wife that:

> our desires
> Are both too fruitful for our barren fortunes.
> How adverse runs the destiny of some creatures:
> Some only can get riches and no children,
> We can only get children and no riches!   (II. i. 8–12)

His wife may be faithful to him, but every time he is unfaithful to her, he begets a bastard (he's managed to produce seven this year). The transformation of this ludicrous generativity into a plot conclusion which is to his family's advantage allows a restoration of balance to the unfair situation he describes, for he earns £400 for his sexual services to a childless couple, the Kixes. This runs against the simplistic view of one of the Puritans at the Christening of Allwit's / Whorehound's child: 'Children are blessings, if they be got with zeal / By the brethren, as I have five at home' (III. ii. 34–5). An economic and balanced approach is seen as better than the ideologically driven fertility of the Puritans, which is subtly undermined by the joking hint here that the brethren may have fathered children communally. Sir Oliver Kix, when his wife is with child, declares, 'I am a man for ever!' (V. iii. 1); this resonant phrase, full of irony as it is in this case, suggests the way in which masculine identity is dependent on paternity, relating a man to a sense of eternity both earthly and even heavenly. It also interestingly echoes the sentiments of Henry VIII in Shakespeare and Fletcher's play. The fact that this is based on self-deception (he was drunk at the time the deal with Touchwood Senior was made, and it is not at all clear that he understood the exact terms) only gives piquancy to this crowing. Who knows? the child just might be his. He has the parish bells rung, and a bonfire lit for good measure – who would begrudge him this?

In Webster and Rowley's *A Cure for a Cuckold* (c. 1624), the title plot, which may be called a subplot, counterpoints a highly romantic main plot which focusses on the exaggeratedly honour-based feelings of aristocrats;[22] this subplot points by contrast to basic or natural feeling in the lower classes, but that natural feeling is not centred on reliable paternity. Compass, a sailor who has been thought lost at sea, returns to his wife and finds that she has had a child by another man; when some boys tell him that the child is three months old, although he has been away four years, he splendidly informs them 'here with us at Blackwall, our children come uncertainly, as the wind serves. Sometimes here we are supposed to be away three or four year together; 'tis nothing so: we are at home and gone again, when nobody knows on't' (II. iii. 50–3).[23] He is content to join the 'company' of 'horners' (line 78), producing his own cheerful fictions about paternity; when his own life at sea has been so uncertain, he has no need to be irritably jealous of uncertain paternity. His wife feels guilty, but he splendidly shrugs this off:

URSE. Alas, husband.
COMPASS. A lass or a lad, wench? I should be glad of both. I did
    look for a pair of Compasses before this day.
URSE. And you from home?
COMPASS. I from home? Why, though I be from home, and other
    of our neighbours from home, it is not fit all should be from
    home, so the town might be left desolate.   (lines 100–6)

The joke here surely alludes to Donne's image of the compass as connecting husband and wife in his great poem of marital separation 'A Valediction: Forbidding Mourning',[24] but Donne's image of union is transformed into cheerful and practical fiction. He sees her as having 'laboured' for him in his absence as he has for her, and views a son as an asset regardless of his own biological input. Remarrying her to legitimize his son becomes, in the terms of this plot, a way of getting one over the cuckold-maker Franckford, who wants to make his 'by-blow' with Urse his heir (I. i. 156); the effect of Compass's acceptance of the child is to make Franckford the cuckold, himself the cuckoo. He splendidly defeats Franckford's attempts to get control of the child, telling him, 'you'll but lose your labour; get as many children as you can, you shall keep none of them' (III. ii. 61–2). Compass's perspective is clearly meant to be unusual, even slightly crack-brained, but the comedy – and these are some of the funniest scenes in Jacobean drama – works because there is something magnificently sane in completely turning around perhaps the most fundamental male anxiety. Here it is accomplished without the vanity of Sir Oliver Kix or Allwit in *A Chaste Maid in Cheapside* (see above). As M. C. Bradbrook notes, Compass is fundamentally a character of 'good sense' – a rarity indeed in the drama.[25] If, as evolutionary psychology tells us, desire for certain paternity is a central drive of male nature, it is all the more wonderful that one can joke one's way out of it. He offers the firmest possible contrast to insistently masculine characters such as the murderous father in *A Yorkshire Tragedy* (1605–8, probably by Middleton), whose insistent fears of 'beggary' are such that he kills two of his three sons, thinking his position is almost heroic – one of 'glory', as he says (vi. 30); such action is an extended suicide through pride that proves his masculinity, and therefore, paradoxically, his paternity. *A Cure for a Cuckold* denies the value of such masculine pride and proof. Franckford insists that he will prove by law that the male is 'the worthier gender' (line 97), implying that paternity is the fundamental basis of all law, but he fails. Compass simply defuses the central issue of the war between the sexes by arguing 'Is not the earth our mother?' (IV. i. 171–2); women are the true ground of nature, and men need to accept this. He plans to blot out the stain of cuckoldry by wooing his wife afresh: 'I will go drink myself dead for an hour; then, when I awake again, I am a fresh new man, and so I go a-wooing' (lines 227–9); this redemption is all that is needed to wash away the sins of the world as founded in problems of paternity.

Whereas *A Chaste Maid in Cheapside* and *A Cure for a Cuckold* present uncertain paternity as enabling happy endings, other plays which deal with higher-caste characters are more anguished, but can still come to happy endings. One of the most tortuous examples of doubt as to paternity comes in Middleton and Rowley's *A Fair Quarrel*, but the complication of the feelings involved here is very revealing. The Captain gets into an argument with his Colonel about their relative merits, during which the Colonel calls his subordinate a son of a whore; such an insult must of course lead to a duel, but the Captain is a man of such punctilious honour that he decides he must check with his mother about the veracity of the charge; his mother initially sets his mind at ease (slapping him for even asking), but when she discovers that her son will therefore run a risk of being killed, she changes tack and slanders her own sexual honour, thus making her son withdraw from the quarrel (until the Colonel calls him a coward, giving him a new and undeniable cause for combat, which the Captain duly wins). In the end, of course, the Captain's mother affirms her sexual honesty, re-securing her son's identity. Convoluted as all this is, the emotional logic involved is powerful: pondering the initial insult, the Captain says 'who lives / That can assure the truth of his conception / More than a mother's carriage makes it hopeful?' (II. i. 14–16) – he immediately makes the leap from the stain on his mother's name to the idea of illegitimacy, as do all his friends (e.g. III. i. 119); a mother's behaviour ('carriage') is the only pointer to hope about identity, a point that Hamlet struggled to accept. Nonetheless, the upshot of the plot is to affirm identity, not least in the Colonel's withdrawal of the insult. That withdrawal comes because the Captain *proves* himself in combat, significantly fighting over the issue of cowardice. The logic of honour is clear: if you're not a coward, then you must be your father's son. Biological paternity seems less important than one's own possession of honour, about which there can be no doubt. It is significant that the father is dead here: he is not even a ghostly presence. The individual secures his own identity by fighting. Patrilineal identity has become much more notional by the mid-Jacobean period, something that one can acquire by one's own efforts.

Webster's *The Devil's Law Case* (c. 1617) centres in a different way on a mother's accusation of her son's bastardy, perhaps with some ironic echoes of *King John* and *The Troublesome Reign* (see Chapter 3, above). Such an accusation seems only dramatically possible after the legal father is dead, but in this case the accusation is false and malicious. The play's other plots also turn on issues of paternity, in ways that suggest a multi-pronged attack on its centrality. Leonora's claim that Romelio is not her husband's son fails due to the presence at court, disguised, of Crispiano, who is able to refute her claim to have slept with him. Though this goes some way to redeeming the villainous Romelio, his acceptance of the general uncertainty of paternity resonates:

> why do I
> Take bastardy so distastefully, when i' th' world
> A many things that are essential parts
> Of greatness are but by-slips, and are fathered
> On the wrong parties;
> Preferment in the world a many times
> Basely begotten?   (IV. ii. 302–8)[26]

This generalization from uncertain paternity to a sense of bastardy in all supposedly essential things suggests that paternity has become a touchstone for wider cultural anxieties; but that means that it is a very abstract notion, detached from individual fathers. The court may be able to negotiate a version of what has gone on in the play, but it doesn't redeem this larger anxiety; there is no Jupiter, as there was in *Cymbeline*, to refute the view that we are all bastards.

This resonates through the other plots. Romelio has his sister cast doubt on the paternity of her child in order to get an inheritance, causing huge legal complication which demonstrates the power of feminine speech; there is no unchallengeable truth about paternity. A third plot-line is still more puzzling, if that were possible, because it is so truncated. Crispiano has returned home in disguise after nearly forty years in the West Indies, and it seems at first that this is to be a belated example of a prodigal plot, but his main role is to deny fathering Romelio; however, there is no great father–son recognition when he reveals himself in the presence of his real son Julio. Early in the play, when Julio was told of his father's death he neither grieved nor rejoiced excessively, and a similar moderation obtains when he sees his father alive:

CRISPIANO. Sirrah, stand you aside;
    I will talk with you hereafter.
JULIO. I never could away with after-reckonings.   (IV. ii. 508–10)

The whole plot is a damp squib, rather as the idea of paternity seems to have become. Recognition, once the most powerful of dramatic moments, has been downgraded to the idea of 'after-reckoning', a pointless kind of score-keeping. When all notions of essential identity have become contingent, plays must tend to the tragicomic – tragedy, for a while at least, seems impossible.

The Honest Lawyer (pub. 1616, by S. S.) begins with the fullest articulation to date of the uncertainties that undermine the supposed primacy of paternal authority. Vaster's opening soliloquy plunges *in medias res* of the paranoid jealousy that leads him to abandon the role of husband and father:

A Cuckold? why now 'tis a common name,
As the shee-Gossips are that give it vs.
Why doth it not deriue, and spread it selfe,
To all the generations we produce?
Why should not euery child of mine be call'd
Cuckold, as well as *Vaster*? Woman, woman!

> Thou sad undoer of the fairest building,
> That euer earth bragg'd to be pauement to.
> Man, man; the pride of heauens creation,
> Abstract of Nature, that in his small volume
> Containes the whole worlds Text, and heauens impression:
> His Makers Image, Angels mate, Earths great wonder;
> Made to guide all, by woman is brought under.   (A3ʳ)[27]

The speech resembles several of Hamlet's, but the challenge to male identity has become so great that tragic dignity is not possible. Standard Humanist praises of man's centrality are undermined here in principle by male dependence on women for continuity. All men are 'deform'd' into cuckolds by the uncertainty of sexual reproduction. Yet in fact Vaster's wife is not unfaithful: it is rather the undermining of his prosperity by the usurer Gripe that really prompts Vaster's despair. Having lost his status due to that usurer, Vaster displaces his anxiety at identity-loss onto his wife, whom he sells into prostitution. His son Robert tries to speak up for his mother, to no avail except to prompt an oddly paradoxical example of attempted male solidarity between father and son:

> if I thought thou wouldst marry, I would unblesse thee, as I haue
>   disinherited thee already: Get bastards, as I would ha' got thee.
>   A woman may serue to lye withal: none good enough to marry.
> ROBERT. Oh were you not my father, I would let
>   This passion out of your impostum'd heart.   (A3ᵛ)

The father doesn't want his son to be a cuckold as he imagines himself, suggesting that he still has some stake in his son, yet the fact that the father is uncertain of his paternity makes him disinherit him (without, notably, removing his blessing), an attitude that prompts the son to want to fight his father for half-denying his paternity, yet because it's only a half-denial, he is constrained not to fight someone who may be his father. This constitutes a proof of virtue, in a roundabout way, and prompts Vaster to express his pleasure that his son is good as he himself is not, being proud of him for not being like him: 'I that had nere lou'd my selfe to be thought good, / Am highly pleasd to see it in my blood' (A4ʳ). The dizzying paradoxes of this recall *The Winter's Tale*, and reflect the fundamental undermining of identity that emerges from the overvaluation of the patrilineal bond.

In this play, fathers seem incapable of having consciences: their sons therefore need to act as proxy-consciences for their fathers, rather as Hamlet tried to do for his mother. On the other hand, there remains the danger that 'The damned father will pervert the son' (C1ᵛ); and the virtuous Robert does at one moment seem to be going in his father's direction, starting to doubt his mother's chastity when he finds her in a brothel, prompting a scene that echoes the mother–son closet confrontation in *Hamlet* (GI^v). Vaster is 'new borne' (K2^r) by the play's end, but not through his own agency. Fathers have neither the dignity of tragic figures nor the redemptive properties of comic fathers in earlier times. Gripe's sycophant Thirsty, when Gripe complains that his 'vrine's stop'd', moralizes on the superiority of sons:

You should drinke, hard, master: all this comes with pinching your selfe of your liquour. This is the reason, that so few Dutchmen are troubled with the stone. Your miserable Churle dribbles like the pissing Conduit: but his iouiall sonne with a streame like Ware-water spout. (FI^r)

The idea that prodigal sons are somehow inherently superior to their fathers (even at pissing) has now taken hold, partly as a result of generic norms, but also reflecting and augmenting an increasing cultural suspicion of paternal authority.

THE TRAGIC RETURN OF THE FATHER

At the very end of the Jacobean period, however, we do see a return of the repressed powers of the father, and this leads to some extraordinary tragic outcomes. Attempts to reassert paternal dignity come at a considerable cost, either to fathers or to those around them. By 1625, tragicomedy seems to have played itself out, and plots which might once have tended towards providentially happy outcomes tend rather to destructive ends, even though the destruction is often configured as redemptive.

Heywood's *The English Traveller* (c. 1626) finds a new kind of dignity for old men, including fathers, yet though the play is superficially tragicomic, it involves suffering as severe as Heywood's much earlier *A Woman Killed with Kindness* (1603).[28] The play sets up and resolves some classic intermasculine tensions; yet for the intergenerational homosocial resolution a woman needs to be sacrificed, as well as a number of other homosocial bonds. The premise of the play's main plot is a curious one: Young Geraldine, the titular traveller, has won the patronal affections of the childless old Wincott, who has made him his heir, but he is a little uneasy on his own father's account, wanting to 'cancell' his obligations:

> Hee [Wincott] studies to engrosse mee to himselfe,
> And is so wedded to my company,
> Hee makes mee stranger to my Fathers house,
> Although so neere a neighbour. (p. 9)[29]

Wincott has become a 'second father' (p. 67). Though they are nominally friends, an odd jealousy between the old men emerges, as if they were rivals over a woman. Old Geraldine mildly complains:

> You have tooke him from me quite, and have I thinke,
> Adopted him into your family,
> He staies with me so seldome.   (p. 41)

Wincott meanwhile explains his motives thus:

> Oh what a happinesse your Father hath,
> Farre above mee, one to inherit after him,
> Where I (Heaven knowes) am childlesse.   (p. 10)

Yet, as Young Geraldine points out in response, heaven has 'supplied' this 'defect' for Wincott in his marrying a young wife. A further tension emerges when we discover that there has been affection between Young Geraldine and this wife – indeed, she vows to marry him should her husband die. We might expect the young man here to cuckold his old patron, but in fact he is honourable, which means that he has to navigate a very tricky course between his two fathers – a unique double bind.

What enables this bind to be resolved is a turn of plot that initially seems a further spanner in the works: Young Geraldine's friend Dalavill betrays him, telling Old Geraldine that his son is only staying with Wincott due to an affair with the young (unnamed) wife. This provokes an extraordinary reaction when father confronts son:

> Oh, that I should live
> To see the hopes that I have stor'd so long,
> Thus in a moment ruin'd: And the staffe,
> On which my old decrepite age should leane;
> Before my face thus broken: On which trusting,
> I thus abortively, before my time,
> Fall headlong to my Grave. *Falls on the earth.*   (p. 48)

The whole tradition of paternity in drama seems summed up here: hope, the idea of a prop or stay, the father's thrift, the notion of familial honour and fame in a social world, the idea of premature death, and the imagery of abortion tearing all this down. Yet Young Geraldine is innocent – no prodigal he. Despite his innocence, though, he is forced into a promise: he can only *prove* his innocence to his father by vowing to stay away from Wincott's house – and he vows this, his father demands, 'upon my blessing' (p. 49).

Honourable as he is, Young Geraldine breaks this vow: he arranges to go and see Wincott, who is upset by his unexplained absence. To this end, he even sneaks in by the back door at night, like an adulterous lover. Once there, having explained what has happened quite frankly, he discovers that Wincott's wife is having an affair with Dalavill. Between friendship, love, and loyalty to his patron, he is therefore in another bind, which he thinks he can only resolve by leaving on his travels again.[30]

The play is an unusual kind of 'Tragi-Comedy' ('To the Reader', p. 5), in that its main body is that of a comedy but it ends with a tragic outcome – at least in some respects. Having found out about the wife's inchastity, Geraldine does not need his father's exhortations to stay away from Wincott's house. Only when his father insists that he take his leave before going travelling does he find himself in another kind of bind. Old Gerald-ine tells him:

> Mee perhaps,
> You may appease, and with small difficulty,
> Because a Father; But how satisfie
> Their deare, and on your part, unmerited love?   (p. 86)

Patronal love must be merited, even if fatherly forgiveness can be taken pretty much for granted. In obeying his father, and going to Wincott's house, however, Young Geraldine finds a way out of all his binds. He rebukes the wife for her inchastity – and she dies of shame, conveniently leaving a letter of confession. This is clearly the tragic element of the tragicomedy, but the virtuous male characters don't really take it as such. They're happy at the resolution, in which Young Geraldine can now be heir to both fathers. This is construed as 'a Marriage of our Love' (p. 94) – a male bonding that works over the sacrifice of a suspect woman. In more standard comedy, father–son relations are subordinated or translated to the happy sphere of marriage, but here the process of translation is reversed. Wincott ends the play saying:

> Wee'le like some Gallants
> That Bury thrifty Fathers, think't no sinne,
> To weare Blacks, without, but other Thoughts within.   (p. 95)

He is referring to his superficial mourning for his wife; real joy is in the father–son bond, and mourning for a wife, not for a father, is the fake emotion. The primacy of paternity is asserted, even as it is dissipated into the unique and paradoxical phenomenon of *two* fathers.

Nowhere else, perhaps, do we encounter so explicitly the idea of the doubleness of fathers, and the play's ending seems like a commentary on the whole tradition of dramatic fathers we have encountered in this book, particularly in the present chapter. The doubling of the fathers expresses the excessive and often contradictory burdens imposed by patriarchy. Where later Jacobean plays had dissipated those burdens by appealing to other loyalties, *The English Traveller* makes filial duty the top priority again, but friendship and romantic love must be sacrificed to it. Though the play seems to endorse this attitude, it is very clear about the human costs involved.

The human cost of an insistence on paternal dignity is even clearer in Webster's *Appius and Virginia* (c. 1624, probably co-written with Heywood), which revises and considerably augments the feeble earlier play on the same subject. Here paternity is utterly certain, but lethal. Though the key event remains the father's killing of his daughter in order to save her from a tyrant's ravishment, the play is also interested in setting up an opposition between a statesman and a soldier, characterizing its central male figures to that end. It is ultimately a very unsubversive work, which refuses to undermine authority figures in any way – even offering mitigation for Appius at the end. Yet the play suggests that the only way to entrench authority is to make it utterly ruthless. We return to the moral world of *Titus Andronicus*, but without Shakespeare's extravagant irony.

The relationship between father and daughter here is powerfully, if conventionally, presented. When giving Virginia away to her proposed husband Icilius (an addition to the plot), Virginius says:

> Here I give up a fathers interest,
> But not a fathers love – that I wil ever
> Wear next my heart, for it was born with her
> And growes still with my age.   (I. iv. 140–3)[31]

As the girl never gets to marry Icilius, Virginius will in fact retain his 'interest' in her, but paternal love is primary, a fact beautifully attested in the following speech, as Virginia is taken away into slavery, his paternity having been denied:

> Farewel my sweet *Virginia*, never, never
> Shall I taste fruit of the most blessed hope
> I had in thee. Let me forget the thought
> Of thy most pretty infancy, when first
> Returning from the Wars, I took delight
> To rock thee in my Target; when my Girl
> Would kiss her father in his burganet
> Of glittering steel hung 'bout his armed neck;
> And viewing the bright mettal, smile to see
> Another fair *Virginia* smile on thee:
> When I first taught thee how to go, to speak:

> And when my wounds have smarted, I have sung
> With an unskilful, yet a willing voice,
> To bring my Girl asleep. O my *Virginia*,
> When we begun to be, begun our woes,
> Increasing still, as dying life still growes. (IV. i. 321–36)

The typical Websterian *sententia* at the end does not undermine the extraordinary power of this, perhaps one of the finest emotional evocations of paternity in the drama of the period. It relies on details that fit Virginius' martial character, yet which also accommodate the child convincingly, and on the various incongruities of war-material being juxtaposed with a female infant – none of which emasculates the father one jot. This father is utterly self-sufficient, yet vulnerable. Ten lines later, he kills his daughter.

Virginius is absent from Rome with his army for much of the play. This is partly due to Appius' scheming, which indicates that Appius is afraid of Virginius, despite his own superior position as one of the *decemviri*: the statesman is afraid of the soldier, we can infer, however high-handedly he treats him, for the soldier is more of a man. The effect of Virginius' absence also reinforces his manliness: he is able to subdue a mutinous army, and his greater concern for martial than domestic matters is intended to be admirably masculine. He is not presented as a neglectful father, though: in his absence, Icilius is able to be admirably defiant to Appius.

Even the trial in which Virginia loses her patrician status does not undermine Virginius' patriarchal authority. Appius' cats-paw Marcus Clodius alleges that Virginia is not really her father's daughter and that she is really the child of one of his (Clodius') slaves. Virginius defiantly turns up at the trial dressed as a slave himself, prompting his brother's comment:

> it ill fits
> Your noble person, or this reverend place.
> VIRGINIUS. Thats true, old man, but it well fits the case
> Thats now in question. If with form and shew
> They prove her slaved, all freedome I'le forgoe. (IV. i. 14–18)

His humble identification with his daughter's interests is only matched by his sense of propriety. He is not to be swayed by allegations that his wife foisted someone else's child on him; his dead wife was a 'sweet Lady', and to be trusted beyond any living witness (line 191). Appius tries to tap into classic male anxieties about the uncertainty of paternity:

> Old man, I am sorry for thee that thy love
> By custome is growne natural, which by nature
> Should be an absolute loathing. Note the Sparrow,
> That having hatch'd a Cucko, when it sees
> Her brood a Monster to her proper kind,
> Forsakes it, and with more fear shuns the nest,
> Then she had care i' th' Spring to have it drest.
> Cast thy affection then behind thy back,
> And think . . .   (lines 196–204)

Despite the great rhetorical power here (Webster's use of animal imagery is characteristically vivid), Virginius cannot be moved, any more than he can be swayed by the Orator's supposedly friendly counsel that soldiers often 'Father strange children' in their absence:

> True: and Pleaders too,
> When they are sent to visit Provinces.
> You my most neat and cunning Orator,
> Whose tongue is Quick-silver – Pray thee good *Janus*
> Look not so many several wayes at once,
> But go to th' point.   (lines 207–13)

Virginius' simple certainty and dignity give him a unity that other Janus-faced figures lack.

Such simplicity of manliness is then carried forward into the play's climax. Appius corruptly judges Virginia to be a slave so that he can sleep with her himself. Virginius accepts the judgement thus:

> Thus I surrender her into the Court   *Kills her.*
> Of all the Gods. And see proud *Appius* see,
> Although not justly, I have made her free.
> And if thy Lust with this Act be not fed,
> Bury her in thy bowels, now shee's dead. (lines 343–7)

The use of imagery of cannibalism here is significant – he has devoured his own substance in killing his only child, but he projects the sin onto Appius.

In the final act, he does seem to lose his nerve somewhat: although he continues to blame Appius as the true murderer, he wavers in his attitude to himself, longing for his soldiers to kill him before they persuade him to vengeance, and appearing feverish and frenzied on his return to Rome – Icilius attributes this to the gods' punishment (V. i. 110–11) and seems to blame him. Nonetheless, he is allowed to be judge over Appius, whom he, however, seems prepared to pardon, as he is contrite. Icilius tries to stir Virginius' vengeance by bringing Virginia's body onto the stage, but it is

Appius himself who now becomes the proper judge, killing himself for his sins. When Clodius refuses to do the same, there is a deliberate contrast with his master – to the latter's advantage. The father, then, is not allowed to be an avenger; he is not to be a Hieronimo or a Titus. This means that he can survive, of course (as avengers almost always must die themselves), but it also indicates the limits of what a father can properly do. He may be able to kill his own daughter, but he cannot take arms effectively against a representative of justice, however corrupt. What dignity he has must stay in the family. Otherwise there will be madness and disorder.

The kind of disorder that may ensue from a father rebelling against his own authority (and then being forced to judge himself) is worked through with devastating force in *The Unnatural Combat* (c. 1624), where Massinger returns to the father–son tensions of the earlier Jacobean period with a vengeance. Malefort here is the worst father in all Renaissance drama and correspondingly suffers the most crushingly tragic of fates. The play's climax has a remarkable power partly because the full range of Malefort's sins is not revealed until the final scene of punishment; until that point, the sins of the father are shady: he is at first a wronged and dignified patriarch, then one who has committed mysterious sins, then a racked soul who resists sin, before ultimately being revealed as having been a terrible sinner all along. The play's structure thereby tears down and utterly deforms the figure of the father more powerfully than anywhere else in the drama of the period, but without destroying his dignity.

The play's starting premise has Malefort on trial for the crimes of his son, who has turned pirate. The magistrates cannot believe that Malefort Junior could be having such success against their shipping without the help of his father, who has been a great naval pillar of the state. The implication of necessary complicity between father and son seems a particularly unjust extension of belief in the unity of patrilineal honour.[32] Malefort's self-defence at this point is powerful and dignified:

> should I now curse him,
> Or wish in th' agonie of my troubled soule,
> Lightning had found him in his mothers womb
> You'll say 'tis from the purpose, and I therefore
> Betake him to the Devill, and so leave him.
> Did never loyall father but my selfe
> Beget a treacherous issue? was't in me
> With as much ease to fashion up his minde,
> As in his generation to forme
> The organs to his body? must it follow
> Because that he is impious, I am false? (I. i. 274–84)

The restraint of the curse and the sense of paternal vulnerability are classic tropes of a tragic father such as we have met throughout this study. As we shall see, there are layers of irony here, particularly in the mention of the mother and of lightning; but we may at this point expect that the play will focus on Malefort's daughter Theocrine heroically trying to save her father, as she is urged to prostitute herself in order to get him off the charges. In the terms of *Measure for Measure*'s Isabella, this would be a 'kind of incest' (III. i. 138) – but Theocrine is determined to save him with honourable pleas (and it helps that her beloved is the son of the governor). However, this adumbrated tragicomic plot (which would be rather Fletcherian) is quickly discarded when Malefort Junior issues a challenge to his father.

That challenge, unnatural though it is, seems to give Malefort a chance to clear himself with the state on his own terms. Yet the basis of the son's challenge muddies the waters: Malefort Junior, even in private talk with his father before they fight, never spells out his reasons, but he does give some hints that haunt the rest of the play. He tells his captains:

> May the cause
> That forces me to this unnatural act,
> Be buried in everlasting silence,
> And I finde rest in death, or my revenge,
> To either I stand equall.   (II. i. 47–51)

There is a touch of Hamlet in this resolve, but it still seems perverse. His father then says:

> Speake thy griefes.
> MALEFORT JUNIOR.   I shall, Sir;
> But in a perplext forme and method, which
> You onely can interpret; would you had not
> A guiltie knowledge in your bosome of
> The language which you force me to deliver,
> So I were nothing. As you are my father
> I bend my knee, and uncompell'd professe
> My life, and all thats mine to be your gift;
> And that in a sonnes dutie I stand bound
> To lay this head beneath your feet, and run
> All desperate hazards for your ease and safetie.
> But this confest on my part, I rise up,
> And not as with a father, (all respect,
> Love, feare, and reverence cast off,) but as
> A wicked man I thus expostulate with you.
> Why have you done that which I dare not speake?

And in the action chang'd the humble shape
Of my obedience, to rebellious rage
And insolent pride? and with shut eyes constrain'd me
To run my Barke of honour on a shelfe,
I must not see, nor if I saw it, shun it?
In my wrongs nature suffers, and lookes backward,
And mankinde trembles to see me pursue
What beasts would flie from.   (lines 116–39)

The horror of filial impiety here is weighed against something else even more unspeakable and unspoken, and both sins are laid at the father's door: Malefort is blamed for his son's need to fight him and possibly kill him. Given Malefort Junior's mysterious discretion as to the *cause*, we cannot help thinking him perversely unfair to his father. We are therefore relieved that the father wins, killing his son, even as we wonder what the issue is. There is a tantalizing hint ('if from the grave / My mother' – lines 191–2), but that is it. The scene ends as an apparent triumph for justice, though a horrible, even tragic one, Malefort saying:

                    they may
Appeare too dearely bought, my falling glories
Being made up againe, and cemented
With a sonnes bloud.   (lines 229–32)

The problem seems to have died with the son.

However, we soon learn that Malefort has another problem: incestuous love for his daughter. So much does this shock dominate the centre of the play that we are bound to think this sinful desire must have been the reason for Malefort Junior's rebellion. Even if it seems hard to think how the son would have known of his father's intentions, we may be as apt as the magistrates to assume some private complicity (founded on identity) between father and son. The first hint of wrongful fatherly love comes when he praises her to her fiancé:

I feast my selfe in the imagination
Of those sweet pleasures, and allowd delights,
I tasted from the mother.   (II. iii. 93–5)

This then leads to him preventing the marriage at the last moment, and some anguished soliloquies, before he gets his friend Montreville to lock the girl up so as to avoid temptation. Killing his rebellious son now comes to seem the least of his troubles (he himself says the killing 'may admit / Some weake defence' (IV. i. 11–12) in comparison to incest).

The play's final movement therefore comes as a considerable surprise. Montreville is a false friend and rapes Theocrine rather than protecting her. It turns out that Montreville has vengeful as well as lustful motives here: Malefort had earlier not only taken his friend's beloved (Theocrine's mother), but had also reneged on a promise to marry Theocrine to his friend in recompense. The fatal antagonism now turns out to be one of long-festering wounds in friendship, which also seems a fair punishment for Malefort's incestuous desires. As Montreville puts it:

> mine was a rape
> And she being in a kinde contracted to me,
> The fact may challenge some qualification:
> But thy intent made natures selfe run backward,
> And done, had caus'd an earth-quake.   (V. ii. 248–52)

This is brutal; but it is not the key surprise.

As soon as an earthquake is mentioned, one happens, and out of it appears the ghost of Malefort Junior. The forgotten son returns – with his mother, who is even more forgotten: plenty of hints about her have appeared, but always in contexts where something else seemed to be at issue (see above). It turns out that the son's motive all along was vengeance for his mother, whom Malefort now admits to having murdered, out of lust for Theocrine's mother. The whole play now seems to have been driven by something like a mirror-image of *Hamlet*'s plot. The ghost does not speak, but his appearance forces Malefort to acknowledge his own crimes, to judge himself – as he says 'thou being my sonne, Were't not a competent judge mark'd out by heaven / For her revenger' (lines 294–5). It may not be true that Hamlet was not a competent judge of his mother in *exactly* this sense, but it may offer one reason why he is told not to contrive anything against her. The father, of course, can *only* judge himself. He is killed with a flash of lightning, as was earlier foreshadowed, and his body is made to stink and is deformed. Though he is not incestuous in fact, his desires in this direction may merely be a symbol of a larger deformation of his paternal identity. However deformed that might be, however, the son cannot judge him. That is the limit of subversion in such tragedy. The son cannot even speak against his father: the rest is silence indeed. As in *Hamlet*, paternal dignity is such that it absorbs all around it.

Conclusion

Fathers end the Jacobean period as a gravitational centre for tragedy, as a black hole absorbing all other human feeling. When their public and private roles are dislocated, far from untangling the tensions of earlier plays, the destructive power of patriarchal ideology is most fully unleashed. Yet in comedy of the same time – such as *A Cure for a Cuckold* – we see a more cheerful acceptance of paternal nullity. Where, in earlier drama, fathers had been everything and nothing, by the beginning of the Caroline period they were everything *or* nothing. And nothing in the end won out: never again would fathers be so central to drama, or to narrative in general. Perhaps only in *The Brothers Karamazov* would a father in subsequent literature be so important, so fraught a figure.[1]

Franco Moretti has argued that Shakespearean tragedy demystifies monarchical absolutism by taking its claims seriously and pushing through to its most paradoxical implications;[2] the same can be said, I think, of Shakespeare's presentation of patriarchy. While Moretti sees this as leading to a loss of a central character focus and a sense of nullity in post-Shakespearean tragedy, the parallel process in the case of fathers is subtler: though characters accept the limitation or loss of their powers, they gain a sense of emotional richness and individuality from the loss.

Fathers haunt the Elizabethan and Jacobean stage. The most memorable father in Shakespeare is obviously the Ghost of Old Hamlet. But sons can do their share of haunting too. As we have seen, Jasper in *The Knight of the Burning Pestle* appears as a ghost to his father, and Sebastian in *The Noble Spanish Soldier* plays a ghostly father to his own father. They have a more purgative role than the Ghost who supposedly comes from Purgatory to make demands on his son. The son's ghost in *The Unnatural Combat* seems not only to catalyse vengeance on his own father, but on all the fathers of the drama. There is something eerie about the idea of paternity, as if it is a role no one is quite comfortable in playing. All sorts of doubleness seem to be involved in taking on that role, suggesting relentless interchanges of identity. Playful though it is, Joyce's Stephen Dedalus is onto something when he gives his famous account of *Hamlet*'s ghost:

> – A father, Stephen said, battling against hopelessness, is a necessary evil. He wrote the play [*Hamlet*] in the months that followed his father's death. If you hold that he, a greying man with two marriageable daughters, with thirtyfive years of life, *nel mezzo del cammin di nostra vita*, with fifty of experience, is the beardless undergraduate from Wittenberg then you must hold that his seventy-year old mother is the lustful queen. No. The corpse of John Shakespeare does not walk the night. From hour to hour it rots and rots. He rests, disarmed of fatherhood, having devised that mystical estate upon his son. Boccaccio's Calandrino was the first and last man who felt himself with child. Fatherhood, in the sense of conscious begetting, is unknown to man. It is a mystical estate, an apostolic succession, from only begetter to only begotten. On that mystery and not on the madonna which the cunning Italian intellect flung to the mob of Europe the church is founded and founded irremovably because founded, like the world, macro- and microcosm, upon the void. Upon incertitude, upon unlikelihood. *Amor matris*, subjective and objective genitive, may be the only true thing in life. Paternity may be a legal fiction. Who is the father of any son that any son should love him or he any son?[3]

In the end, Stephen seems to suggest, the son creates his own father, but this is not quite the same thing as Freud's superego. In creating the father he creates the notion of a fully realized self (more like Freud's ego), and then, crucially, defers or displaces it onto someone else. He does this because the idea of the father, though necessary, is ultimately conceived as evil; though it embodies an idea of virtue, it makes one aware that virtue, or manliness, is a fiction.

Yet Joyce also raises the question of love, an issue that is central to the best drama of our period. Love for the father is not strong in Greek tragedy, or in Joyce's model *The Odyssey*, but *Ulysses* works its way to that end. So, in the end, does Shakespearean drama.[4] Yet *amor patris* (that is, the love of or for the father) is truly the love that dares not speak its name in the Renaissance. Hamlet, replying 'Oh God!' to his father's mention of love, and Cordelia's 'Love, and be silent' are key instances of this. A love that is both compulsory and supposedly natural is bound to create difficulties of articulation when it actually exists.

In the end, the plots of the various genres we have explored in this book constitute an articulation or formalization of feeling that cannot be expressed in simple speech. The emotional connections involved in recognitions always seem a problem for men, because they are so estranging, as we have seen. Yet most forms of feeling are hard for fathers to assert in the drama of the period. Any feeling *for* him needs to be filtered through his offspring, as in cases like Macduff's loss of his children. The danger in feeling for someone is that it unmans them. One of the simplest presentations of a son in Shakespeare is that of Young Martius in *Coriolanus*, of whom Valeria reports the following:

A' my word, the father's son. I'll swear 'tis a very pretty boy. A' my troth, I look'd upon him a' Wednesday half an hour together; h' as such a confirmed counten-ance. I saw him run after a gilded butterfly, and when he caught it, he let it go again, and after it again, and over and over he comes, and up again; catch'd it again: or whether his fall enrag'd him, or how 'twas, he did so set his teeth and tear it. O, I warrant, how he mammock'd it!

There is real affection here – the kind of affection that cannot be felt by or about Coriolanus himself. To this Volumnia sagely and approvingly replies 'One on's father's moods' (I. iii. 57–66). In some ways this is yet another example of female speech confirming masculine paternity, but there's also a degree of absurdity in the exchange which seems to under-mine masculinity. The boy's futile, repetitive rage in chasing a butterfly may undermine in advance the great heroic deeds of his father in the next scenes and indeed throughout the play.[5] Proving manliness is a futile activity, a kind of mammocking as silly as Lear's desire to 'laugh / At gilded butterflies' (V. iii. 12–13). Male emotions are not really taken seriously, perhaps because to be emotional is to be unmanned: Coriolanus himself will become a 'boy of tears' later on (V. vi. 100). Coriolanus' own attitude to his son is very distant: he is more interested in Rome than in his own family, saying 'I do love / My country's good with a respect more tender, / More holy and profound, than mine own life, / My dear wife's estimate, her womb's increase, / And treasure of my loins' (III. iii. 111–15), but even in saying so he makes the son abstract; as is typical for Roman plays, disinterested patriotism is signalled by a lack of interest in family. Public and private roles are dislocated even where they are assumed to be allied. The father can only express personal feeling by disavowing it.

The one thing that the father has over his son is the idea of his sacredness, but even that is never quite owned. If the father can only feel when he disclaims feeling, his ownership of his sacredness is compromised by his inability to lay it aside. There is therefore an element of self-alienation in the father, partly based on the son being guarantor of his status, but also based on the doubleness of his selfhood. He is both a time-bound individual and a possessor of the idea of sacred continuity, both a private and a public self. Though the modern division between public and private had not quite emerged by our period, there was a sense of distinct spheres available. Later culture would begin to separate these spheres,[6] and thus perhaps to clarify and simplify the conflict between them, but in Shakespeare's time the spheres overlapped uncomfortably, creating real pressure on the individual father – the figure who most fully embodied the tension.

What emerges, then, from the drama of Elizabethan and Jacobean England is the figure of a father who remains valorized and retains his sacred qualities, but who is also treated in the end as a fundamentally human, ordinary man, with all the indignity that entails. This, I think, is a crucial development of modern selfhood: such a man is embedded in society, but has an ultimate and irreducible freedom and autonomy. This paradoxical self is inevitably masculine – we shall have to wait until Richardson's *Clarissa*, at least, for an equivalently complex woman – and that self is the key to the formal tensions of a period of great drama.

For Shakespeare and his contemporaries, if a self is realized in drama it is through a recognition of dependence and limitation, not of personal growth. Broadly sympathetic as I am to Peter Holbrook's portrayal of Shakespeare as a radical individualist,[7] some qualification is needed in order to understand the power of his plays. Shakespeare does allow each individual within his plays a radical freedom to determine his identity, and clearly prefers those who take that opportunity to those who do not.[8] The pattern of the plays does not, however, wholly license individualism, which is compromised in two major ways: on the one hand, more dispiritingly, moments of individual freedom are ultimately defeated by the larger pattern of political/historical necessity, even if the forces of necessity, which are in some senses incommensurable with the feeling of freedom, cannot wholly do away with the momentary feeling; on the other hand, more positively, Shakespeare very much understands that the human desire to identify with someone else may lead to the limitation of individuality. Coriolanus, confronted with his wife, son, and mother as he prepares to attack Rome, says:

> I'll never
> Be such a gosling as to obey instinct, but stand
> As if a man were author of himself,
> And knew no other kin.   (V. iii. 34–7)

This is, firstly, an attempt to deny his mother, but it also denies his son: not only would he believe that he made himself, but that the only thing he has made is himself. But, just as he must recognize his mother in the end, he must recognize his son. In the end, Coriolanus is not author of himself, nor is anyone: but in being a gosling he can save both his city and those whom he loves.[9] The son is his 'poor epitome' (says Volumnia – line 68), a 'brave boy' for kneeling to him (line 77). Yet he says little else to Young Martius, whose only lines in the play are "A shall not tread on me; / I'll run away till I'm bigger, but then I'll fight' (lines 127–8); in essence, this is a deferred threat to fight his father rather than be trampled by him, and it clarifies the enormity of the father's treason. Once dissuaded from his invasion, Coriolanus addresses his mother and his wife, but not his son; it is as if he is embarrassed to have backed down in front of him. Paradoxically, in recognizing his family he seals his fate. The individual cannot exist without such connections, even if they destroy him.

The plays show, in the end, that a desire for radical autonomy and self-creation like Coriolanus' is as unattainable as a desire to identify completely with another. Fathers focalize the opposition between these desires very powerfully, being at the same time objects of reverence, symbols of the larger patterns of history, and objects with whom their children can identify, yet also being individuals themselves. As such, they are the pivots of some of the world's greatest drama; they define its limits, and therefore enable subtle and humane encroachment on those limits. Prospero, at the very end of *The Tempest*, gives final commands to his proxy son Ariel, his 'chick', 'Then to the elements / Be free, and fare thou well' (V. i. 317–19). He abandons his connection with the magical perfect son, so that 'what strength I have's mine own, / Which is most faint' (Epilogue, 2–3). It is in such moments of dispossession that we touch closest to the quick of dramatic selves, and yet even as Prospero says 'Please you, draw near' we may feel that he is at the greatest distance from us.

Notes

1 INTRODUCTION

1 John Aubrey, *Brief Lives*, ed. John Buchanan-Brown (London: Penguin, 2000), p. 261.

2 Judith Haber, *Desire and Dramatic Form in Early Modern England* (Cambridge University Press, 2009), p. 1.

3 Simon Palfrey and Tiffany Stern, *Shakespeare in Parts* (Oxford University Press, 2007).

4 'Fiction and Friction', in Stephen Greenblatt, *Shakespearean Negotiations: The Circulation of Social Energy in Renaissance England* (Oxford: Clarendon Press, 1988), pp. 75–6.

5 Fred B. Tromly, *Fathers and Sons in Shakespeare: The Debt Never Promised* (University of Toronto Press, 2010).

6 Lisa Jardine, *Still Harping on Daughters: Women and Drama in the Age of Shakespeare*, 2nd edn (London: Harvester Wheatsheaf, 1989), p. 6 and Chapter 3.

7 Linda Bamber, *Comic Women, Tragic Men: A Study of Gender and Genre in Shakespeare* (Stanford University Press, 1982), p. 154.

8 See Bruce R. Smith, *Shakespeare and Masculinity* (Oxford University Press, 2000), p. 138.

9 Peter Erickson, *Patriarchal Structures in Shakespeare's Drama* (Berkeley: University of California Press, 1985), p. 3.

10 Catherine Belsey, *Shakespeare and the Loss of Eden: The Construction of Family Values in Early Modern Culture* (London: Macmillan, 1999), p. 25.

11 See Robin Headlam Wells, *Shakespeare on Masculinity* (Cambridge University Press, 2000).

12 The term was, at least vaguely, available to Elizabethan writers: Sir John Harington, discussing the Aristotelian validity of *Orlando Furioso*, seems to elide it partly with '*Peripetia*, which I interpret an agnition of some unlooked for fortune either good or bad, and a sudden change thereof' ('A Brief Apology of Poetry', prefaced to *Orlando Furioso* (London, 1591)). The word 'agnition' means both recognition and acknowledgement (*OED*).

13 Northrop Frye, *Fables of Identity: Studies in Poetic Mythology* (New York: Harcourt, Brace, 1963), p. 25.

14 This may help account for the quality of 'scandal' that Terence Cave sees in the history of the term – see his *Recognitions: A Study in Poetics* (Oxford: Clarendon Press, 1988), p. 24; Cave's book, undoubtedly the most capacious and subtlest discussion of *anagnorisis*, demonstrates that the pleasures of recognition are always in danger of destroying our sense of coherence and plausibility in fiction. Cave, rightly preoccupied as he is by formal matters, can sometimes dismiss the importance of familial recognition, even though he does emphasize the tensions between nature and artifice that are so often aspects of a recognition scene (e.g. pp. 20–1).

15 Aristotle, *Poetics* – in D. A. Russell and M. Winterbottom (eds.), *Classical Literary Criticism*, revised edn (Oxford University Press, 1989), p. 59.

16 See A. D. Nuttall, *Why Does Tragedy Give Pleasure?* (Oxford: Clarendon Press, 1996).

17 Though the element of suspense and/or surprise in *anagnorisis*, of course, is very controversial, see Cave, *Recognitions, passim*. Shakespeare, at least, is more interested in creating *wonder* than surprise, as we shall see in later chapters.

18 See ibid., p. 231: 'coherence is assured by a first-person pronoun having a function at once singular and plural: the "I" of the present rediscovers the "I" of the past and imposes meaning on it'.

19 In the psychoanalytic tradition, the transition is often managed through relations to objects – see D. W. Winnicott, *Playing and Reality* (Hove: Brunner-Routledge, 1991); in this light, it is significant that comedic (and some other) recognitions can be mediated by objects, particularly children's toys. In Plautus' *The Rope*, for instance, the lost daughter Palaestra is recognized through listing the toys she carried with her – she even goes so far as to refer to these toys as her 'parents' (line 1145). Unless otherwise stated, references to classical texts are to the Loeb editions.

20 Lorna Hutson's groundbreaking work in *The Invention of Suspicion: Law and Mimesis in Shakespeare and Renaissance Drama* (Oxford University Press, 2007) suggests that late Tudor theatrical audiences had become more sceptical and searching in their assessment of evidence, and that they were much more attuned to the differences between recognition and identification – see especially p. 116.

21 I therefore find it hard to agree with Frye's contention that recognition is essentially a comic matter, or even 'the archetypal theme' of comedy – see Northrop Frye, *Anatomy of Criticism: Four Essays* (Princeton University Press, 1957), p. 192; when Frye extends the idea of recognition, though, he is more convincing: e.g. 'In the greatest moments of Dante and Shakespeare, in say *The Tempest* or the climax of the *Purgatorio*, we have a feeling of converging significance, the feeling that here we are close to seeing what our whole literary experience has been about, the feeling that we have moved into the still center of the order of words' (*Anatomy*, p. 117); the theological abstraction here only just blurs what could be a central *human* experience. Cave, looking at this from a different angle, sees 'an ineradicable – but

also seductive – asymmetry between the recognizer and the recognized'
(*Recognitions*, p. 270).

22 This is perhaps based on the empathetic bonds created by oxytocin: see
H. J. Lee, A. H. Macbeth, J. H. Pagani, and W. S. Young, 'Oxytocin: The
Great Facilitator of Life', *Progress in Neurobiology* 88 (2009): 127–51.

23 Ian McAdam, *Magic and Masculinity in Early Modern English Drama*
(Pittsburgh: Duquesne University Press, 2009).

24 See Stanley Cavell, *Disowning Knowledge in Seven Plays of Shakespeare*,
updated edn (Cambridge University Press, 2003), for some of the problems
associated with acknowledgement in Shakespeare's plays.

25 References to *The Dramatic Works in the Beaumont and Fletcher Canon*, ed.
Fredson Bowers *et al.*, 10 vols. (Cambridge University Press, 1966–89).

26 Tromly, *Fathers and Sons in Shakespeare*, p. 20 argues that the paternal
blessing was becoming 'old-fashioned in Shakespeare's time', but the evidence of the drama is for its continuing and indeed increasing importance;
perhaps the drama preserved a ritual that was falling out of favour in life.

27 *Totem and Taboo*, in *The Standard Edition of the Complete Psychological
Works of Sigmund Freud*, 24 vols. (London: Hogarth Press and the Institute
of Psycho-Analysis, 1953–74), XIII: 141–2; he concludes 'It seems to me a most
surprising discovery that the problems of social psychology . . . should prove
soluble on the basis of one single concrete point – man's relation to his
father' (p. 157); it is, of course, all about men. The myth is redeveloped in
Moses and Monotheism (in *The Standard Edition*, vol. XXIII), where Moses is
the murdered leader.

28 *Totem and Taboo*, p. 145.

29 See Tom MacFaul, *Poetry and Paternity in Renaissance England: Sidney,
Spenser, Shakespeare, Donne and Jonson* (Cambridge University Press, 2010),
pp. 5–6, 39–40.

30 References to Ben Jonson, *Works*, ed. C. H. Herford, Evelyn Simpson and
Percy Simpson, 11 vols. (Oxford: Clarendon Press, 1925–52).

31 Unless otherwise stated, references are to *The Dramatic Works of Thomas
Heywood*, 6 vols. (London: J. Pearson, 1874). The edition has no line
numbers.

32 All references to Middleton's plays and *dubia* are to Thomas Middleton, *The
Collected Works*, ed. Gary Taylor and John Lavagnino (Oxford University
Press, 2007).

33 Coppélia Kahn, *Man's Estate: Masculine Identity in Shakespeare* (Berkeley:
University of California Press, 1981), p. 1.

34 Despite the recognition by the likes of Benedick in *Much Ado about Nothing*
that the end of romantic love is to people the world, it is rare for lovers to
produce offspring within the action of a play. *The Family of Love* (c. 1603,
possibly by Middleton, though serious doubts have been cast on his author-
ship) is unusual in having its romantic hero impregnate his beloved; an
obvious comparison is *Measure for Measure*, though Claudio is less central
there, and the impregnation is a starting premise rather than a central event

of the dramatic action (Bertram's impregnating of Helena in *All's Well that Ends Well* is still more of a plot device).

35 See Keith Thomas, *The Ends of Life: Roads to Fulfilment in Early Modern England* (Oxford University Press, 2009); Elizabeth Foyster, *Manhood in Early Modern England: Honour, Sex and Marriage* (London: Longman, 1999).

36 Alexandra Shepard, *Meanings of Manhood in Early Modern England* (Oxford University Press, 2003), p. 250.

37 See Mark Breitenberg, *Anxious Masculinity in Early Modern England* (Cambridge University Press, 1996).

38 For a more detailed analysis of analogues between Greek and Shakespearean tragedy, see Adrian Poole, *Tragedy: Shakespeare and the Greek Example* (Oxford: Basil Blackwell, 1987); A. D. Nuttall, 'Action at a Distance: Shakespeare and the Greeks', in Charles Martindale and A. B. Taylor (eds.), *Shakespeare and the Classics* (Cambridge University Press, 2004), argues that 'Shakespeare never looks steadily at the Greeks, but he does, on occasion, look with Greek eyes' (p. 220), in that many of his dramatic structures have qualities reminiscent of Greek literature; Laurie Maguire, *Shakespeare's Names* (Oxford University Press, 2007), pp. 97–104 gives convincing circumstantial evidence that Euripides' plays, at least, were familiar to writers of Shakespeare's time.

39 Aeschylus, *The Oresteia*, trans. Robert Fagles (London: Penguin, 1977), *The Eumenides* lines 628, 665–71 (lines 618, 657–61 in the original Greek). On the wider cultural implications in Athens of the devaluation of women's role in reproduction, see Simon Goldhill, *Reading Greek Tragedy* (Cambridge University Press, 1986), p. 59.

40 I am aware that the examples given here are from late Euripides and therefore may not be particularly orthodox ones; however, I think that they are representative examples of a tendency we can see throughout Greek tragedy.

41 In Euripides' *Heracles*, the titular hero has to be insane to kill his children.

42 Michael Silk has argued that the absence of the god–human–hero continuum is a crucial difference between Shakespeare and Greek tragedy – 'Shakespeare and Greek Tragedy: Strange Relationship', in Martindale and Taylor (eds.), *Shakespeare and the Classics*, pp. 243–4.

43 Compare Cordelia's 'no cause' – see Chapter 4, below.

44 Marianne L. Novy, *Love's Argument: Gender Relations in Shakespeare* (Chapel Hill, NC: The University of North Carolina Press, 1984), p. 98.

45 Or perhaps, in modern terms, he's *the* man.

46 For more details of this, see David Cressy, *Birth, Marriage and Death: Ritual, Religion and the Life-Cycle in Tudor and Stuart England* (Oxford University Press, 1997).

47 See Eve Keller, *Generating Bodies and Gendered Selves: The Rhetoric of Reproduction in Early Modern England* (Seattle: University of Washington Press, 2007).

48 See Alan Macfarlane, *The Origins of English Individualism: The Family, Property and Social Transition* (Oxford: Basil Blackwell, 1978). For a fuller discussion of all these matters, see MacFaul, *Poetry and Paternity*, Chapter 2.

49 Charles Taylor, *Sources of the Self: The Making of Modern Identity* (Cambridge University Press, 1989), p. 13.

50 Ibid., p. 15.

51 See E. H. Kantorowicz, *The King's Two Bodies: A Study in Mediaeval Political Theology* (Princeton University Press, 1957).

52 Alastair Fowler, *Renaissance Realism: Narrative Images in Literature and Art* (Oxford University Press, 2003), pp. 102, 111 (in the latter case referring specifically to *Hamlet* and its eponymous hero).

53 See Jean-Pierre Maquerlot, *Shakespeare and the Mannerist Tradition: A Reading of Five Problem Plays* (Cambridge University Press, 1995).

54 Alexandra Shepard, *Meanings of Manhood*, p. 23.

55 D. M. Palliser, *The Age of Elizabeth: England under the Later Tudors 1547–1603*, 2nd edn (London: Longman, 1992), pp. 70–1.

56 Anthony Fletcher, *Gender, Sex and Subordination in England 1500–1800* (New Haven, CT: Yale University Press, 1995), p. 402.

57 Ibid., p. 98.

58 See Ibid., p. 220.

59 See MacFaul, *Poetry and Paternity*, p. 25, and Taylor, *Sources of the Self*, *passim*.

60 References to *The Dramatic Works of Thomas Dekker*, ed. Fredson Bowers, 4 vols. (Cambridge University Press, 1953–61).

61 Ben Jonson, satirized in this play, seems to remember this moment twenty-five years later in *The Staple of News*, where Pennyboy Canter is revealed to have 'had the chiefest part in the play' (IV. Int. 6).

62 References to *Wily Beguiled*, ed. W. W. Greg (Oxford University Press for the Malone Society, 1912).

63 For the absence of fathers in *The Faerie Queene*, see MacFaul, *Poetry and Paternity*, Chapter 4.

64 Janet Adelman argues that the presence of mothers is a sign of tragedy in Shakespeare, but I would suggest that this is not so true of other dramatists; see Janet Adelman, *Suffocating Mothers: Fantasies of Maternal Origin in Shakespeare's Plays, Hamlet to The Tempest* (London: Routledge, 1992), p. 35.

65 In Fletcher's *The Night Walker* (c. 1611, pub. 1640), Hartlove tells the mother of his beloved Maria (whom he supposes dead) that 'love unites more than the tie of blood', adding 'No matter for the empty voyce of mother' (V. ii. 46–7). As the Jacobean period goes on – after around 1611–13 – fathers become increasingly irrelevant. At the end of Middleton's *More Dissemblers besides Women* (1614), for instance, the duchess can secure Aurelia's marriage without reference to paternal consent: she simply says 'though your father / Be not in presence, we'll assure his voice' (V. ii. 261–2).

66 Interestingly, drama almost never presents three male generations simultaneously: so powerful and supposedly unique is the father–son bond that to double it up would cause intolerable confusion. *Titus Andronicus* is a rare exception; though grandsons of Bajazeth appear in *Selimus*, the first is a son of a deceased father, and the others only appear after Bajazeth's death; in

Thomas, Lord Cromwell, the hero's son and father both appear, though not simultaneously.

67 Harry Berger, Jr, *Making Trifles of Terrors: Redistributing Complicities in Shakespeare* (Stanford University Press, 1997), p. 291.

68 Sometimes, as in the case of King Lear, a daughter; see Chapter 4, below.

69 See the discussions in Lawrence Danson, *Shakespeare's Dramatic Genres* (Oxford University Press, 2000), pp. 30–2, and Martin Wiggins, *Shakespeare and the Drama of His Time* (Oxford University Press, 2000), p. 25.

2 STAYING FATHERS IN EARLY ELIZABETHAN DRAMA: *GORBODUC* TO *THE SPANISH TRAGEDY*

1 It is later used repeatedly in the laments for Edward IV in Shakespeare's *Richard III* (II. ii. 74–6).

2 See Kevin Dunn, 'Representing Counsel: *Gorboduc* and the Elizabethan Privy Council', *English Literary Renaissance* 33 (2003): 279–308.

3 References to Ashley Thorndike (ed.), *The Minor Elizabethan Drama*, 2 vols. (London: J. M. Dent, 1910).

4 See Barbara Heliodora Carneiro De Mendonça, 'The Influence of *Gorboduc* on *King Lear*', *Shakespeare Survey* 13 (1966): 41–8.

5 For a more sympathetic treatment of the play, see Peter Happé, 'Tragic Themes in Three Tudor Moralities', *SEL* 5 (1965): 207–27.

6 References to R. B., *Apius and Virginia*, ed. R. B. McKerrow (London: The Malone Society, 1911).

7 References to Alexander Nevyle, *The Lamentable Tragedie of Oedipus* (London, 1563).

8 This is a literal translation of Seneca's original, 'siste, ne in matrem incidas' (line 1051), but has more of a comic ring in English, which lacks the compression of the Latin.

9 References to George Gascoigne, *A Hundreth Sundrie Flowres*, ed. G. W. Pigman III (Oxford: Clarendon Press, 2000).

10 See J. E. Phillips, 'A Revaluation of *Horestes*', *Huntington Library Quarterly* 18 (1955): 227–44, and Howard Erskine-Hill, *Poetry and the Realm of Politics: Spenser to Dryden* (Oxford University Press, 1996), pp. 21–2.

11 References to John Pikerying, *The Interlude of Vice (Horestes)*, ed. Daniel Seltzer (London: Oxford University Press for the Malone Society, 1962).

12 References to Theodore Beza, *A Tragedie of Abrahams Sacrifice*, trans. A. G. (London, 1575).

13 References to Thomas Garter, *The Most Virtuous and Godly Susanna*, ed. B. Ifor Evans (London: Oxford University Press for the Malone Society, 1936).

14 References to Nathaniel Woodes, *The Conflict of Conscience*, ed. Herbert Davis and F. P. Wilson (Oxford University Press for the Malone Society, 1952).

15 See Frances E. Dolan, 'The Subordinate(s) Plot: Petty Treason and the Forms of Domestic Rebellion', *Shakespeare Quarterly* 43 (1992), 317–40.

16 References to Gascoigne, *A Hundreth Sundrie Flowres*.

17 See Gillian Beer, *The Romance* (London: Methuen, 1970), and Helen Cooper, *The English Romance in Time: Transforming Motifs from Geoffrey of Monmouth to Shakespeare* (Oxford University Press, 2004).

18 See Peter T. Hadorn, '*Sir Clyomon and Sir Clamydes*: A Revaluation', *Journal of the Rocky Mountain Medieval and Renaissance Society* 12 (1991): 85–102.

19 References to Anon., *Clyomon and Clamydes*, ed. W. W. Greg (Oxford University Press for the Malone Society, 1913).

20 In Plautus' play, the father Daemones is not quite so weak, despite his exile: he is able to protect the daughter he unwittingly rescues because he has strong slaves.

21 References to *Common Conditions*, ed. Tucker Brooke (New Haven, CT: Yale University Press, 1895).

22 This is not *quite* certain: the unfinished play does not make the revelation of Leostines' identity, but it is obvious enough.

23 See Susan Doran, *Monarchy and Matrimony: The Courtships of Elizabeth I* (London: Routledge, 1996), and the same author's 'Why Did Elizabeth Not Marry?', in Julia M. Walker (ed.), *Dissing Elizabeth: Negative Representations of Gloriana* (Durham, NC: Duke University Press, 1998).

24 The speech is actually given to Leostines, but Tucker Brooke's note to the line is surely right to suggest that this is nonsense: it must be Nomides arriving to resolve the plot.

25 Anon., *The Rare Triumphs of Love and Fortune* (London: 1589).

26 See Walter Fischer, 'Shakespeares *Sturm* und *The Rare Triumphs of Love and Fortune*', in Helmut Viebrock (ed.), *Festschrift zum 75. Geburtstag von Theodor Spira* (Heidelberg: C. Winter, 1961), pp. 144–51.

27 References to Anon., *Guy of Warwick*, ed. Helen D. Moore (Manchester University Press for the Malone Society, 2006).

28 References to John Lyly, *Galathea and Midas*, ed. George Hunter and David Bevington (Manchester University Press, 2000).

29 See Hutson, *The Invention of Suspicion*, p. 296 for the peculiar standards of paternal proof that obtain in the play.

30 *A Knack to Know a Knave*, ed. G. R. Proudfoot (Oxford University Press for the Malone Society, 1963).

31 See David J. Houser, 'Purging the Commonwealth: Marston's Disguised Dukes and *A Knack to Know a Knave*', *PMLA* 89 (1974): 993–1006.

32 For a discussion of the play's genre, see Paul Dean, 'Shakespeare's Henry VI Trilogy and Elizabethan "Romance" Histories: The Origins of a Genre', *Shakespeare Quarterly* 33 (1982): 34–48.

33 King James VI and I, *Political Writings*, ed. Johann P. Sommerville (Cambridge University Press, 1994), p. 39.

34 References to Robert Greene, *The Scottish History of James the Fourth*, ed. Norman Sanders (London: Methuen, 1970).

35 See McAdam, *Magic and Masculinity*.

36 Richard A. McCabe, *Incest, Drama and Nature's Law 1550–1700* (Cambridge University Press, 1993), p. 126.

37 See Andrew King, 'Dead Butchers and Fiend-Like Queens: *The Misfortunes of Arthur and Macbeth*', in *The Scots and Medieval Arthurian Legend*, ed. Rhiannon Purdie and Nicola Royan (Cambridge: Boydell and Brewer Press, 2005), pp. 121–34.

38 Thomas Hughes and others, *The Misfortunes of Arthur* (London: Tudor Facsimile Texts, 1911).

39 Francis Bacon, '*In Felicem Memoriam Elizabethae Angliae Reginae*', in Francis Bacon, *The Works of Francis Bacon*, ed. J. Spedding, R. L. Ellis, and D. D. Heath, 7 vols. (London: Longman's, 1857–74), VI: 296.

40 References to *Shakespeare's Edmund Ironside: The Lost Play*, ed. Eric Sams (Aldershot: Wildwood House, 1986). The play is almost certainly not Shakespeare's.

41 The David–Henry analogy had been common: see Greg Walker, *Writing under Tyranny: English Literature and the Henrician Reformation* (Oxford University Press, 2005).

42 References to *The Minor Elizabethan Drama*, vol. I.

43 Christopher Marlowe, *Tamburlaine*, ed. J. S. Cunningham (Manchester University Press, 1981).

44 See Michael Witmore, *Pretty Creatures: Children and Fiction in the English Renaissance* (Ithaca: Cornell University Press, 2007).

45 References to Robert Greene, *Alphonsus King of Aragon*, ed. W. W. Greg (London: Oxford University Press for the Malone Society, 1926).

46 *The Countess of Pembroke's Arcadia (The New Arcadia)*, ed. Victor Skretko-wicz (Oxford: Clarendon Press, 1987), p. 175.

47 Scott McMillin and Sally-Beth MacLean, *The Queen's Men and Their Plays* (Cambridge University Press, 1998), p. 158 see *Selimus* as part of an 'anti-Marlowe' campaign, demonstrating the moral perils of the *Tamburlaine* model – that may be the intention but, by taking things further, the play is if anything more subversive; Mark Hutchings, 'The End of *II Tamburlaine* and the Beginnings of *King Lear*', *Notes and Queries* 245 (2000): 84–6 argues that *Selimus* is a 'corrective' to *Tamburlaine*'s optimism that the Turks can be defeated (p. 85) and to the too-easy transfer of power with which Marlowe's play ends; Shakespeare, in this reading, was more persuaded by *Selimus*'s pessimism about inheritance than Marlowe's optimism.

48 See Tom MacFaul, *Male Friendship in Shakespeare and His Contemporaries* (Cambridge University Press, 2007), chapter 3.

49 References to *The Tragical Reign of Selimus* (London: Chiswick Press, 1908; reprinted Oxford University Press, 1964).

50 Alan Macfarlane, *Marriage and Love in England 1300–1840* (Oxford: Basil Blackwell, 1986), p. 232 notes William Harvey's later theory of 'telegony', i.e. the idea 'that the womb of a woman was like a clay mould: it would be shaped by the first child, and all subsequent children would bear the imprint of the first'; although the idea was not common, if applied to Tamora's womb, it would imply that her conception by the Moor would affect any future offspring by Saturninus.

51 References to Thomas Kyd, *The Spanish Tragedy*, ed. Philip Edwards (London: Methuen, 1959).

52 Lukas Erne, *Beyond The Spanish Tragedy: A Study of the Works of Thomas Kyd* (Manchester University Press, 2001), pp. 90–2 is sceptical about the importance of anti-Spanish feeling to the play's popularity, emphasizing rather the appeal of the play's expression of hierarchical frustration, but while it is true that the play does not demonize the Spanish, it is surely right to see some *Schadenfreude* at imaginary Spanish misfortunes as being important to its impact.

53 Erne, *Beyond The Spanish Tragedy*, p. 67 argues that the play was probably intended to be in five acts, but the structural effect of inaction at that crucial stage remains.

54 References to Thomas Kyd, *The Spanish Tragedie with The First Part of Jeronimo*, ed. Emma Smith (London: Penguin, 1998).

55 As John Kerrigan points out, Hieronimo is not even able to act the role of revenger in his play – *Revenge Tragedy: Aeschylus to Armaggedon* (Oxford: Clarendon Press, 1996), p. 181.

3   IDENTIFICATION AND IMPASSE IN DRAMA OF THE 1590s: *HENRY VI* TO *HAMLET*

1 For the way the genre developed by blending protestant propaganda modes with the new inwardness of Kyd's and Marlowe's styles, see McMillin and MacLean, *The Queen's Men and Their Plays*, pp. 167–8.

2 Lawrence Danson, *Shakespeare's Dramatic Genres*, pp. 89–90.

3 Thomas Nashe, *Pierce Pennilesse his Supplication to the Diuell*, in Thomas Nash, *The Works of Thomas Nashe*, ed. Ronald B. McKerrow, corr. F. P. Wilson, 5 vols. (Oxford: Basil Blackwell & Mott, 1957), I: 212.

4 It is ironic, then, as Tromly points out – *Fathers and Sons in Shakespeare*, pp. 43–4 – that Shakespeare has erased Talbot's other sons, who are mentioned in his sources.

5 See Jean E. Howard and Phyllis Rackin, *Engendering a Nation: A Feminist Account of Shakespeare's English Histories* (London: Routledge, 1997), pp. 61–4.

6 In Lodge and Greene's *A Looking Glass for London and England* (?1592), the arriviste royal favourite Radagon repudiates his impoverished and starving parents, for which crime he is promptly swallowed up into the earth. Other than Joan, I can think of no one who curses their *father* so specifically.

7 See Giorgio Melchiori (ed.), *King Edward III* (Cambridge University Press, 1998), Introduction, pp. 16–24.

8 As David Womersley points out in *Divinity and State* (Oxford University Press, 2010), p. 145, 'the fact that Edward triumphs through his son ... creates an audacious parallelism between the governance of England and of heaven'.

9 This is to say that patricide here is not really dramatized; significant as these figures are, they do not constitute a representation of the unthinkable murder of a father (or indeed of a son). It is important that these figures are unnamed, and therefore do not constitute figures of pathos.

10 Catherine Belsey, 'Little Princes: Shakespeare's Royal Children', in Kate Chedgzoy, Susanne Greenhalgh, and Robert Shaughnessy (eds.), *Shakespeare and Childhood* (Cambridge University Press, 2007), pp. 40, 43.

11 See, further, my discussion of this moment in *Poetry and Paternity*, pp. 59–60.

12 References to Christopher Marlowe, *Edward the Second*, ed. Charles R. Forker (Manchester University Press, 1994).

13 Haber, *Desire and Dramatic Form*, p. 36.

14 See Heather Dubrow, *Shakespeare and Domestic Loss: Forms of Deprivation, Mourning and Recuperation* (Cambridge University Press, 1999), p. 153.

15 As Bamber, *Comic Women, Tragic Men*, p. 153 observes, 'Prince Hal enacts perfect, almost studied consciousness of the separation between father and son' in his control of his plot.

16 Howard and Rackin, *Engendering a Nation*, p. 30 point out that women are radically marginalized from the business of dynasty- and nation-building in the second tetralogy.

17 See, for instance, Theseus and Hippolyta's famous discussion of shadows in *A Midsummer Night's Dream*, V. i. 1–25. The phrase 'shadow of succession' may fit with the general sense in Shakespeare's plays of the inadequacy of dominant modes of mimetic representation, whether those be artistic or patrilineal; see Pauline Kiernan, *Shakespeare's Theory of Drama* (Cambridge University Press, 1996), particularly p. 190, where she discusses the problem of shadows as opposed to the power of dramatic embodiment.

18 Valerie Traub, *Desire and Anxiety: Circulations of Sexuality in Shakespearean Drama* (London: Routledge, 1992), p. 59 sees the mother as associated with death, and Falstaff as a grotesque imagining of motherhood – in choosing his father, then, as a better model than the fat knight, Hal is opting against a feminine world.

19 As Tromly points out – *Fathers and Sons in Shakespeare*, pp. 135–6 – in Shakespeare's sources, including *The Famous Victories*, the prince takes the crown, but does not put it on.

20 See MacFaul, *Male Friendship*, p. 131.

21 References to *The Famous Victories of Henry the Fifth*, ed. Chiaki Hanabusa (Manchester University Press for the Malone Society, 2007); see also lines 514–15. 'The young prince' is the title repeatedly given by other characters, though the speech headings call him Henry V even before his father's death.

22 Cf. *Henry VI Part 2*, IV. ii. 8–9.

23 This is an example of the 'anxiety for narrative completeness' characteristic of the Queen's Men's plays – see McMillin and MacLean, *The Queen's Men and Their Plays*.

24 Erickson, *Patriarchal Structures*, p. 43.

25 What a modern reader might see as an Oedipal tension is therefore turned into a mode of political discourse, as Berger suggests – *Making Trifles of Terrors*, p. 218.

26 See Harold Bloom, *Shakespeare: The Invention of the Human* (New York: Riverhead Books, 1998), p. 55.

27 References to *The Troublesome Raigne of King John* (London: C. Praetorius, 1888).

28 Shakespeare uses the idea of Phaethon very differently, as a way of thinking about the fundamental non-equivalence of fathers and sons; see Kiernan, *Shakespeare's Theory of Drama*, p. 29.

29 In fact, *The Troublesome Reign* has Queen Eleanor doubt Richard's paternity; as Howard and Rackin, *Engendering a Nation*, p. 133 point out, 'Only in Shakespeare is [the Bastard] required to receive his paternity from the hands of women.'

30 For the influence of Marlowe in the play, see McMillin and MacLean, *The Queen's Men and Their Plays*, p. 84. The repeated use of the name 'Cordelion' also has a Marlovian ring (one also wonders if it might have later inspired Shakepeare, in *King Lear*, to revise the name Cordella to Cordelia).

31 See Peter Holbrook, *Shakespeare's Individualism* (Cambridge University Press, 2010), p. 121 for a fine discussion of the Bastard as self-creator.

32 References to *Look about You*, ed. W. W. Greg (London: Oxford University Press for the Malone Society, 1913); in fact only three sons are presented, Geoffrey being absent.

33 References to Henry Porter, *The Two Angrie Women of Abington*, ed. W. W. Greg (London: Oxford University Press for the Malone Society, 1912).

34 Kiernan Ryan, *Shakespeare's Comedies* (Basingstoke: Palgrave Macmillan, 2009), p. 9 also treats this misrecognition as being a profound mark of 'time's dominion' in this play.

35 It is also ironic, given his name, which echoes that of Theseus' father who died as a result of his son's neglect, that his son will help to save him. L. Maguire, *Shakespeare's Names*, pp. 79–80, discussing Egeus in *A Midsummer Night's Dream*, points out that Theseus was often considered a parricide in his failure to announce his return from Crete by hoisting white sails. One might also argue, though, that the classical Aegeus could have been more patient in waiting for confirmation/true recognition before killing himself.

36 As Ewan Fernie points out, the shame for Hero's supposed misdeeds is mostly felt by Leonato; it is mostly a masculine, paternal matter – *Shame in Shakespeare* (London: Routledge, 2002), p. 86.

37 See Lynda E. Boose, 'The Father and the Bride in Shakespeare', *PMLA* 97 (1982): 325–47.

38 Bamber, *Comic Women, Tragic Men*, p. 116 argues that 'salvation and damnation are subjects for witty repartee' in Jessica's case; yet such banter has serious potential.

39 References to Christopher Marlowe, *The Jew of Malta*, ed. N. W. Bawcutt (Manchester University Press, 1978).

40 Similarly, when Barabas plays the evil stage Jew in front of Ithamore (II. iii. 176ff.) he may become stuck in this role.

41 She makes Bernadine her 'ghostly father' (III. vi. 12), but he is no better than her real one, betraying the secrets of the confessional, and seeming to lust after her once she's dead.

42 See the discussion of this moment in Ryan, *Shakespeare's Comedies*, p. 133, where it is treated as an indication of the real problems of *kind*ness in the play.

43 References to *Englishmen for My Money*, ed. W. W. Greg (London: Oxford University Press for the Malone Society, 1912).

44 Unless otherwise stated, references to Marston are to *The Plays of John Marston*, ed. H. Harvey Wood, 3 vols. (Edinburgh: Oliver & Boyd, 1934–9); the edition has no line numbers.

45 Heywood, *Dramatic Works*, vol. ii.

46 References to *The Plays of George Chapman: The Comedies*, ed. Allan Holaday assisted by Michael Kiernan (Urbana, IL: University of Illinois Press, 1970).

47 *Shakespeare and the Drama of His Time*, p. 72.

48 See my discussion of the play in *Poetry and Paternity*, pp. 190–3.

49 See Tom MacFaul, 'Friendship in Sidney's *Arcadias*', *Studies in English Literature* 49 (2009): 17–33.

50 Anticipating *The Winter's Tale*, the apparently dead Prince Ferdinand pretends to be a statue in front of the penitent princess who has mistreated him, coming to life in order to offer forgiveness. Shakespeare's changes to this scene – reversing the gender dynamic, not bringing us in on the plan, stretching the timescale of the penitence – are of course crucial, interrelated developments, bringing a new set of meanings to the device.

51 See Gillian Woods, 'The Contexts of *The Trial of Chivalry*', *Notes and Queries* 54 (2007): 313–18.

52 Anon., *The Trial of Chivalry* (London: 1605).

53 Anon., *The Blind Beggar of Bednall Green* (London: 1659).

54 Anon., *The Wisdom of Doctor Dodypoll* (London: 1600).

55 References to *The Weakest Goeth to the Wall*, ed. W. W. Greg (London: Oxford University Press for the Malone Society, 1912).

56 Ryan, *Shakespeare's Comedies*, p. 220.

57 See Alciati, *Emblems*, 195, and Whitney, *Emblems*, p. 163; cf. Alciati 161, which represents *mutuum auxilium* (mutual help), also used by Whitney. The Alciati emblems can be conveniently seen at www.mun.ca/alciato. Whitney's emblems are available at www.emblem.libraries.psu.edu/whitntoc. htm. The image eventually became comic: in Beaumont and Fletcher's *Cupid's Revenge* (c. 1607–8, pub. 1615), Duke Leontius is flattered as an Aeneas, but really 'lookes like his olde father upon his backe' (II. vi. 70).

58 Many editors assign this line to Celia – but see the discussion by Juliet Dusinberre in her notes: *As You Like It*, ed. Juliet Dusinberre (London: Arden Shakespeare, 2006).

59 Bamber, *Comic Women, Tragic Men* observes in passing that 'We do not judge Rosalind by her loyalty to Duke Senior' (p. 109); we may not judge her positively on this account, but there is at least the potential to judge her negatively.

60 A. D. Nuttall, *Shakespeare the Thinker* (New Haven, CT: Yale University Press, 2007), p. 237.

61 *As You Like It*, ed. Dusinberre, Appendix 1.

62 References to *The Tragedy of Locrine* (Oxford University Press for the Malone Society, 1908).

63 See Palfrey and Stern, *Shakespeare in Parts*.

64 See Chapter 2, above, for a discussion of why *The Misfortunes of Arthur* is the exception to the rule of not representing patricide in the non-Islamic world.

65 References to Thomas Lodge, *The Wounds of Civil War*, ed. Joseph W. Houppert (London: Edward Arnold, 1970).

66 E.g. *Arden of Faversham* and Robert Yarington's *Two Lamentable Tragedies* (both early 1590s).

67 Pressures on memory are also accentuated by the ambiguity as to whether Old Hamlet's Ghost comes from Hell or Purgatory – see Stephen Greenblatt, *Hamlet in Purgatory* (Princeton University Press, 2001), and Michael Neill, *Issues of Death: Mortality and Identity in English Renaissance Tragedy* (Oxford: Clarendon Press, 1997), pp. 243–61.

68 References to John Marston, *The Malcontent and Other Plays*, ed. Keith Sturgess (Oxford University Press, 1997).

69 On the crucial importance of memory in *Hamlet*, see Kerrigan, *Revenge Tragedy*, p. 192.

70 For the key Oedipal readings of *Hamlet*, see *The Interpretation of Dreams*, in Freud, *The Standard Edition*, vols. IV–V; and Ernest Jones, *Hamlet and Oedipus* (London: Gollancz, 1949).

71 Nuttall, *Shakespeare the Thinker*, p. 194.

72 As Tromly points out – *Fathers and Sons in Shakespeare*, p. 161 – 'Hamlet's most thorough work of repression centres on his ghostly father rather than his carnal father'. In the end, Hamlet 'aveng[es] himself against his father and . . . against his own succession'.

73 Peter Alexander, *Hamlet: Father and Son* (Oxford: Clarendon Press, 1955), p. 35; see also Holbrook, *Shakespeare's Individualism*, p. 77.

74 There is also the shadowy issue of Denmark being apparently an elective monarchy, which, as Philippa Berry points out, 'obliquely calls a patrilineal transmission of royal power into question' – *Shakespeare's Feminine Endings: Disfiguring Death in the Tragedies* (London: Routledge, 1999), p. 57.

75 *The First Quarto of Hamlet*, ed. Kathleen O. Irace (Cambridge University Press, 1998), scene 14.

76 Hamlet's desire to drink 'hot blood' (III. ii. 390) probably derives from this play (line 1054).

77 Jasper Heywood, in 1560, translates thus: 'Truth of th' uncertain seed / By such a practice may be tri'd: – if it refuse they shall, / Nor of debate will bearers be, if they him uncle call – / He is their father.' References to Jasper Heywood (trans.), *Thyestes*, ed. Joost Daalder (London: Ernest Benn, 1982), II. 154–7.

78 Heywood translates: 'now even children born to me / I count; and now of bridebed chaste the faith I do repair' (V. iii. 130–1). As Daalder points out in his notes to these lines, Heywood appears to imply that Atreus' sons'

involvement in the plot has assured him of his paternity; for Seneca, however, the vindication is more abstractly the result of the revenge.

79 See Patricia Parker, 'Black Hamlet: Battening on the Moor', *Shakespeare Studies* 31 (2003): 127–64.

80 On the pressure to differentiate between Old Hamlet and Claudius, see Janet Adelman, *Suffocating Mothers*, p. 13.

81 Emrys Jones, *Scenic Form in Shakespeare* (Oxford: Clarendon Press, 1971), pp. 105–6 notes the structural importance of the heroes' waiting to take on fathers' roles in both *Hamlet* and *Henry IV Part 2*.

82 In Beaumont and Fletcher's *Love's Cure* (c. 1606), Vitelli needs to take vengeance for his uncle's murder, but would not take revenge on 'a weak woman' (the murderer's wife) and her daughter, but now sees 'the father, and his hopefull son' as worthy quarries 'to make me man' (I. i. 121–6); his gendered self-realization is crucial to revenge drama, even though this play is ultimately a tragicomedy, where familial tensions are resolved by love. This play, with its effeminate son and its masculine daughter, both of whom need to find their proper gender roles, sums up a tradition of gender trouble in revenge drama.

83 See McCabe, *Incest, Drama and Nature's Law*, p. 167.

84 Polonius, in fact, is very much a symbol of domesticity, given that we are presented with so many scenes of his familial dealings.

85 Alternatively, if the play comes after *Hamlet*, that hint of Shakespeare's might have been enough to inspire the whole play.

86 The play was printed as Marlowe's.

87 References to Dekker, *Dramatic Works*, vol. IV.

88 See Alastair Fowler's reading of the play in *Renaissance Realism* (pp. 100–20).

89 Simon Palfrey, *Doing Shakespeare*, 2nd edn (London: Methuen Drama, 2011), p. 44.

90 Leonard Tennenhouse has argued that a major shift takes place in drama's representation of patriarchal power around 1600 (he identifies *Hamlet* as a pivot) – *Power on Display: The Politics of Shakespeare's Genres* (London: Methuen, 1986), particularly pp. 37, 62, 79, 85.

4 LIMITING THE FATHER IN THE 1600s: THE WAKE OF *HAMLET* AND *KING LEAR*

1 Some of them were discussed in the previous chapter, but difficulties of chronology may mean that those plays were models rather than imitations.

2 References to Henry Chettle, *The Tragedy of Hoffman*, ed. Harold Jenkins (London: Oxford University Press for the Malone Society, 1951).

3 See Duke Pesta, 'Articulating Skeletons: *Hamlet, Hoffman* and the Anatomical Graveyard', *Cahiers Elisabéthains* 69 (2006): 21–39.

4 A similar loss of identity can be found in *The Revenger's Tragedy* (c. 1607, probably by Middleton), but here there is less attention to women's power and to the process of taking revenge for a father. Vindice is more motivated

by revenge for his beloved than for his father, and perhaps that explains why he loses his identity so radically in the course of the play.

5 As they are in having the Ophelia figure Lucibella take an active part in vengeance for her father and fiancé.

6 Indeed, such phraseology had become a perversely paradoxical proverb for happiness – see Chapter 1, above.

7 References to Cyril Tourneur, *The Atheist's Tragedy*, ed. Brian Morris and Roma Gill (London: A&C Black, 1989).

8 For the importance of the genre of 'disguised ruler' plays, see Wiggins, *Shakespeare and the Drama of His Time*, pp. 106–10.

9 References to Samuel Rowley, *When You See Me, You Know Me*, ed. F. P. Wilson (Oxford University Press for the Malone Society, 1952).

10 The text actually reads 'first'.

11 References to Barnabe Barnes, *The Devil's Charter*, ed. Jim C. Pogue (New York: Garland, 1980).

12 L. C. Knights, *How Many Children Had Lady Macbeth? An Essay in the Theory and Practice of Shakespeare Criticism* (Cambridge: G. Fraser, The Minority Press, 1933).

13 Ironically, as Robin Headlam Wells points out, *Macbeth* is full of 'images of springtime, procreation, and harvest', most notably, the 'procreant cradle' (I. vi. 8) of the birds at Macbeth's castle – *Shakespeare on Masculinity*, p. 136.

14 As Bamber observes, *Comic Women, Tragic Men*, p. 107 'Macbeth is neither a father nor a son; the dialectic in this play is between Macbeth's individualism and the social cohesion of the world of the fathers and sons'.

15 Tennenhouse, *Power on Display*, p. 131 argues that 'all the elements of nature … join to put Malcolm on the throne'.

16 See Alexander Leggatt, *Shakespeare's Tragedies: Violation and Identity* (Cambridge University Press, 2005), pp. 201–4.

17 Shakespeare may deliberately invite the comparison to Heywood's play when Macbeth compares his murderous intentions to 'Tarquin's ravishing strides' (II. i. 55).

18 For the continental tradition, see John Doebler, 'Beaumont's *The Knight of the Burning Pestle* and the Prodigal Son Plays', in *Studies in English Literature* 5 (1965): 333–44. For the English tradition, see Alan R. Young, *The English Prodigal Son Plays: A Theatrical Fashion of the Sixteenth and Seventeenth Centuries* (Salzburg: Institut für Anglistik und Amerikanistik, Universität von Salzburg, 1979).

19 Richard Helgerson, *The Elizabethan Prodigals* (Berkeley: University of California Press, 1976).

20 References to *The Shakespeare Apocrypha*, ed. C. F. Tucker Brooke (Oxford: Clarendon Press, 1987).

21 See my discussion of the play in *Poetry and Paternity*, pp. 190–3.

22 References to Thomas Heywood, *Three Marriage Plays*, ed. Paul Merchant (Manchester University Press, 1996).

23 John Day, *Law Tricks*, ed. John Crow (London: Oxford University Press for the Malone Society, 1949).

24 The text actually reads the nonsensical 'your sonne'.

25 Compare Falstaff's excuse for running away at Gad's Hill – *Henry IV Part 1*, II. iv. 267–75.

26 References to *Dramatic Works of Thomas Dekker*.

27 An idea ultimately deriving from Plato's *Lysis*.

28 Though she is not unchaste, she is rather eager for her husband's sexual services; there is also some sexual licence in the prodigal apprentice Quicksilver – of whom the language of the prodigal son is used (I. i. 115–17); references to George Chapman, Ben Jonson, and John Marston, *Eastward Ho*, ed. R. W. van Fossen (Manchester University Press, 1979).

29 It is just possible that the influence works the other way, and that Jonson (probable author of this scene) was mocking *King Lear*, but that would require us to postulate a very early date for Shakespeare's play.

30 References to *The Collected Works of Robert Armin* (New York: Johnson Reprint Corporation, 1972).

31 John Jones, *Shakespeare at Work* (Oxford: Clarendon Press, 1995), pp. 208–39 argues that the Folio version of *Lear* is a revision which is contemporaneous with the late romances/tragicomedies, and relates to their themes.

32 References to *King Leir*, ed. Tiffany Stern (London: Nick Hern Books, 2002).

33 In addition to being slang for the vagina, 'nothing' is often, paradoxically, a supplement for Shakespeare: in Sonnet 20, for instance, Nature gives the young man 'one thing to my purpose nothing' (line 12).

34 As Curtis Perry points out, this has a clear political dimension, acting as a complex critique of King James's fantasies of rule: 'It is possible ... to read in the language of Lear's abdication a kind of *reductio ad absurdum* of the normative ideal of royal bounty as free-flowing and limitless: once the kingdom itself is given away it becomes evident that royal magnificence is not finally as abundant as grace' – Curtis Perry, *The Making of Jacobean Culture: James I and the Renegotiation of Elizabethan Literary Practice* (Cambridge University Press, 1997), p. 126. He also sees the absence of Lear's wife as a component of 'an ideal of autonomous patriarchal rule' (p. 130).

35 Gadding (capricious wandering about) was a supposed vice for which women were particularly criticized – see Laura Gowing, *Domestic Dangers: Women, Words, and Sex in Early Modern London* (Oxford: Clarendon Press, 1996), p. 87.

36 If, as Tennenhouse suggests, the play is concerned to restore supposedly natural patriarchy against a more feminized order of things (*Power on Display*, p. 142), it is at the cost of all these other values. Margreta de Grazia argues that there is no true superfluity in *Lear*, that everything returns to its normal course, but that is to focus on the social at the expense of the emotional – 'The Ideology of Superfluous Things: *King Lear* as Period Piece', in Margreta de Grazia, Maureen Quilligan, and Peter Stallybrass (eds.),

Subject and Object in Renaissance Culture (Cambridge University Press, 1996), pp. 17–42.

37 It is perhaps instructive that Orwell thought Edgar 'a superfluous character' (he also believed that 'One wicked daughter would have been quite enough') – 'Lear, Tolstoy, and the Fool', in *The Complete Works of George Orwell*, 20 vols. (London: Secker & Warburg, 1986–98), xix: 59.

38 In Harry Berger's brilliant discussion of the play, what is discovered (or revealed) is fear – specifically the fear that one does not deserve love: see *Making Trifles of Terrors*, pp. 25–69, especially p. 33; that discovery may lead to a deeper discovery, though: that one *cannot* deserve love, that there can be no sufficient cause for it.

39 Goulart, *The Wise Vieillard*, cit. Shepard, *Meanings of Manhood*, p. 41.

40 Shepard, *Meanings of Manhood*, pp. 241–3.

41 See Stephen Greenblatt, *Will in the World: How Shakespeare Became Shakespeare* (London: Jonathan Cape, 2004), pp. 356–61.

42 John Bayley, *Shakespeare and Tragedy* (London: Routledge & Kegan Paul, 1981), p. 21.

43 This point, and some of what follows, chimes with Stanley Cavell's argument in *Disowning Knowledge*, pp. 45–51.

44 The phrase, fascinatingly, originates in *King Leir*, where Cordella tells her husband Gallia that he has 'no cause' to worry about her grief (IV. iv. 9); he goes on to say that Cordella should not worry too much about her father, given that she is 'now graft in another stock' (line 17); this is an essentially *comic* attitude.

45 As Novy points out, the need for the overly masterful, like Lear, to be forgiven, is a crucial way of blending emotional mutuality into a hierarchical world – *Love's Argument*, pp. 150–1, 160.

46 Tromly is surely right to see 'a note of the human sublime' here, but I think him wrong to suggest that there is 'no space for filial ambivalence' in the scene – *Fathers and Sons in Shakespeare*, p. 209.

47 The footprints etc. that, in *The Libation Bearers*, rather ridiculously allow Orestes and Electra to recognize one another; Euripides mocked this form of recognition in his *Electra*.

48 Wallace Stevens refers, in 'An Ordinary Evening in New Haven', to 'the intricate evasions of as' – *Collected Poems* (London: Faber and Faber, 1955), p. 486. There is no finer literary example of the serendipitous virtue of such evasions than Lear's 'as I am a man'.

49 I think that Terence Cave finds too much here, when he says that what Lear recognizes here is 'a moral or spiritual quality rather than a genealogy' (*Recognitions*, p. 275); that may be true at first, but the spiritual gives way to the simply human.

50 *King Leir's* Cordella puts this double duty in a more patly aphoristic manner: 'Ah, good old father, tell to my thy grief; / I'll sorrow with thee if not add relief' (V. iv. 124–5).

51 The Quarto reads 'when did you die?'

52 Helen Small, *The Long Life* (Oxford University Press, 2007), p. 81.

53 For a fine discussion of apocalyptic finality in *King Lear*, see Frank Kermode, *Shakespeare's Language* (London: Allen Lane, 2000), pp. 183–200. De Grazia, however, sees the play's sense of an ending as a 'chiliastic tease' – 'The Ideology of Superfluous Things', p. 31.

54 See Small, *The Long Life*, p. 87.

55 Of course, tragicomedy begins before *King Lear*, but its entrenchment as the key late Jacobean genre has a great deal to do with Shakespeare having taken tragedy to its limits in that play. For the roots and development of the genre, see Eugene M. Waith, *The Pattern of Tragicomedy in Beaumont and Fletcher* (New Haven, CT: Yale University Press, 1952), G. K. Hunter, 'Italian Tragicomedy on the English Stage', in his *Dramatic Identities and Cultural Traditions* (Liverpool University Press, 1978), and Nancy Klein Maguire (ed.), *Renaissance Tragicomedy* (New York: AMS Press, 1987).

56 References to Heywood, *Dramatic Works*, vol. vi.

57 It may have been performed as early as 1608, but was licensed as a new play in 1622; see *ODNB* entry for William Rowley.

58 References to *The Shakespeare Apocrypha*.

59 References to Edward Sharpham, *Cupid's Whirligig*, ed. Allardyce Nicoll (Waltham Saint Lawrence, Berkshire: The Golden Cockerel Press, 1926).

60 See Kevin Sharpe, *Image Wars: Promoting Kings and Commonwealths in England 1603–1660* (New Haven, CT: Yale University Press, 2010), chapter 4.

61 References to *Nero & Other Plays*, ed. Herbert P. Horne, H. Ellis, A. Symons, and A. Verity (London: Vizetelly & Co., 1888).

62 There is some havering over what happens to Helvetius: the performance version adds a short scene which indicates plans to free him as he is 'The honourable father of the state' (IV. iia. 9), but does not bring him back. The original has no such scene, but does bring him on at the end to validate Govianus' succession.

63 Robin Headlam Wells, *Shakespeare on Masculinity*, p. 37 argues that 'Having anatomized the Herculean hero in a series of tragedies, Shakespeare turns, at the end of his writing career, to an entirely different kind of leader' – that is, the Orphic figure of Prospero.

64 See Caroline Bicks, 'Midwiving Virility in Early Modern England', in Naomi J. Miller and Naomi Yavneh (eds.), *Maternal Measures: Figuring Caregiving in the Early Modern Period* (Aldershot: Ashgate, 2000).

65 McCabe, *Incest, Drama and Nature's Law*, p. 190.

66 Kiernan, *Shakespeare's Theory of Drama*, p. 90 suggests that Prospero's acknowledgement of Caliban has to do with him acknowledging his own *natural* humanity, for Prospero's art was not potent enough to deal with such natural issues as finding food and water on the island.

67 Lyne, *Shakespeare's Late Work*, p. 89 argues that in Shakespeare's late plays 'the central characters are reconciled to their own mortality by embracing the existence and growth of the next generation'.

68 Bamber, *Comic Women, Tragic Men*, pp. 171, 191 rightly emphasizes the implicit grief involved in the play's difference from *The Winter's Tale*, in the fact that 'Prospero's wife stays dead'.

69 Tennenhouse, *Power on Display*, p. 186 argues that the late romances introduce a new, more distant and alienated image of patriarchal power, but it is also coloured by sadness and self-effacement; compare Holbrook, *Shakespeare's Individualism*, for a rather different, but complementary account of the kind of freedom Prospero arrives at.

70 It is, however, interesting to speculate: did Shakespeare start off with the idea that Antonio would think his son dead after the shipwreck, or did he even plan to have that son die as Prospero's vengeance? If the latter, Shakespeare's failure to suppress the plot strand completely fits nicely with the gritted teeth of Prospero's forgiveness.

71 See my discussion of these lines in *Poetry and Paternity*, p. 16.

72 McCabe, *Incest, Drama and Nature's Law*, p. 180.

73 Valerie Traub may be right to argue that the recovery of Hermione is 'wish-fulfillment for Leontes' rather than 'a victory for the wronged heroine' (*Desire and Anxiety*, p. 45), but to get his wish fulfilled in the purging of female sexuality, Leontes has to lose his primary masculine attribute, a son.

74 The play may also have been placed last in the Folio as its last word 'peace' nicely accords with James I's motto *Beati Pacifici* – blessed are the peace-makers; the effect is to ally the ideology of the reigning monarch with the national playwright. Given the outbreak of what would become the Thirty Years War, that ideology was increasingly controversial by 1623, and had been quite controversial in Shakespeare's own lifetime.

75 Sir A[ntony] W[eldon], *The Court and Character of King James* (London: 1651).

76 Novy, *Love's Argument*, p. 170.

77 References to William Shakespeare, *Pericles*, ed. Suzanne Gossett (London: Arden Shakespeare, 2004) – for once, given the play's seriously problematic text, it seems best to use this edition, which reflects the latest scholarship, rather than the *Riverside*.

78 Cave, *Recognitions*, p. 289.

79 Introduction to Arden edition, pp. 46–8.

5   AFTER *THE TEMPEST*

1 Of the other children born in Shakespeare's plays, Perdita and Mariana are born in decidedly troubling situations – one in gaol, the other after a storm – and Tamora's son by Aaron is hardly the most promising figure.

2 See, further, my discussion of *Henry VIII* in *Poetry and Paternity*, pp. 56–7.

3 Henry Peacham, *The Compleat Gentleman* (London, 1622), p. 32.

4 See Gordon McMullan, *The Politics of Unease in the Plays of John Fletcher* (Amherst: University of Massachusetts Press, 1994), pp. 106–8.

5 See Paul Salzman, *Literary Culture in Jacobean England: Reading 1621* (London: Palgrave Macmillan, 2002), p. xvii.

6 Though the play may announce itself as 'nor *Comody*, nor *Tragedy*, / Nor *History*' (Prologue, 6–7), it is clearly more the first than anything else.

7 References to Thomas Heywood, *The Captives*, ed. Arthur Brown (Oxford University Press for the Malone Society, 1953).

8 See Lawrence Stone, *The Crisis of the Aristocracy 1558–1641* (Oxford: Clarendon Press, 1965), and Mervyn James, *English Politics and the Concept of Honour 1485–1642* (Oxford: Past and Present Society, 1978).

9 As the play was included in the Beaumont and Fletcher Folio of 1647, I refer to the *Dramatic Works*, ed. Bowers.

10 It is worth noting that Erota, in attempting to seduce Antinous, tells him 'looke what honour thou dost gaine by me, / I cannot lose by it' (III. iii. 3–4); this point about marriage ought to apply to the father–son bond too.

11 Anon., *The Costlie Whore* (London: 1633).

12 There is also a very similar scene of paternal lamentation (E4^v–FI^r) in John Day's *The Knave in Grain* (also c. 1625), perhaps indicating that there was a new vogue for *The Spanish Tragedy* at around that stage – but, in the case of Day's play, the son is not really dead.

13 William Sampson, *The Vow-Breaker: or, the Fair Maid of Clifton* (London: 1636).

14 It is probably no coincidence that Hamlet's use of a picture is also in a scene that presents a ghost.

15 W. Smith, *The Hector of Germany, or The Palsgrave, Prime Elector* (London: 1615). The author is almost certainly William Smith, a herald.

16 It may be a reworking of an earlier play, and it does seem to fit better with the mode of early Jacobean tragedy than with later Jacobean tragicomedy, but it has elements of both. References are to Dekker, *Dramatic Works*.

17 In this respect the play is tragicomic in the later Jacobean manner: were it a play of around 1600–8, there would surely be a bloodbath.

18 The play also contains some very interesting reflections on Ireland and Wales – as various characters pretend to be from those nations. It deserves deeper study on this front, but this is not the place; nonetheless, it suggests that the play is reflecting on the special character of the British Isles.

19 It is surely no coincidence that King James had in his youth written an epic poem about this battle.

20 Anon., *Swetnam the Woman-Hater* (Amersham: Tudor Facsimile Texts, 1914).

21 References to Middleton, *Collected Works*: Taylor's text here emends to 'curse' rather than the 'course' of the original, on the basis that it is not an idiom typical of Middleton, but that reading makes rather less sense.

22 For a discussion of the romantic plot see MacFaul, *Male Friendship*, pp. 86–8.

23 References to John Webster, *The Duchess of Malfi and Other Plays*, ed. René Weis (Oxford University Press, 1996).

24 Rowley, who was responsible for the Compass plot, would have to have seen Donne's poem in manuscript, as it was not published until 1633, but that is entirely possible, given the circulation of Donne's texts.

25 M. C. Bradbrook, *John Webster: Citizen and Dramatist* (London: Weidenfeld and Nicolson, 1980), p. 177.

26 Webster, *The Duchess of Malfi and Other Plays.*

27 S. S., *The Honest Lawyer* (Amersham: Tudor Facsimile Editions, 1914).

28 Richard Rowland, in his fine discussion of the play, argues that it is 'concerned with the instability of generic conventions' – *Thomas Heywood's Theatre 1599–1639: Locations, Translations, and Conflict* (Farnham: Ashgate, 2010), p. 206.

29 References to Heywood, *Dramatic Works*, vol. IV.

30 The comic elements of the main plot are pointed up by a commonplace enough prodigal-son subplot, in which Young Lionel is (rather ineptly) helped by his foxily cunning servant Reginald to conceal his boozing and whoring during the father's absence.

31 References to *The Complete Works of John Webster*, ed. F. L. Lucas, 4 vols. (London: Chatto & Windus, 1927).

32 As Ira Clark, *The Moral Art of Philip Massinger* (Lewisburg: Bucknell Unversity Press, 1993), p. 178 suggests, Massinger is concerned here to attack the 'blind egoism' of aristocratic values.

CONCLUSION

1 Some of the great Modernists – Lawrence, Woolf, Joyce, for instance – do engage very strikingly with fathers, handling them with what Philip Larkin calls 'a son's harsh patronage', but mothers are so much more important in *Sons and Lovers, To the Lighthouse*, and even *Ulysses* that the power of the father is quite easily dissipated.

2 Franco Moretti, 'The Great Eclipse: Tragic Form as the Deconsecration of Sovereignty', trans. David Miller, in *Signs Taken for Wonders: On the Sociology of Literary Forms* (London: Verso, 2005), pp. 42–82.

3 James Joyce, *Ulysses* (Harmondsworth: Penguin, 1992), pp. 265–6.

4 As Alexander Leggatt observes, 'Shakespeare's people, like the people of no other dramatist, care for each other' – *English Drama: Shakespeare to the Restoration: 1590–1660* (Harlow: Longman, 1988), p. 97.

5 The Volscians later follow Coriolanus 'Against us brats [Romans] with no less confidence / Than boys pursuing summer butterflies' (IV. vi. 93–4).

6 For a comprehensive discussion of this development, see Michael McKeon, *The Secret History of Domesticity: Public, Private and the Division of Knowledge* (Baltimore, MD: Johns Hopkins University Press, 2005).

7 *Shakespeare's Individualism.*

8 See Stephen Greenblatt, *Shakespeare's Freedom* (The University of Chicago Press, 2010) for a fine account of Shakespeare's devotion to 'the singular' (p. 6), and the limitations of this devotion.

9 Geese, we may remember, saved Rome from invasion after Coriolanus' time (Livy, *Ab Urbe Condita*, V. 47–9).

Bibliography

PRIMARY WORKS

Aeschylus, *The Oresteia*, trans. Robert Fagles (London: Penguin, 1977)
Anon., *The Blind Beggar of Bednall Green* (London: 1659)
    The Costlie Whore (London: 1613)
    Clyomon and Clamydes, ed. W. W. Greg (Oxford University Press for the Malone Society, 1913)
    Common Conditions, ed. Tucker Brooke (New Haven, CT: Yale University Press, 1895)
    Englishmen for My Money, ed. W. W. Greg (London: Oxford University Press for the Malone Society, 1912)
    The Famous Victories of Henry the Fifth, ed. Chiaki Hanabusa (Manchester University Press for the Malone Society, 2007)
    Guy of Warwick, ed. Helen D. Moore (Manchester University Press for the Malone Society, 2006)
    King Leir, ed. Tiffany Stern (London: Nick Hern Books, 2002)
    A Knack to Know a Knave, ed. G. R. Proudfoot (Oxford University Press for the Malone Society, 1963)
    Look about You, ed. W. W. Greg (London: Oxford University Press for the Malone Society, 1913)
    The Rare Triumphs of Love and Fortune (London: 1589)
    Shakespeare's Edmund Ironside: The Lost Play, ed. Eric Sams (Aldershot: Wildwood House, 1986)
    Swetnam the Woman-Hater (Amersham: Tudor Facsimile Texts, 1914)
    The Tragedy of Locrine (Oxford University Press for the Malone Society, 1908)
    The Trial of Chivalry (London: 1605)
    The Troublesome Raigne of King John (London: C. Praetorius, 1888)
    The Two Noble Ladies, ed. Rebecca G. Rhoads (Oxford University Press for the Malone Society, 1930)
    The Weakest Goeth to the Wall, ed. W. W. Greg (London: Oxford University Press for the Malone Society, 1912)
    Wily Beguiled, ed. W. W. Greg (Oxford University Press for the Malone Society, 1912)
    The Wisdom of Doctor Dodypoll (London: 1600)

Armin, Robert, *The Collected Works of Robert Armin* (New York: Johnson Reprint Corporation, 1972)

Aubrey, John, *Brief Lives*, ed. John Buchanan-Brown (London: Penguin, 2000)

Bacon, Francis, *The Works of Francis Bacon*, ed. J. Spedding, R. L. Ellis, and D. D. Heath, 7 vols. (London: Longman's, 1857–74)

Barnes, Barnabe, *The Devil's Charter*, ed. Jim C. Pogue (New York: Garland, 1980)

Beaumont, Francis, and Fletcher, John, *The Dramatic Works in the Beaumont and Fletcher Canon*, ed. Fredson Bowers *et al.*, 10 vols. (Cambridge University Press, 1966–89)

Beza, Theodore, *A Tragedie of Abrahams Sacrifice*, trans. A. G. (London, 1575)

Chapman, George, *The Plays of George Chapman: The Comedies*, ed. Allan Holaday assisted by Michael Kiernan (Urbana, IL: University of Illinois Press, 1970)

Chapman, George, Jonson, Ben, and Marston, John, *Eastward Ho*, ed. R. W. van Fossen (Manchester University Press, 1979)

Chettle, Henry, *The Tragedy of Hoffman*, ed. Harold Jenkins (London: Oxford University Press for the Malone Society, 1951)

Daborne, Robert, *The Poor Man's Comfort*, ed. Kenneth Palmer (Oxford University Press for the Malone Society, 1955)

Day, John, *Law Tricks*, ed. John Crow (London: Oxford University Press for the Malone Society, 1949)

Dekker, Thomas, *The Dramatic Works of Thomas Dekker*, ed. Fredson Bowers, 4 vols. (Cambridge University Press, 1953–61)

Garter, Thomas, *The Most Virtuous and Godly Susanna*, ed. B. Ifor Evans (London: Oxford University Press for the Malone Society, 1936)

Gascoigne, George, *A Hundreth Sundrie Flowres*, ed. G. W. Pigman III (Oxford: Clarendon Press, 2000)

Greene, Robert, *Alphonsus King of Aragon*, ed. W. W. Greg (London: Oxford University Press for the Malone Society, 1926)

Friar Bacon and Friar Bungay, ed. J. A. Lavin (London: Ernest Benn, 1969)

The Scottish History of James the Fourth, ed. Norman Sanders (London: Methuen, 1970)

[?] *The Tragical Reign of Selimus* (London: Chiswick Press, 1908; reprinted Oxford University Press, 1964)

Harington, John, *Orlando Furioso* (London, 1591)

Heywood, Jasper (trans.), *Thyestes*, ed. Joost Daalder (London: Ernest Benn, 1982)

Heywood, Thomas, *The Captives*, ed. Arthur Brown (Oxford University Press for the Malone Society, 1953)

The Dramatic Works of Thomas Heywood, 6 vols. (London: J. Pearson, 1874)

Three Marriage Plays, ed. Paul Merchant (Manchester University Press, 1996)

King James VI and I, *Political Writings*, ed. Johann P. Sommerville (Cambridge University Press, 1994)

Jonson, Ben, *Works*, ed. C. H. Herford, Evelyn Simpson and Percy Simpson, 11 vols. (Oxford: Clarendon Press, 1925–52)

Kyd, Thomas, *The Spanish Tragedy*, ed. Philip Edwards (London: Methuen, 1959)

The Spanish Tragedie with The First Part of Jeronimo, ed. Emma Smith (London: Penguin, 1998)

Lodge, Thomas, *The Wounds of Civil War*, ed. Joseph W. Houppert (London: Edward Arnold, 1970)

Lyly, John, *Galathea and Midas*, ed. George Hunter and David Bevington (Manchester University Press, 2000)

Mother Bombie (Oxford University Press, 1948)

Marlowe, Christopher, *Edward the Second*, ed. Charles R. Forker (Manchester University Press, 1994)

The Jew of Malta, ed. N. W. Bawcutt (Manchester University Press, 1978)

Tamburlaine, ed. J. S. Cunningham (Manchester University Press, 1981)

Marston, John, *The Malcontent and Other Plays*, ed. Keith Sturgess (Oxford University Press, 1997)

The Plays of John Marston, ed. H. Harvey Wood, 3 vols. (Edinburgh: Oliver & Boyd, 1934–9)

Massinger, Philip, *The Plays and Poems of Philip Massinger*, ed. Philip Edwards and Colin Gibson, 5 vols. (Oxford: Clarendon Press, 1976)

Middleton, Thomas, *The Collected Works*, ed. Gary Taylor and John Lavagnino (Oxford University Press, 2007)

Nashe, Thomas, *The Works of Thomas Nashe*, ed. Ronald B. McKerrow, corr. F. P. Wilson, 5 vols. (Oxford: Basil Blackwell & Mott, 1957)

Nero & Other Plays, ed. Herbert P. Horne, H. Ellis, A. Symons, and A. Verity (London: Vizetelly & Co., 1888)

Nevyle, Alexander, *The Lamentable Tragedie of Oedipus* (London, 1563)

Peacham, Henry, *The Compleat Gentleman* (London, 1622)

Pikerying, John, *The Interlude of Vice (Horestes)*, ed. Daniel Seltzer (London: Oxford University Press for the Malone Society, 1962)

Porter, Henry, *The Two Angrie Women of Abington*, ed. W. W. Greg (London: Oxford University Press for the Malone Society, 1912)

R. B., *Apius and Virginia*, ed. R. B. McKerrow (London: The Malone Society, 1911)

Rowley, Samuel, *When You See Me, You Know Me*, ed. F. P. Wilson (Oxford University Press for the Malone Society, 1952)

Russell, D. A., and M. Winterbottom, M. (eds.), *Classical Literary Criticism*, revised edn (Oxford University Press, 1989)

S. S., *The Honest Lawyer* (Amersham: Tudor Facsimile Editions, 1914)

Sampson, William, *The Vow-Breaker: or, the Fair Maid of Clifton* (London: 1636)

Shakespeare, William, *As You Like It*, ed. Juliet Dusinberre (London: Arden Shakespeare, 2006)

The First Quarto of Hamlet, ed. Kathleen O. Irace (Cambridge University Press, 1998)

Pericles, ed. Suzanne Gossett (London: Arden Shakespeare, 2004)

The Sonnets and A Lover's Complaint, ed. John Kerrigan (London: Penguin, 1986)

The Shakespeare Apocrypha, ed. C. F. Tucker Brooke (Oxford: Clarendon Press, 1918)

Sharpham, Edward, *Cupid's Whirligig*, ed. Allardyce Nicoll (Waltham Saint Lawrence, Berkshire: The Golden Cockerel Press, 1926)

Sidney, Philip, *The Countess of Pembroke's Arcadia (The New Arcadia)*, ed. Victor Skretkowicz (Oxford: Clarendon Press, 1987)

Smith, W., *The Hector of Germany, or The Palsgrave, Prime Elector* (London: 1615)

Thorndike, Ashley (ed.), *The Minor Elizabethan Drama*, 2 vols. (London: J. M. Dent, 1910)

Tomkis, Thomas, *Albumazar: A Comedy*, ed. Hugh G. Dick (Berkeley: University of California Press, 1944)

Tourneur, Cyril, *The Atheist's Tragedy*, ed. Brian Morris and Roma Gill (London: A&C Black, 1989)

Webster, John, *The Complete Works of John Webster*, ed. F. L. Lucas, 4 vols. (London: Chatto & Windus, 1927)

The Duchess of Malfi and Other Plays, ed. René Weis (Oxford University Press, 1996)

W[eldon], Sir A[ntony], *The Court and Character of King James* (London: 1651)

Wilmot, Robert, *The Tragedie of Tancred and Gismund* (London: 1591)

Woodes, Nathaniel, *The Conflict of Conscience*, ed. Herbert Davis and F. P. Wilson (Oxford University Press for the Malone Society, 1952)

Yarington, Robert, *Two Lamentable Tragedies* (Amersham: Tudor Facsimile Texts, 1913)

SECONDARY WORKS

Adelman, Janet, *Suffocating Mothers: Fantasies of Maternal Origin in Shakespeare's Plays, Hamlet to The Tempest* (London: Routledge, 1992)

Alexander, Peter, *Hamlet: Father and Son* (Oxford: Clarendon Press, 1955)

Bamber, Linda, *Comic Women, Tragic Men: A Study of Gender and Genre in Shakespeare* (Stanford University Press, 1982)

Bayley, John, *Shakespeare and Tragedy* (London: Routledge & Kegan Paul, 1981)

Beer, Gillian, *The Romance* (London: Methuen, 1970)

Belsey, Catherine, 'Little Princes: Shakespeare's Royal Children', in Kate Chedgzoy, Susanne Greenhalgh, and Robert Shaughnessy (eds.), *Shakespeare and Childhood* (Cambridge University Press, 2007)

Shakespeare and the Loss of Eden: The Construction of Family Values in Early Modern Culture (London: Macmillan, 1999)

Berger, Harry Jr, *Making Trifles of Terrors: Redistributing Complicities in Shakespeare* (Stanford University Press, 1997)

Berry, Philippa, *Shakespeare's Feminine Endings: Disfiguring Death in the Tragedies* (London: Routledge, 1999)

Bicks, Caroline, 'Midwiving Virility in Early Modern England', in Naomi J. Miller and Naomi Yavneh (eds.), *Maternal Measures: Figuring Caregiving in the Early Modern Period* (Aldershot: Ashgate, 2000)

Bloom, Harold, *Shakespeare: The Invention of the Human* (New York: Riverhead Books, 1998)

Boose, Lynda E., 'The Father and the Bride in Shakespeare', *PMLA* 97 (1982): 325–47

Bradbrook, M. C., *John Webster: Citizen and Dramatist* (London: Weidenfeld and Nicolson, 1980)

Braunmuller, A. R., and Hattaway, Michael, *The Cambridge Companion to English Renaissance Drama*, 2nd edn (Cambridge University Press, 2003)

Breitenberg, Mark, *Anxious Masculinity in Early Modern England* (Cambridge University Press, 1996)

Carneiro De Mendonça, Barbara Heliodora, 'The Influence of *Gorboduc* on *King Lear*', *Shakespeare Survey* 13 (1966): 41–8

Cave, Terence, *Recognitions: A Study in Poetics* (Oxford: Clarendon Press, 1988)

Cavell, Stanley, *Disowning Knowledge in Seven Plays of Shakespeare*, updated edn (Cambridge University Press, 2003)

Clark, Ira, *The Moral Art of Philip Massinger* (Lewisburg: Bucknell University Press, 1993)

Cooper, Helen, *The English Romance in Time: Transforming Motifs from Geoffrey of Monmouth to Shakespeare* (Oxford University Press, 2004)

Cressy, David, *Birth, Marriage and Death: Ritual, Religion and the Life-Cycle in Tudor and Stuart England* (Oxford University Press, 1997)

Danson, Lawrence, *Shakespeare's Dramatic Genres* (Oxford University Press, 2000)

de Grazia, Margreta, 'The Ideology of Superfluous Things: *King Lear* as Period Piece', in Margreta de Grazia, Maureen Quilligan, and Peter Stallybrass (eds.), *Subject and Object in Renaissance Culture* (Cambridge University Press, 1996), pp. 17–42

Dean, Paul, 'Shakespeare's *Henry VI* Trilogy and Elizabethan "Romance" Histories: The Origins of a Genre', *Shakespeare Quarterly* 33 (1982): 34–48

Doebler, John, 'Beaumont's *The Knight of the Burning Pestle* and the Prodigal Son Plays', in *Studies in English Literature* 5 (1965): 333–44

Dolan, Frances E., 'The Subordinate(s) Plot: Petty Trenson and the Forms of Domestic Rebellion', *Shakespeare Quarterly* 43 (1992), 317–40.

Doran, Susan, *Monarchy and Matrimony: The Courtships of Elizabeth I* (London: Routledge, 1996)

  'Why Did Elizabeth Not Marry?', in Julia M. Walker (ed.), *Dissing Elizabeth: Negative Representations of Gloriana* (Durham, NC: Duke University Press, 1998)

Dubrow, Heather, *Shakespeare and Domestic Loss: Forms of Deprivation, Mourning and Recuperation* (Cambridge University Press, 1999)

Dunn, Kevin, 'Representing Counsel: *Gorboduc* and the Elizabethan Privy Council', *English Literary Renaissance* 33 (2003): 279–308

Erickson, Peter, *Patriarchal Structures in Shakespeare's Drama* (Berkeley: University of California Press, 1985)

Erne, Lukas, *Beyond The Spanish Tragedy: A Study of the Works of Thomas Kyd* (Manchester University Press, 2001)

Erskine-Hill, Howard, *Poetry and the Realm of Politics: Spenser to Dryden* (Oxford University Press, 1996)

Fernie, Ewan, *Shame in Shakespeare* (London: Routledge, 2002)

Fischer, Walter, 'Shakespeares *Sturm* und *The Rare Triumphs of Love and Fortune*', in Helmut Viebrock (ed.), *Festschrift zum 75. Geburtstag von Theodor Spira* (Heidelberg: C. Winter, 1961), pp. 144–51

Fletcher, Anthony, *Gender, Sex and Subordination in England 1500–1800* (New Haven, CT: Yale University Press, 1995)

Fletcher, Hattie, and Novy, Marianne, 'Father–Child Identification, Loss and Gender in Shakespeare's Plays', in Kate Chedgzoy, Susanne Greenhalgh, and Robert Shaughnessy (eds.), *Shakespeare and Childhood* (Cambridge University Press, 2007)

Fowler, Alastair, *Renaissance Realism: Narrative Images in Literature and Art* (Oxford University Press, 2003)

Foyster, Elizabeth, *Manhood in Early Modern England: Honour, Sex and Marriage* (London: Longman, 1999)

Freud, Sigmund, *The Standard Edition of the Complete Psychological Works of Sigmund Freud*, 24 vols. (London: Hogarth Press and the Institute of Psycho-Analysis, 1953–74)

Frye, Northrop, *Anatomy of Criticism: Four Essays* (Princeton University Press, 1957)
  Fables of Identity: Studies in Poetic Mythology (New York: Harcourt, Brace, 1963)

Goldhill, Simon, *Reading Greek Tragedy* (Cambridge University Press, 1986)

Gowing, Laura, *Domestic Dangers: Women, Words, and Sex in Early Modern London* (Oxford: Clarendon Press, 1996)

Greenblatt, Stephen, *Hamlet in Purgatory* (Princeton University Press, 2001)
  Shakespearean Negotiations: The Circulation of Social Energy in Renaissance England (Oxford: Clarendon Press, 1988)
  Shakespeare's Freedom (The University of Chicago Press, 2010)
  Will in the World: How Shakespeare Became Shakespeare (London: Jonathan Cape, 2004)

Haber, Judith, *Desire and Dramatic Form in Early Modern England* (Cambridge University Press, 2009)

Hadorn, Peter T., '*Sir Clyomon and Sir Clamydes*: A Revaluation', *Journal of the Rocky Mountain Medieval and Renaissance Society* 12 (1991): 85–102

Happé, Peter, 'Tragic Themes in Three Tudor Moralities', *SEL* 5 (1965): 207–27

Helgerson, Richard, *The Elizabethan Prodigals* (Berkeley: University of California Press, 1976)

Holbrook, Peter, *Shakespeare's Individualism* (Cambridge University Press, 2010)

Houser, David J., 'Purging the Commonwealth: Marston's Disguised Dukes and *A Knack to Know a Knave*', *PMLA* 89 (1974): 993–1006

Howard, Jean E., and Rackin, Phyllis, *Engendering a Nation: A Feminist Account of Shakespeare's English Histories* (London: Routledge, 1997)

Hughes, Thomas, and others, *The Misfortunes of Arthur* (London: Tudor Facsimile Texts, 1911)

Hunter, G. K., *Dramatic Identities and Cultural Traditions* (Liverpool University Press, 1978)

  English Drama 1586–1642: The Age of Shakespeare (Oxford: Clarendon Press, 1997)

Hutchings, Mark, 'The End of *II Tamburlaine* and the Beginnings of *King Lear*', *Notes and Queries* 245 (2000)

Hutson, Lorna, *The Invention of Suspicion: Law and Mimesis in Shakespeare and Renaissance Drama* (Oxford University Press, 2007)

  The Usurer's Daughter: Male Friendship and Fictions of Women in Sixteenth-Century England (London: Routledge, 1994)

James, Mervyn, *English Politics and the Concept of Honour 1485–1642* (Oxford: Past and Present Society, 1978)

Jardine, Lisa, *Still Harping on Daughters: Women and Drama in the Age of Shakespeare*, 2nd edn (London: Harvester Wheatsheaf, 1989)

Jones, Emrys, *Scenic Form in Shakespeare* (Oxford: Clarendon Press, 1971)

Jones, Ernest, *Hamlet and Oedipus* (London: Gollancz, 1949)

Jones, John, *Shakespeare at Work* (Oxford: Clarendon Press, 1995)

Kahn, Coppélia, *Man's Estate: Masculine Identity in Shakespeare* (Berkeley: University of California Press, 1981)

Kantorowicz, E. H., *The King's Two Bodies: A Study in Mediaeval Political Theology* (Princeton University Press, 1957)

Keller, Eve, *Generating Bodies and Gendered Selves: The Rhetoric of Reproduction in Early Modern England* (Seattle: University of Washington Press, 2007)

Kermode, Frank, *Shakespeare's Language* (London: Allen Lane, 2000)

Kerrigan, John, *Revenge Tragedy: Aeschylus to Armaggedon* (Oxford: Clarendon Press, 1996)

Kiernan, Pauline, *Shakespeare's Theory of Drama* (Cambridge University Press, 1996)

King, Andrew, 'Dead Butchers and Fiend-Like Queens: *The Misfortunes of Arthur* and *Macbeth*', in Rhiannon Purdie and Nicola Royan (eds.), *The Scots and Medieval Arthurian Legend* (Cambridge: Boydell and Brewer Press, 2005)

Knights, L. C., *How Many Children Had Lady Macbeth? An Essay in the Theory and Practice of Shakespeare Criticism* (Cambridge: G. Fraser, The Minority Press, 1933)

Lee, H. J., Macbeth, A. H., Pagani, J. H. and Young, W. S. 'Oxytocin: The Great Facilitator of Life', *Progress in Neurobiology* 88 (2009): 127–51

Leggatt, Alexander, *Shakespeare's Tragedies: Violation and Identity* (Cambridge University Press, 2005)

Macfarlane, Alan, *Marriage and Love in England 1300–1840* (Oxford: Basil Blackwell, 1986)

The Origins of English Individualism: The Family, Property and Social Transition (Oxford: Basil Blackwell, 1978)

MacFaul, Tom, 'Friendship in Sidney's *Arcadias*', *Studies in English Literature* 49 (2009): 17–33

Male Friendship in Shakespeare and His Contemporaries (Cambridge University Press, 2007)

Poetry and Paternity in Renaissance England: Sidney, Spenser, Shakespeare, Donne and Jonson (Cambridge University Press, 2010)

Maguire, Laurie, *Shakespeare's Names* (Oxford University Press, 2007)

Maguire, Nancy Klein (ed.), *Renaissance Tragicomedy* (New York: AMS Press, 1987)

Maquerlot, Jean-Pierre, *Shakespeare and the Mannerist Tradition: A Reading of Five Problem Plays* (Cambridge University Press, 1995)

Martindale, Charles, and Taylor, A. B. (eds.), *Shakespeare and the Classics* (Cambridge University Press, 2004)

McAdam, Ian, *Magic and Masculinity in Early Modern English Drama* (Pittsburgh: Duquesne University Press, 2009)

McCabe, Richard A., *Incest, Drama and Nature's Law 1550–1700* (Cambridge University Press, 1993)

McKeon, Michael, *The Secret History of Domesticity: Public, Private and the Division of Knowledge* (Baltimore, MD: Johns Hopkins University Press, 2005)

McMillin, Scott, and MacLean, Sally-Beth, *The Queen's Men and Their Plays* (Cambridge University Press, 1998)

McMullan, Gordon, *The Politics of Unease in the Plays of John Fletcher* (Amherst: University of Massachusetts Press, 1994)

Mills, Laurens J., *One Soul in Bodies Twain: Friendship in Tudor Literature and Stuart Drama* (Bloomington, IN: Principia Press, 1937)

Moretti, Franco, *Signs Taken for Wonders: On the Sociology of Literary Forms*, trans. David Miller (London: Verso, 2005)

Neill, Michael, *Issues of Death: Mortality and Identity in English Renaissance Tragedy* (Oxford: Clarendon Press, 1997)

Novy, Marianne L., *Love's Argument: Gender Relations in Shakespeare* (Chapel Hill, NC: The University of North Carolina Press, 1984)

Nuttall, A. D., 'Action at a Distance: Shakespeare and the Greeks', in Martindale and Taylor (eds.), *Shakespeare and the Classics*

Shakespeare the Thinker (New Haven, CT: Yale University Press, 2007)

Why Does Tragedy Give Pleasure? (Oxford: Clarendon Press, 1996)

Orwell, George, *The Complete Works of George Orwell*, 20 vols. (London: Secker & Warburg, 1986–98)

Palfrey, Simon, *Doing Shakespeare*, 2nd edn (London: Methuen Drama, 2011)

Palfrey, Simon, and Stern, Tiffany, *Shakespeare in Parts* (Oxford University Press, 2007)

Palliser, D. M., *The Age of Elizabeth: England under the Later Tudors 1547–1603*, 2nd edn (London: Longman, 1992)

Parker, Patricia, 'Black Hamlet: Battening on the Moor', *Shakespeare Studies* 31 (2003): 127–64

Perry, Curtis, *The Making of Jacobean Culture: James I and the Renegotiation of Elizabethan Literary Practice* (Cambridge University Press, 1997)

Pesta, Duke, 'Articulating Skeletons: *Hamlet, Hoffman* and the Anatomical Graveyard', *Cahiers Élisabéthains* 69 (2006): 21–39

Phillips, J. E. 'A Revaluation of *Horestes*', *Huntington Library Quarterly* 18 (1955): 227–44

Poole, Adrian, *Tragedy: Shakespeare and the Greek Example* (Oxford: Basil Blackwell, 1987)

Rowland, Richard, *Thomas Heywood's Theatre 1599–1639: Locations, Translations, and Conflict* (Farnham: Ashgate, 2010)

Ryan, Kiernan, *Shakespeare's Comedies* (Basingstoke: Palgrave Macmillan, 2009)

Salzman, Paul, *Literary Culture in Jacobean England: Reading 1621* (London: Palgrave Macmillan, 2002)

Shannon, Laurie, *Sovereign Amity: Figures of Friendship in Shakespearean Contexts* (University of Chicago Press, 2002)

Sharpe, Kevin, *Image Wars: Promoting Kings and Commonwealths in England 1603–1660* (New Haven, CT: Yale University Press, 2010)

Selling the Tudor Monarchy: Authority and Image in Sixteenth-Century England (New Haven, CT: Yale University Press, 2009)

Shepard, Alexandra, *Meanings of Manhood in Early Modern England* (Oxford University Press, 2003)

Silk, Michael, 'Shakespeare and Greek Tragedy: Strange Relationship', in Martindale and Taylor (eds.), *Shakespeare and the Classics*

Small, Helen, *The Long Life* (Oxford University Press, 2007)

Smith, Bruce R., *Shakespeare and Masculinity* (Oxford University Press, 2000)

Stone, Lawrence, *The Crisis of the Aristocracy 1558–1641* (Oxford: Clarendon Press, 1965)

Stevens, Wallace, *Collected Poems* (London: Faber and Faber, 1955)

Taylor, Charles, *Sources of the Self: The Making of Modern Identity* (Cambridge University Press, 1989)

Tennenhouse, Leonard, *Power on Display: The Politics of Shakespeare's Genres* (London: Methuen, 1986)

Thomas, Keith, *The Ends of Life: Roads to Fulfilment in Early Modern England* (Oxford University Press, 2009)

Traub, Valerie, *Desire and Anxiety: Circulations of Sexuality in Shakespearean Drama* (London: Routledge, 1992)

Tromly, Fred B., *Fathers and Sons in Shakespeare: The Debt Never Promised* (University of Toronto Press, 2010)

Walker, Greg, *Writing under Tyranny: English Literature and the Henrician Reformation* (Oxford University Press, 2005)

Waith, Eugene M., *The Pattern of Tragicomedy in Beaumont and Fletcher* (New Haven, CT: Yale University Press, 1952)

Wells, Robin Headlam, *Shakespeare on Masculinity* (Cambridge University Press, 2000)

Wiggins, Martin, *Shakespeare and the Drama of His Time* (Oxford University Press, 2000)

Winnicott, D. W., *Playing and Reality* (Hove: Brunner-Routledge, 1991)

Witmore, Michael, *Pretty Creatures: Children and Fiction in the English Renaissance* (Ithaca: Cornell University Press, 2007)

Womersley, David, *Divinity and State* (Oxford University Press, 2010)

Woods, Gillian, 'The Contexts of *The Trial of Chivalry*', *Notes and Queries* 54 (2007): 313–18

Young, Alan R., *The English Prodigal Son Plays: A Theatrical Fashion of the Sixteenth and Seventeenth Centuries* (Institut. für Anglistik und Amerikanistik, Universität von Salzburg, 1979)

Index

Note: Plays which receive frequent mention or detailed analysis are indexed by title; works receiving only passing reference appear as subheadings under the author's name (where known).

CPSIA information can be obtained
at www.ICGtesting.com
Printed in the USA
LVHW011749121119
637142LV00013B/389